Praise for *Behind the 8-Ball*

"This book offers a helpful support and guide for anyone who knows a troubled gambler or who . . . is having difficulty in coping with someone in the family who is gambling over his or her head."

—Sirgay Sanger, M.D., Assistant Clinical Professor of Psychiatry, Columbia University College of Physicians & Surgeons, President, National Council on Problem Gambling

"An excellent, step-by-step recovery guide. . . . I am very pleased to recommend and praise this book because it moves on to detail an excellent plan for recovery—helping the family to understand gambling as an addiction, reaching out for support groups and experienced therapists, and looking inward for strength of a personal faith."

—Msgr Joseph A. Dunne, M.P.A., C.A.C., founder and President Emeritus, National Council on Problem Gambling

"It is rare that a text can be both a primer and a definitive work. *Behind the 8-Ball* has accomplished this feat. This book is . . . intelligible and enlightening to the novice, yet professionals who have expertise in human behavior can benefit greatly from the case histories and psychological explanations of the bewildering phenomenon of destructive gambling."

—Rabbi Abraham Twerski, M.D., founder and Medical Director, Gateway Rehabilitation Centers, and author of *Addictive Thinking*

Behind the 8-Ball is an absolutely fascinating book. It is must reading for anyone working with an individual who has a gambling problem—family member, social worker, twelve-step group, the gamblers themselves."

—Frank Riessman, Ph.D., Director, National Self-Help Clearinghouse

"Berman and Siegel make a significant and lucid contribution to understanding the plight of the gambler's family. Their book will be invaluable to families who suffer as they try to hide, understand, or deal with the gambler in their midst."

—Judith S. Seixas, M.A., C.A.C.,
coauthor of *Children of Alcoholism: A Survivor's Manual*

BEHIND THE 8-BALL

A Guide for Families of Gamblers

**Linda Berman, M.S.W.,
and Mary-Ellen Siegel, M.S.W.**

iUniverse, Inc.
San Jose New York Lincoln Shanghai

Behind the 8-Ball: A Recovery Guide for the Families of Gamblers

Authors Choice Press
an imprint of iUniverse, Inc.

For information address:
iUniverse, Inc.
5220 S. 16th St., Suite 200
Lincoln, NE 68512
www.iuniverse.com

ISBN: 1-58348-046-3

Printed in the United States of America

With much love
To my friends and family
Most of all Mike, Michael, and Deborah
LB

With love always
To my family
Past, Present, and Future
MES

Acknowledgments

Westchester Jewish Community Services, a nonsectarian not-for-profit family mental health agency, provided me with the clinical experience to write this book. I am extremely grateful to the entire staff and particularly thank Ron Gaudia, the deputy executive director. His vision and the special fund grants from UJA-Federation of New York made possible my work with gamblers and their families.

LB

As always, my colleagues in the Department of Social Work Services at the Mount Sinai Medical Center, and the Department of Community Medicine (Social Work) at the Mount Sinai School of Medicine provided encouragement and assistance. I especially thank Dr. Susan Blumenfield, Dr. Helen Rehr, and Dr. Gary Rosenberg.

MES

Many people shared their experiences and perceptions with us: some were gamblers; most were spouses, parents, siblings, or adult children of gamblers. Our social work colleagues and other mental health professionals shared their personal and professional experiences. We are particularly indebted to those pioneers in the field of gambling, addictions, and recovery whose scholarly and clinical studies and observations inspired and educated us in our own work.

Jean Chasen-Falzon, executive director of the National Council on Problem Gambling and her staff, and Judy Cornelius of the Institute for the Study of Gambling and Commercial Gaming were particularly helpful and supportive. We greatly appreciate it.

Toni Sciarra's enthusiasm was encouraging, and Sheila Curry's editing was immensely helpful. We thank them both.

LB and MES

Addiction. Dependence characterized by chronicity, compulsiveness, and uncontrollable urges to use a substance or to perform an activity. The attempt to cut down, control, or stop the activity or use causes severe emotional, mental, and/or physiological reactions. Tolerance develops, prolonging or increasing use of the substance or performance of the activity. Addictions interfere with important social, occupational, or recreational activities.

Behind the 8-Ball. A colloquial expression, derived from pool, meaning a troubled situation from which it is difficult to extricate oneself.

Gamble. To risk money or something of value on the outcome of an unpredictable chance event or contest.

Gambler. A person who plays at games of chance for money or something of value; a person who takes chances on the outcome of a particular event.

Addictive Gambler. *See* Compulsive Gambler.

Compulsive Gambler. A person with an impulse disorder, who suffers from a chronic and progressive psychological disease that is often unrecognized because of its hidden nature. Also called Addictive or Pathological gambler.

Pathological Gambler. *See* Compulsive Gambler.

Problem Gambler. A person who invests considerable time and emotional energy in gambling or planning to do so, and who plays for stakes that are higher than he or she can afford. Problem gamblers may become compulsive gamblers, but some are able to stop or cut down on their gambling if circumstances warrant it.

Recreational Gambler. *See* Social Gambler.

Social Gambler. A person who gambles for a predetermined amount of time and with a fixed amount of money and is able to restrict gambling at any time.

Authors' Note

With the exception of the references to Mary-Ellen Siegel's own family and certain public figures, all the individuals discussed in this book are fictional. Although the authors have drawn on their clinical experiences in creating such fictional composites, any resemblance to a real person alive or dead is purely coincidental.

To eliminate awkwardness of style, the masculine pronoun has been used when referring to the gambler, and the feminine pronoun has been used when referring to the spouse or to a person affected by the gambler's behavior. However, as demonstrated in many examples in this book, a growing number of problem and compulsive gamblers are women, and many of those affected by gambling are men.

Contents

PART FOUR
RECOVERY

Foreword to the 1999 Edition

When we first began to consider writing a book to help those who had been affected by someone who gambled too much there were still a limited number of ways to gamble. Sports betting, card playing, horse racing and a handful of casinos, local bingo parlors as well as the old "numbers game" were the major outlets for those who wished to gamble. Only the so-called sophisticated gambler "bet" on the stock-market, and gambling on the Internet was unknown. Most gamblers were men, with women, teens and seniors still lagging behind.

The picture has changed radically in just ten years.

Two-income producing families have proliferated, giving women more access to funds. Teens are finding that the illegal sports gambling is available to them at their local, traditional "hang-outs", and seniors are lured to casinos by enticing offers of bus-rides, buffets and entertainment. Since a certain number of those who gamble will become "hooked" on it, the actual numbers of problem and compulsive gamblers have grown.

Attitudes towards gambling have changed considerably in recent times. No longer perceived as a shameful activity, gambling is more liked to be referred to as "gaming" as it has blended into the entertainment field. The gambler is no longer restricted to a "backroom" somewhere, as modern casinos can be found throughout the country beckoning everyone to participate: the factory worker, the retiree on a fixed income, the middle-manager, the high-rolling executive and the rich and famous.

Stock market gambling has become more and more common as people have become more acquainted with this form of investing. The union worker who has seen his retirement fund grow due to investments in equities, and the moderate or even conservative investor who has made money in the market have been tempted to make riskier investments.

Buying and selling stocks has been made so easy on the Internet that without the advice of a trained financial advisor, many people have become reckless in their trading. This gambler is not socially stigmatized in the way that a racing track aficionado or back-room poker player might be. Such an individual is made to seem even more socially acceptable by the number of books and seminars with titles like, *How to Invest in the Stock Market; How to Double Your Money Every Month; Introduction to Commodities; Learn How to Become A Profitable Day Trader: The Secrets of Electronic Day Trading* and *The Electronic Day Trader*. The list continues.

Reliable predictions that half of all retail trades in stock shares may be online by the year 2001, it is likely before long just about everyone with access to a credit card and a computer will be able to buy and sell stock. Some people are seduced by the excitement of their new found ability to go in and out of the market from minute to minute. Others, not wanting to consult with a traditional broker, or understanding the research they may or may not have done online, will buy and sell stock with total abandon. When people "bet" on the Internet, whether it is the stock market or the illegal gambling still available there, their sense of reality can become blurred and the excitement and "living on the edge" can take over.

Studies have shown that many of those people with other addictions have undiagnosed gambling problems, and the various gambling hot-lines report that those who call have greater debts than callers in previous years, and that more women, seniors and teens are being affected.

Despite the numbers of gamblers, particularly in vulnerable age groups, we are disappointed that there is still insufficient attention to the problem from mental health professionals. We are heartened that there are a growing number of professionals who are bringing gambling out of the shadows of other addictions as they identify gambling as the underlying cause of much misery and tragedies in families.

In the meantime many questions still exist: Will the secrecy around money in some families continue as an outgrowth of their psychological needs? Will the general public continue to look away when someone gambles too much? Will the gaming industry continue to find ways to entice new participants, who may eventually have major problems with gambling? Will the gaming industry begin to move further in the direction of working to help prevent out-of-control gambling and to educate the public?

We are encouraged by some movement towards prevention in schools and businesses and we are hopeful that this attention will increase and that the government will take stronger measures to prevent illegal gambling on the Internet.

If you are a mental professional or educator who is reading this book, we hope it will help you to identify gamblers, and those affected by gambling so that they can find the help they need.

If you find yourself "Behind the 8-Ball", in a troubled situation from which you are having difficulty in extricating yourself, we have confidence that when you read this book you, like so many other readers, will find yourself empowered with knowledge and strength to come out from Behind the 8-Ball.

Linda Berman, MSW
Mary-Ellen Siegel, MSW
November, 1998

Introduction

We are all gamblers of one kind or another. Sometimes we take an emotional or spiritual risk, like a leap of faith, or drive ourselves to the extent of, or even beyond, our physical capacities. These kinds of risks can enhance and enrich our lives.

Games of chance in which money is at risk hold a special fascination for most of us; they offer fun, excitement, a change of pace, and an opportunity to try our luck at improving our lots in life. Each toss of the dice, blackjack hand, lottery ticket, or bet on a sporting event can make you feel special and lucky. The list of ways to gamble is endless: cards, horse racing, bingo, office sports pools, mah-jongg, slot machines, illegal "numbers," and, of course, the financial markets.

Most of us gamble for excitement or simply in response to availability and seductive advertisements. For example, two young mothers saw a sign announcing a huge lottery jackpot while shopping for party favors for their babies' first birthday parties. They impulsively decided to buy a lottery ticket, combining the babies' birthdates and the locker number they shared in high school. They had fun filling in the numbers, and forgot the drawing date until one of them heard the result on television the following week. The two young women had become multi-millionaires!

Gambling can be fun, and sometimes very profitable. Some people, however, become problem or compulsive gamblers and are unable to stop whether they are winning or losing.

Many famous people have been such gamblers. Arnold Rothstein, the man who fixed the World Series in 1919, was thought by most people to be a winner, but he has been reported to have died penniless, murdered for reneging on a $250,000 bet! Performer Debbie Reynolds states in her autobiography that she was married to two compulsive gamblers—each lost not only his own money but hers too! Band leader Woody Herman died destitute in 1987, in considerable debt to the IRS because his trusted business manager was reportedly a compulsive gambler who had siphoned off the band's profits and failed to file tax returns.

The gambling problems of baseball superstar Pete Rose were heavily publicized by the media. Ultimately convicted of tax evasion and sentenced to prison, Rose became a symbol of the havoc that gambling can create. During a 1990 interview with Barbara Walters on "20/20," he discussed his predicament: "I thought you had to gamble every day to have a problem. And I didn't really start thinking about any kind of problem until they took the game of baseball away from me. Then I had to wake up."

Pete Rose isn't the only athlete to succumb to the lure of gambling. Chet Forte, star athlete and Emmy award–winning director of "Monday Night Football," was faced with a series of tax and fraud charges and lost his $1.5 million house, had his Mercedes repossessed, and couldn't even afford a lawyer despite annual earnings of more than $500,000, making him eligible for representation by a public defender.

Gambling too much has become a problem for a growing number of people each year, and is now the third major addiction in the United States. It affects not only the gambler but those who care about him and are forced to stand by helplessly while he slowly but surely digs his own financial and emotional grave, losing his family, friends, livelihood, and self-respect, perhaps ending up in jail or dying prematurely of a stress-related illness. It is easy to understand why gamblers commit suicide at a far greater rate than the population at large.

If someone in your life has a gambling problem, you may be in more trouble than you realize. You *know* what he is like in your gut, even if you can't sort it all out. You know that you feel trapped, betrayed, helpless, and that your life is unmanageable. You feel that you're in a difficult situation, behind the 8-ball, and sometimes life looks totally hopeless. You know that you need to learn a way to survive and rebuild your life, but it seems like an insurmountable task.

This book is a guide to *your* financial, legal, and emotional freedom and to rebuilding your life.

In it you will learn:

• how to identify the problem and the compulsive gambler and to realistically assess the financial and emotional damage he is causing the family
  • why some people lose control of their gambling
  • how to survive—emotionally and financially—when you are involved with a gambler
    • why *you* can't control someone else's gambling
    • how to encourage the gambler to seek help
    • how to get your relationship back on track if your gambler gets help
    • how—when all efforts to urge the gambler to rehabilitate have failed—to disengage or detach yourself from the gambler
    • how to rebuild your life after you have been involved with a gambler

We have been able to help others, and we have been able to help ourselves.

LINDA'S STORY

Rosalyn D. would often say to me, "I either wear all my jewelry or carry it in my purse."

She simply couldn't trust her gold necklace, bracelet, watch, and pearls at home with her husband.

This extraordinary statement marked the beginning of my education about what it is like for people who live with someone who gambles too much.

Rosalyn first came to see me in 1979. I had just earned my master's degree in social work and had joined the staff of a large family mental health agency in Westchester County, New York. Before graduate school, I had worked for several years in an inner-city alcohol and drug prevention program, conducting and teaching group counseling.

In those years, the public had just begun to recognize that no income group or community was immune to drug problems. The recovery movement as we know it today was in its infancy, but gaining momentum. Compulsive gambling, however, continued to be largely overlooked, even though it had been officially recognized by the mental health profession as a psychological disorder.

By the time Rosalyn came to me for therapy, her life was in

ruins and she blamed it on her husband's gambling. I was immediately struck by Rosalyn's rage and bitterness. She reminded me of other patients who had been either cruelly exploited or abused by those close to them. Like those women, Rosalyn felt deeply betrayed.

In addition to Rosalyn's frazzled and angry, yet passive, demeanor (the result of having lived with someone who had gambled away their money and self-respect), she was troubled by her sixteen-year-old daughter, Stacy. Stacy was talking about dropping out of school. Rosalyn suspected that Stacy, whom she described as obese and unattractive because she had "let herself go," was using drugs and drinking, influenced, Rosalyn felt, by her nineteen-year-old "born loser" boyfriend.

Problems with Stacy brought Rosalyn to my office. "I can't expect my husband to be helpful or cooperative," she said. "He just takes the easy way out of everything, indulging and spoiling Stacy, as if he were a fond uncle rather than a parent. I'm so exhausted from trying to get him to act like a grown-up father that I feel ready to throw in the towel myself."

Rosalyn described herself as having changed during her marriage of twenty-three years from a lighthearted, fun-loving, attractive woman to a lonely shrew. Occasional sleep problems had become full-blown insomnia, and she was beginning to rely on pills to fall asleep.

"I'm beginning to sound and look a lot like my mother," she said one day. Rosalyn's parents fought a lot over her father's stinginess with the family and his frequent drinking binges and absences from home. He was a womanizer, and there was always "someone else" in his life. But he also had many good qualities that Rosalyn liked; he would take Rosalyn and her siblings to ball games and have fun with them, and he could be very warm and loving. Often Rosalyn thought that her mother's shrewlike behavior had driven her father out of the house and to drinking and other women.

When Rosalyn married Joel, she thought her life was going to be very different from her mother's. Joel was funny and lovable like her father, but he also was unlike him: Joel never drank and was generous and totally devoted to Rosalyn. She thought he would make an ideal husband and father. Indeed, the first few years with him more than met her expectations. He became a teacher in the late 1950s and was loved by his students. When his father died, Joel took over the family's dry-cleaning business. His father had barely eked out a living from it, but Joel soon made it thrive, and became so busy he gave up teaching. Even before Stacy was born money was plentiful, and Rosalyn, with Joel's encouragement, spent freely and easily on their home.

How different this was for Rosalyn, whose mother had always counted the pennies, and whose faded furniture was a source of embarrassment to her when friends stopped by after school. Now Rosalyn had the home and family of her dreams.

Soon gambling played a central role in their social lives. Card games, junkets to Caribbean casino hotels, and weekly dinners at the track made up their vacations and entertainment. On Sundays their home sounded like an appliance store. Radios and televisions blasted and telephones and doorbells rang as Joel's gambling buddies constantly checked in.

Rosalyn thought the gambling was fun and enjoyed the glamour and the constant tumult of people around them. How different Joel was from her father, she thought. Her husband always wanted to include her in his activities. After Stacy was born, Rosalyn preferred to stay home with her. She wished Joel would also stay home on weekends, but he began to go off on junkets and to the track without her, and as Stacy grew into childhood and needed her less, Rosalyn felt left behind by both of them.

Joel began to talk about money problems, blaming them on "the poor business climate caused by all those wash-and-wear clothes" and on Rosalyn's extravagant tastes for herself and Stacy. Still, he was generous with gifts and dining out. But as time went by, payment of ordinary bills was delayed. Arguments over money became part of Rosalyn's daily life. They rarely enjoyed sex, which had once been so good.

Calls from friends and strangers about loans became commonplace. Rosalyn began to see Joel's gambling activities as a rival for his time and attention. She would try to convince herself that she was far better off than her mother had been. "He doesn't drink or run around with other women, so why am I complaining?"

But she was beginning to suspect that his gambling was at the root of their financial problems. Joel, however, continued to blame their circumstances on Rosalyn's spending and his business "setback." She would badger him to stay home, constantly nagging him to become more involved in Stacy's care. He would turn this around and claim her nagging drove him out of the house to seek "a little relaxation" that gambling offered.

Stacy saw her mother just as Rosalyn had viewed *her* mother— a "crazy witch" who was driving her father away. And Rosalyn was beginning to believe it too.

The debts mounted. Their car and Rosalyn's jewelry disappeared with inadequate explanations. Rosalyn found herself constantly checking on Joel.

"I felt like a detective looking for clues. I just couldn't understand why our life was unraveling. But the more questions I asked Joel, the more lies he told me," she said.

One day quite by accident, Rosalyn discovered that Joel had become a bookmaker and ran the illegal business from the dry-cleaning store. She lived in constant fear and yelled at and threatened him. At this point in their relationship, there was no sex or affection left: only anger and spitefulness. "Joel lived at the end of the telephone, talking to strangers who also began to appear at the door." She considered ending the marriage.

Rosalyn told me about Joel's gambling over a number of sessions as she discussed her concerns about Stacy's possible drug and alcohol use and her threats to quit school. Stacy agreed to see one of my colleagues at the agency, and this allowed Rosalyn to focus more on her problems with Joel.

One day Joel was arrested for selling football sheets. "For four days, he has been just sitting around the house in his pajamas. He even refuses to let me get him a lawyer, and he won't talk about what will happen if he goes to jail or about the thousands owed to loan sharks, the banks, and now the IRS. And, do you believe this, he's still blaming me and not the gambling." At that point Rosalyn started to sob. "Maybe he's right. If I hadn't expected so much from him, maybe he never would have started gambling."

I felt sorry for her. But I also found myself blaming her, although for different reasons. Why hadn't she known that Joel was gambling too much years ago? Didn't she know how much he was losing? If he wouldn't stop, why didn't she walk out? I also found it hard to believe that only Joel's gambling was making her life so miserable. And I questioned Rosalyn's descriptions of herself and Joel when they were younger. Had she ever been that fun-loving, happy young woman? She had a hard, tight-lipped quality that made her look older than her forty-five years. Had Joel really been such a nice guy? He sounded more like a small-time hoodlum to me. I was becoming increasingly irritated with Rosalyn. She wasn't an "innocent bystander" in this embattled marriage, I thought. She was intelligent. Why hadn't she been able to see where her life was heading?

Just by chance, an in-service training workshop on compulsive gambling was offered at my agency. I attended in hope of finding new understanding so that I could be more helpful to Rosalyn.

That workshop turned out to be a turning point for not only my work with Rosalyn but also my career. It was the catalyst that brought together my work in the addiction field, my personal experiences with gamblers of all types, and my interests as a psychotherapist.

I learned that a problem gambler's desire to gamble is so intense that it is difficult for him to make the choice to stop, that compulsive gambling is a progressive, addictive illness as severe as any other addiction, and that Rosalyn was as much a victim of this disease as was her husband. I learned how an addiction to gambling can change the personality of the gambler and any person involved with the gambler. I realized then that I had really failed Rosalyn by not fully understanding the enormous emotional toll that living with a compulsive gambler had taken on her life, her dreams, and her hopes.

After that workshop I was able to understand Rosalyn's situation more fully, give her hope, and help her restructure her own life despite living with a severely depressed and almost nonfunctioning husband. She stayed with Joel for several years, and in time she began to recover from the pain caused by the gambling. Rosalyn also healed her relationship with her daughter, who went on to achieve her own recovery.

Since then I have worked with hundreds of gamblers and their families. Each one has a different story, a different experience, a different outcome. But all of them share some issues, and most of them say, in their own words, that they feel as if they lived behind the 8-ball. They saw no chance of becoming free of the problems that gambling caused. With time, they saw how they could reorder their lives and move on.

As program director of the compulsive gambling program for

my agency, I run many workshops on the subject and give talks to professionals and the general public. I keep discovering people who are either living with the impact of gambling or still experiencing its aftermath. It was at one of these meetings that I met Mary-Ellen Siegel, a social worker on the faculty of the Mount Sinai School of Medicine in New York City. She told me about her psychotherapy practice and of her interest in the subject, and that she had written a number of books and had often thought about writing a book for families of people who gamble too much. This book grew out of our professional and personal relationship.

If Rosalyn had read this book, she would have realized early that Joel's gambling was out of control, that she wasn't crazy or inadequate—the situation was. She wouldn't have felt so isolated and would have sought help sooner. She also would have understood the dynamics of her daughter's problems, and she would have prepared herself for eventual independence: socially, emotionally, and financially.

MARY-ELLEN'S STORY

Life is a gamble. I know that. You know that.

Sometimes we have to take a chance.

But I never liked to take a chance. At least not with money. It took me years to believe that my money was safe in a money market. I wanted it in the bank so I would have a bankbook that I could hide someplace and always know how much I had, and I wanted to know no one could ever touch it but me.

I had another quirk. I never thought adults should play, unless they were playing with children. I spent hours with my kids: sitting on the floor building with blocks, helping them bathe and dress their dolls, riding bikes, dodging the waves in the ocean, playing checkers and board games, and often just sitting in the park or around the pool watching them.

But if I just sat and read a novel, went swimming myself, played tennis, relaxed outdoors on a beautiful day while they were in school, or did anything that had no *real* purpose I was overwhelmed with anxiety and guilt. I didn't know why.

But I do now. It was related to my feelings on those days when I returned from elementary school and my mother would be play-

ing mah-jongg or cards with some ladies who were so intent on
their games they barely looked up to say hello to me.

I remembered driving cross-country with my parents right
after World War II. When we got to Nevada, my mother and I
discovered slot machines at the gas station. My father stood by
tolerantly and rather bemusedly while Mom and I tried our luck.
When I didn't win, I quickly lost interest. But Mother was fasci-
nated and was reluctant to give up.

My mother, who died of cancer at the age of seventy-four, was
more than *just* a social gambler. Gambling was a part of her
identity, but it is only recently that I have recognized or acknowledged it. She was always there when we needed her, and was able
to put aside any cardplaying plans if my sister or I asked her to
baby-sit or if anyone else in the family needed her. However,
wagering and being in action was such a vital part of her life that
she missed it if she was away from it for too long. Knowing this
doesn't diminish the love I had for her, or how much I miss her
today. I wish we had once discussed gambling, and how I felt
about it. I feel she is at my shoulder today, encouraging me to
write this book and wishing me well with it.

Before I was twenty, I married a charming, warm, intelligent
young man who had many talents: He could have been a physician
like his father, a fine writer, or found success as a stand-up come-
dian. But he chose business, and that was just fine with me. He
loved to play cards and watch sports on television. It seemed to
me he was mesmerized by both the games and the outcome. He
loved his evenings out with the "boys," playing poker. I felt very
left out and I was sure that if I was prettier, smarter, better
educated, and more fun-loving he would prefer the children's and
my company to his cardplaying friends and television viewing. In
typical codependent style, I used to nag and complain and I made
many scenes but I never told anyone, even my best friends or
sister how I felt.

For many years we belonged to a summer beach club much like
the one my parents joined when I was a child. The pool and tennis
courts were seldom crowded and there was plenty of room to
stretch out on the beach because most of the adults were sitting
under umbrellas (or sometimes in the air-conditioned card rooms)
playing cards. Everyone, even the youngest children, knew that
you didn't go over to a certain section of the cardplaying area,

where the cardplayers looked so intense, as if nothing would divert their attention from the cards.

Many of those cardplayers started early in the morning, continuing until the pool area closed at six o'clock, never stopping long enough to watch their children swim.

I hated the whole scene, but it never occurred to me to tell anyone or protest. I would alternate between acting like a martyr, somehow getting satisfaction in the virtue of being such a "good" (albeit smothering) mother, and like a noisy shrew. Later I would feel ungrateful and unreasonable. Didn't I have everything I wanted? A nice home, three terrific kids, a lovely place to swim, and a husband who provided well for us all.

Yet somehow I felt as if I were living on a ledge and that any day my whole precious world would topple. No matter how much I had, I always felt as if the children and I were "second place" to the cardplaying and the sports scores.

Around that time I had returned to college and was majoring in sociology. I came across material on the sociological aspects of gambling and began to explore the topic more fully for a term paper. The more I read, the more I became convinced that my husband was a problem gambler. From what I was learning, I felt that he might remain a problem gambler, stop gambling, or progress to becoming a compulsive gambler. I chose not to wait and find out, and, by the time I had finished graduate school and become a social worker, we separated.

In the mid-1980s, happily remarried, and with children grown and settled in their careers, I thought I had put memories of the gambling environment all behind me.

Then one rainy day while on vacation my husband and I saw the movie *The Flamingo Kid*. It's the story of a working-class boy who gets a job at a beach club similar to the one where I had belonged. There's a scene in which a cardplayer shoos a kid away. It's a small scene, probably not noticed by most people. But it shook me up, piercing my defenses and forcing me to face my feelings about my experiences.

I came out of the theater in a daze. "That's a terrible movie," I said. My husband and the people we were with looked at me as if I were a little crazy. It's a good movie, they insisted.

And then I began to sob. "Those cardplaying scenes could have come right out of my life. That's what I let happen to me. And that's what I did to my kids. Didn't I see what was going on? Why didn't I?"

As I calmed down, I realized that although I was familiar with all the problems of gambling and knew how to help people cope with a gambler in their life, I clearly had *not* recovered from my experiences.

Later, sitting in a local coffee shop, waiting for the rain to stop, one of our friends suggested, "That should be the subject for your next book. Write a guide for people who are involved with gamblers. Tell them how to spot the problem early on, what can happen, and teach them how to get on with their lives."

"You mean the way I did?" I asked.

"Precisely," he said.

"But I'm still dealing with the impact of gambling on my life— or that movie wouldn't have gotten to me the way it did."

"Listen," said this wise man, "you're a therapist. If you can't figure out how to achieve 'recovery,' find an expert on gambling problems—someone who has worked with both gamblers and their families, and coauthor the book." With a wink, he added, "You'll get a little therapy on the side, and I bet writing the book will help you achieve all the recovery you need."

Luck was on my side. A few months later I met Linda Berman. And our collaboration began. Before we ever put a word on paper we talked. And talked. She shared many of the experiences of the gamblers and their families she had helped, and she helped jog my memory of all the gamblers and the families I had known.

The more we talked, the more I realized I had grown up thinking everyone gambles, and only *much* later did I notice that some people gamble too much. And I understood that recovery can be a very long process, and that I was *still* recovering from loving people who gambled too much.

As I read everything that has been written about gambling problems, and as we talked with researchers and listened to members of Gamblers Anonymous and Gam-Anon (the group for those closely involved with the gambler), the more we recognized the need for a step-by-step guide for families, friends, and others associated with someone who gambles too much.

This book is a true collaboration, reflecting Linda Berman's wide professional experience and expertise and my personal experience as well as professional perspective.

If you are even just a little bit worried about someone's gambling or if you care about someone or work with someone who is gambling too much, this book will tell you everything you need to know.

This book is about personal growth and recovery, but it's *much* more. Because gambling problems are so often unrecognized, even by those living with the gambler, we first help you identify the problem and look for the subtle signs that gambling is getting out of hand. Then we focus on the emotional, financial, and legal consequences of gambling—both to the gambler and to you. Next, we explain the essential techniques needed to survive *in* or *out* of your relationship with the gambler. It doesn't matter whether the gambler is your spouse, close friend, sibling, parent, child, or grandchild. You need all the help you can get. And you will get it in these pages. The last section of the book is devoted to recovery, the gambler's and yours.

You'll learn to not blame yourself for having gotten involved with a gambler, or for letting things escalate. You will learn how to reconstruct your life financially, legally, and emotionally, even if the gambler continues to gamble. And you may—as we have often seen—discover that the gambler in your life will seek help when you change.

This book and the steps we outline have worked for the many people whom Linda has helped. And, after almost twenty years, it has allowed me to walk into a place where people are gambling without my eyes filling up or getting a lump in my throat. And I can watch my grandchildren play games of chance without getting knots in my stomach.

I wish Lisa could have had this book. Recently I ran into her. I hadn't seen her since 1969, my last summer at the beach club. I remembered that her husband, Hank, was one of the big "players" at the club. He used to go on junkets to Las Vegas (that was before Atlantic City had gambling) and owned a large retail carpet and floor-covering chain. They lived in a large, beautiful house with a swimming pool in an expensive New York suburb. When I told Lisa about my current activities she told me about her life. She remained married to Hank until two years ago when he was killed after crashing his car into an embankment. And then she discovered that, unknown to her, he had remortgaged the house and had no life insurance and more personal and business debts than she ever thought possible, including several to Atlantic City casinos. The business was sold to meet some of the debts, the house was repossessed by the bank, and only the "innocent spouse" law kept her from going to jail for tax evasion. She's living with her sister and brother-in-law now and working as a part-time salesperson in the posh store where she used to shop.

She said, "I would have bailed out long ago, but there was no parachute. I'm not sure whether I couldn't find it, was afraid to look, or just couldn't figure out how to open it."

We promise you that after you read this book you will know where your parachute is, have the courage to use it, and know how to fly freely, even if you don't want to bail out.

Lisa's story could have been mine. Don't let it be yours.

PART ONE

KNOWING THE SCORE

Recognizing Gambling in Your Life

CHAPTER 1

Inside Track

Understanding the Gambler

Scott, a successful owner of a large suburban photographic supply store, and his wife, Grace, who sells insurance, have three married children who live nearby. They belong to a country club and have always had a wide circle of personal and business friends. Scott served on the school board when his children were younger, and Grace was president of the PTA. They have one major interest outside of work. Every two months they go to the Caribbean or Las Vegas for four days and nights of nonstop gambling. Both of them say it gives them a needed rest from their pressured everyday lives. But in the last three years they have lost all their savings and deferred needed repairs on their house. Lately they socialize less with friends and family, for they are working longer hours to allow them the time to get away on their little "vacations," and it is hard for them to get their mind off their financial situation. They both have lost control over their gambling.

Why would anyone like Scott and Grace gamble more than they can afford to lose? Why would some people spend so much time gambling, or planning to gamble that both family and work responsibilities would be neglected? Why would people invest so much emotional energy into gambling that there would be little left over for social, family, or work activities? And although this has not yet happened to Scott and Grace, why in the world would anyone allow gambling to threaten or destroy their relationships with everyone: family, friends, and coworkers?

Why indeed?

GAMBLERS ARE PUZZLING CONTRADICTIONS

Such gamblers aren't out of their minds, but they *do* suffer from a disorder, and they view the world differently than the rest of us. It's not easy to get the inside track on what goes on in the mind of these gamblers, for they are a puzzle to themselves and others.

As one accountant who was arrested for embezzling, the money being needed to pay gambling debts, explained, "I certainly understand the laws of probability, and I intellectually knew I was unlikely to win the lottery, yet I continued to spend five hundred dollars a week on tickets. Somehow, I felt that eventually I would have to win."

DIFFERENT KINDS OF GAMBLERS

People gamble for many reasons: enjoyment, excitement, making money, hoping to get something for nothing. Like alcohol or drugs, gambling can temporarily change a person's mood. It can heighten excitement to the point of euphoria. It has the potential to alleviate anxiety and depression, permitting people to remain out of touch with feelings that they consciously or unconsciously perceive as dangerous. Gambling can raise some people's self-esteem and give them a sense of identity. Those who begin as social or recreational gamblers are at risk of becoming problem or compulsive gamblers if they experience the gambling as a mood-changing "drug" *and* have an extraordinary need to change their mood. Anyone who is already abusing alcohol or drugs or is in recovery is also at risk.

There are three types of gamblers.

• *The social or recreational gambler* is a person who gambles for a predetermined amount of time and with a fixed amount of money and is able to restrict gambling at any time. Social gamblers use their winnings to buy something for themselves or others or save the money.

• *The problem gambler* is a person who invests considerable time and emotional energy in gambling or planning to do so. The stakes may be higher than he or she can afford, and often the gambling causes social, family, or work problems. Problem gamblers may get carried away, unaware of their spiraling losses, and they may become compulsive gamblers. Some are able to stop or cut down on their gambling if circumstances warrant it. Winnings are often used for more gambling.

• *The compulsive (addictive or pathological) gambler* is a person who suffers from a chronic and progressive psychological disease that is often unrecognized because of its hidden nature. The urge to gamble is triggered by an impulse (an irresistible craving) and the accompanying compulsivity and mental preoccupation are similar to those of other addictions, such as abuse of alcohol and drugs. As in all addictions, tolerance develops, and higher or more frequent bets are required to obtain the same mood state as before. As the addiction progresses, the urge to gamble intensifies, making it more difficult to resist. Eventually, gambling interferes with functioning in almost every aspect of life, yet the activity continues. When gambling is unavailable or attempts are made to cut down, some gamblers may suffer the characteristic symptoms of withdrawal: cravings, anxiety attacks, depression, or extreme restlessness. Compulsive gamblers usually reserve winnings for more gambling.

GAMBLERS' CHARACTERISTICS

Although the ratio of male to female compulsive gamblers is five to one, the gap is closing. Women are increasingly encouraged to participate in risk-taking activities like gambling. Because of changing values and life-styles, women of all ages now have the time, money, and access to legal and illegal gambling. Women turn to gambling for the same reasons as men: to alter their moods, especially if they have suffered a loss or major blow to self-esteem.

People who gamble too much begin at all ages. Women tend to start gambling as adults; most male compulsive gamblers discover gambling as youngsters and never stop, although a few don't take it up until they are seduced by lottery advertisements or their senior center charters a bus to a casino. Like alcoholics and drug addicts, compulsive gamblers will tell you that their first experience left them with a special intoxication that they immediately recognized. They then sought to return to this artificial paradise. Many gamblers can graphically describe their first wager, or relive, in the telling, their first big win, like Tom D., a recovering compulsive gambler.

I'll never forget that first time I went to the track. I was only
fourteen but looked older. I went with my friend Jack and his older
brother. I had $10 to play with and on impulse bet the daily double.
I'll never forget it. I bet $2 on Lucky Belle and Valentine Beau, both
long shots. The double paid off $268. By the ninth race I had won a
couple of other races but overall I had given back about $140. No bet
has ever been as exciting as that double even though I have won
thousands. And lost much, much more.

Gamblers come from all levels of society. Although personality
types vary, gamblers share certain character traits and emotional
vulnerabilities that make them susceptible to addictive activities
and taking mood-altering drugs. Most have chronic low self-
esteem, underlying depression, and difficulty in coping with their
own and others' feelings. Often gamblers feel defeated in life
(despite outward successes) and have felt different from early
childhood; as a result, they become alienated from others. They
tend to believe that money causes and is the solution to all of their
problems.

Excessive gambling is often associated with the kinds of personalities popularized and romanticized in literature and the
movies. Indeed, some gamblers fit the stereotype of the riverboat
gambler or of a fast-talking Damon Runyon character. Often they
are extremely competitive, independent, and aggressive in every
area of their lives, but their bravado actually belies their insecurities and vulnerabilities. They seem to thrive on risk and do
most things, especially gambling, in excess.

Paradoxically many gamblers are shy, unassuming, reserved,
subdued, and conservative (even spartan) in their dress and life-
style, fitting Hollywood's image of an uptight bank officer or
librarian. They may be hard workers, have a regular routine (even
to the point of rigidity), and be pragmatic in many aspects of their
lives. Some are people you would hardly notice—introverted
loners. Although they don't seem to be people who are likely to
gamble too much, they are "acting out" their repressed and
unconscious feelings through gambling.

All of these gamblers—those who fit and those who defy the
stereotypes—are quite fearful, especially of the unknown or of
uncertainty. Gambling offers them an opportunity to symbolically
overcome these fears.

You will understand the gambler better if you picture the small child who tells you that scary monsters (representing anxieties about other things or people) live under his bed or come in the window, yet plays with the latest monster toys. The youngster finds that "flirting with danger" helps him master normal fears. But an adult who continuously flirts with Lady Luck to deal with the monsters in his life (without addressing those monsters directly) creates new problems instead of mastering the old ones.

Many gamblers, even the shy, retiring ones, are often appealing and friendly and may be willing to lend a sympathetic ear. The facade of sophistication, bravado, or warm charm (especially that of the compulsive gambler) is misleading, for it hides their immaturity and self-absorption. You may have known the gambler for some time before you became aware of the traits that are at the core of his or her character, but once you do, you will begin to understand why he or she gambles. These traits result from being raised in an environment that hindered emotional growth. Regardless of economic situations, gamblers as children were emotionally deprived, neglected, or traumatized in some way, *or* they were so indulged or overprotected that they never learned to cope with or properly tolerate frustration, anger, stress, or disappointments.

While we are all self-absorbed to some extent, gamblers are even more narcissistic. Although it is easy to become angry and frustrated with them, we need to recognize that their narcissism is a way of coping with anger, fear, and the great hurt they experienced early in childhood.

Gamblers have some (but usually not all) of the following narcissistic characteristics:

• *Grandiosity.* Grandiose people may behave as if they are "special" or they may secretly believe it or fantasize about it. They expect and "need" to be recognized that way. The gambling industry recognizes this, and that is why casinos offer perks such as complimentary rooms or meals, limos, and even helicopters for the "high rollers."

They also have a sense of self-importance that leads them to exaggerate or embellish their achievements and/or abilities. This helps to explain why gamblers love to boast about winnings and play down losses. At the same time, they sometimes set unrealistically high standards for themselves. Their grandiosity, which may offend people, should be recognized as a way to counteract their feelings of unworthiness and fear of rejection.

• *Exploitative tendencies.* Narcissists tend to "use" people to meet their own ends and goals. They may try to befriend someone who is prominent or choose as a mate someone who is extremely attractive, all in an attempt to bolster their own faltering self-image.

• *Poor reaction to criticism.* They eagerly seek approval and react poorly to criticism, sometimes with outward rage or indifference, dismissing it as erroneous or inappropriate. Inwardly they tend to feel ashamed, hurt, and humiliated. This helps to explain why gamblers become so enraged when confronted about their excessive gambling. Many will avoid all confrontations to escape dealing with these uncomfortable feelings.

• *Sense of entitlement.* Their sense of entitlement is startling. They feel that they should get special treatment from everyone, acquaintances and the boss alike, and display anger or hurt when they don't. They are often disappointed that life hasn't dealt them a better hand. Gamblers have a long list of things to which they feel entitled, ranging from time to gamble (even at the expense of family or work) to bailouts.

• *Recurrent fantasies of unlimited success.* They might be preoccupied with fantasies of unlimited success, often as a substitute for the hard work necessary for achievement. If success does occur (*even* as a result of hard work), it is taken for granted, and so it doesn't *really* offset their basic insecurities. Success pales compared to both the fantasies and reality of wagering and winning.

• *Chronic feelings of envy.* Gamblers are envious of those who have achieved or "lucked into" more than they have. These chronic feelings result from feelings of inadequacy; no matter what they have or what they have accomplished, it is never enough.

• *Lacking in empathy.* They have difficulty recognizing and experiencing how others feel (as well as recognizing their *own* feelings), although an empathetic manner may conceal this.

• *Craving attention and admiration.* Their constant craving for attention and admiration may manifest itself in many ways. They may seem exceedingly vain; be exhibitionist; have a flashy demeanor, clothes, or possessions; be big tippers; or behave generously. Some are "people pleasers" and seek approval by offering unlimited favors or doing good deeds.

• *Feelings of uniqueness.* Often they believe that their problems are unique—perhaps even extraordinary and intriguing—so that they can only be understood by exceptional people. Sadly, compulsive gamblers report that they hadn't sought help for their gambling problems because they thought no one would ever understand them.

• *"All or nothing" tendencies.* Many such individuals oscillate between extreme overidealization and devaluation of others, seeing people as being all good or all bad. They may see someone, or themselves, as being either a "winner" or a "loser," seldom anything in-between. And yet, their rationalizations prevent them from seeing their own contradictory messages and behavior.

Passive aggressiveness is another character trait that is common to gamblers. Like narcissism, this trait is frequently misunderstood by those involved with the gambler. Passive-aggressive people, like narcissists, experienced great hurts in childhood and are frightened of their own anger and self-assertiveness. They resist many normal demands made on them, often without directly saying so. Instead they indirectly manage to get out of what they have been asked or are expected to do by procrastinating; forgetting; being sullen, irritable, incompetent, or argumentative; or criticizing the task. This behavior is a means of coping with their fears of domination, rejection, dependency, or with other conflicts.

Although you may understand and feel sympathetic toward people with these traits, you will find it difficult to form a truly mature relationship with them. Gamblers, especially compulsive gamblers, are so fearful of their own vulnerability and dependency that the one risk they seldom take is getting too close to anyone, even a spouse.

Other gamblers suffer from an antisocial personality disorder and have little or no regard for others or for the rules of society. They have no regrets about their transgressions unless they have to face personal consequences. They seem to have no conscience, and are often criminals.

Many confuse these criminal types with gamblers who, desperate to stay in action, turn to illegal activities for funds but feel guilt and remorse about their actions. Rather than face their guilt, they often use elaborate rationalizations to explain their wrongdoing to themselves and others. They anticipate returning the money when they "hit it big." When they disappoint someone to whom they should be emotionally or otherwise available, they sincerely believe they will make up for it later.

THE GAMBLER AS THE GREAT ESCAPE ARTIST

Problem and compulsive gamblers are especially threatened by situations that arouse their underlying feelings of powerlessness, inferiority, helplessness, or dependency, so they do whatever they can to avoid these feelings. Gambling is one way they cope with their discomfort, but when gambling losses cause *more* discomfort, they become skilled escape artists with an amazing ability to deceive themselves as well as everyone else.

These deceptions usually take the form of lies of omission or commission. The lies may be believable, so many times you're frustrated because you just don't know whether the gambler is telling the truth. Other times the lies may defy all credibility. If you challenge gamblers, they will persist in their lies, seldom backing down. They can be so convincing that you begin to think *you're* crazy. That's what we call "gaslighting." In the movie *Gaslight* a husband carefully and methodically instills doubt in his wife's perception of reality.

Why do gamblers lie?

- To keep people from knowing they are gambling too much
- To avoid confrontation, rejection, or criticism
- To avoid responsibilities
- To avoid doing anything they don't want to do
- To maintain a facade
- To manipulate others
- To enjoy thinking they are "putting one over" on someone
- To keep people (including family or close friends) at a distance
- To satisfy the need to regularly and repeatedly lie, which has become a habit

Gamblers also lie because they so desperately need to feel full of self-worth, which they interpret as Big, Important, and Powerful. By lying, they hope to get others to "join in" their pretenses. Many compulsive gamblers become pathological liars who have a compulsive need to regularly and repeatedly lie. This trait is probably one of the most infuriating and stressful for those close to a compulsive gambler to deal with.

These escape artists rely on illusions to make them feel safe and protected. This illusion system leads them to believe that they will win (sooner or later!) and that no matter what happens, everything will work out for them. When gamblers *win*, the illusion is confirmed and strengthened. When they *lose* and problems mount, they maintain the illusions by denying, minimizing, and rejecting pieces of reality. For example, when they lose a lot, they may stop keeping track of losses, so they can dismiss the loss and not have to think about the inevitable consequences. If the losses cannot be denied, they will find a way to rationalize them as insignificant. When even *this* denial is impossible, to avoid giving up their illusions they will convince themselves that the losses will be magically restored.

Magical thinking is an important part of the inner world of the gambler. It is left over from earliest childhood when there is little understanding of cause and effect. As the child comes to understand reality, he relies less on his magical notions of how things and people really are. Of course, when his objective perception of reality causes too much discomfort, magical thoughts can be quite comforting. Gamblers, however, rely too much on magical solutions because the real world makes them feel so impotent.

With a burning desire to feel invincible and powerful, gamblers test fate and challenge Lady Luck. Through gambling they set out to reassure themselves and to prove to others that they are omnipotent. These feelings and fantasies are mainly unconscious and are a defense against the terror of feeling helpless and vulnerable. A win reinforces gamblers' omnipotent feelings. A loss is a blow to the pride they feel regarding their gambling skills and is a significant threat to their illusion of omnipotence. The omnipotence that keeps them feeling safe is also accompanied by awesome responsibility, which leads to excessive guilt and fear.

Like magical thinking, omnipotence is a remnant of early emotional life when children believe that their thoughts, actions, or wishes can influence and control the universe.

Omnipotence can be seen in the behavior of Mimi. Mimi's mother was in the habit of putting her toddler in pajamas and robe after her bath at about six o'clock every evening, just before Mimi's daddy came home. Mimi began to associate her robe with Daddy's arrival, and sometimes she would toddle over to get the robe because she thought wearing it would bring Daddy home. Imagine her panic when the robe was still in the washing machine one evening and she couldn't wear it. She thought that Daddy wouldn't come home. Mimi believed that Daddy would come back only if she were wearing her robe.

As you can see, this omnipotent feeling, which was once comforting, can also become terrifying.

Regardless of their intellectual development, gamblers are emotionally stuck at that early part of emotional development and continue to rely on magical solutions. This unrealistic view of life keeps them in action long after the social gambler stops betting.

HOW DOES GAMBLING BEHAVIOR GET STARTED?

Culture can have a major impact on attitudes toward gambling. Gambling may be associated with religious holidays, church or synagogue fund-raisers, family occasions, or the way in which adults socialized with friends and neighbors. Some people may begin gambling because some significant member of their family or neighborhood gambled.

Often gamblers remember "special" experiences during childhood in which gambling played a part. Others may have "happened" into a gambling situation and just felt as if they "belonged." It may provide them with a feeling of excitement and of being alive in a way that nothing else has done before.

In families where money is an important means of achieving status, having security, solving problems, or showing love, children grow up with a sense that money is equated with self-esteem, power, prestige, control, a solution to all problems, or love. Many times parents who have "taught" this to children are also depressed and emotionally unavailable, increasing the possibility that the children will grow up to become gamblers. Children who have grown up in an atmosphere where they haven't learned to defer gratification will find gambling especially attractive because of its promise of instant reward.

Thus, some people are at risk of becoming gamblers long before they pick up a card or enter a casino, racetrack, or bingo parlor.

GAMBLING AS AN ADDICTION

At one time people who lost all control over their gambling were seen as being morally weak and *unwilling* rather than *unable* to stop. Now these people are recognized by the mental health profession as having an addictive disease; their attraction to gambling is so great that the urge to continue to gamble is all-consuming.

"Nick the Greek" (also called the "King of Gamblers") understood this attraction to action. In 1928, he reputedly lost the largest stud poker pot up to that time to racketeer Arnold Rothstein. Nick is supposed to have said, "The next best thing to gambling and winning is gambling and losing."

Like other addictions, gambling addiction takes on a life of its own. From the initial attraction to the discovery that the substance or activity can provide an escape from unpleasant feelings or situations, a psychological dependency commences and escape is sought whenever the person feels "uncomfortable." Tolerance for discomfort disappears and before too long the addictive pattern is established. The addiction becomes the person's best friend and confidante, and soon healthy and normal relationships with people and other activities become less important. Each gambler has his or her own addictive cycle. Some gamble daily, others weekly, and still others go on occasional "binges." To be considered an addictive or compulsive gambler a person needs (1) to demonstrate tolerance that leads him to gamble more to gain the same desired effect on his mood, (2) to be emotionally dependent on gambling, (3) to experience discomfort if he stops gambling, and (4) to have jeopardized family, career, or social life by gambling.

Because of the chronic and progressive nature of addiction, the stresses from the consequences of gambling are piled on top of the internal anxieties that propelled the person to escape into the world of gambling. The only way to erase the pain the gambler now feels is either to try to cut down or to escape into *more* gambling. The gambler may make great efforts to stop—he even succeeds for a time—but because the underlying causes of the addiction are not addressed, the gambler returns to the action and continues to gamble with even greater intensity. Alcohol or drugs may be substituted or added to this arsenal of escape weapons.

The cycle continues as the addiction feeds on itself. The craving increases and so more time, money, and emotions are invested into gambling. Eventually the addiction leads to spiritual erosion. Principles, values, and morality are abandoned. It is not unusual for a wife to say, "He's no longer the man I married," or for a parent to say, "She no longer seems like the daughter I raised."

The late Robert Custer, M.D., a psychiatrist who is the acknowledged modern pioneer in the diagnosis and treatment of gambling disorders, described the addiction in three phrases: the Winning Phase, the Losing Phase, and the Desperation Phase.

These phases are not carved in stone because someone may win, lose, win again and even be ahead, or lose again and be behind for many years. The gambler may even have periods of abstinence before reaching the desperation phase in which he is mentally, emotionally, and financially exhausted. On the verge of losing his family and career and perhaps facing homelessness or jail, he continues to believe that if *only* he had enough money all his problems would be solved. At one time it was thought that gamblers, like alcoholics and drug addicts, could only be "helped" when they became desperate and hit bottom. Now it is recognized that friends, family, or colleagues can bring the bottom up by intervening long before the desperation phase and his own, family, or career disasters occur. (In part 4 we discuss interventions.)

THEORIES ABOUT GAMBLING

Gambling is a risk-taking activity that helps meet our normal desire for a variety of experiences. Unfortunately *some* people get hooked. Fyodr Dostoyevsky, himself a compulsive gambler, knew this. In 1866, he wrote in *The Gambler*:

> I am sure vanity was half responsible for this; I wanted to astonish the spectators by taking senseless chances and—a strange sensa-

tion—I clearly remember that even without any promptings of vanity I really was suddenly overcome by a terrible craving for risk. . . .

In one of his letters he confesses, "The main point is the game itself. On my oath, it is not greed for money, despite the fact that I need money badly."

Dostoyevsky's wife understood omnipotence and magical thinking. In 1877, she wrote in her diary:

Fedja took eighty gulden, gambled and lost. He took the same sum once more and lost. . . . He fetched the last forty gulden and promised me *unconditionally* that he would bring home my earrings and my ring which he had pawned for 170 francs. He said that *in a tone of complete conviction, as if his winning or not winning depended on him alone.* Of course that conviction did not help him; he lost the last forty gulden too. [Emphasis in original.]

Freud viewed gambling as a form of self-punishment. He described Dostoyevsky as follows:

He never rested until he had lost everything. For him gambling was a matter of self-punishment. . . . When his sense of guilt was satisfied by the punishments he had inflicted on himself, the inhibition upon his work became less severe and he allowed himself to take a few steps along the road to success.

In 1957, Edmund Bergler, M.D., a psychiatrist renowned for his work with gamblers, wrote *The Psychology of Gambling*, which became the standard work on the subject. Bergler believed that the gambler wants to lose to free himself from unconscious guilt. Most recently, experts have disavowed this "unconscious wish to lose" theory as the *chief* cause of gambling. Sirgay Sanger, M.D., assistant clinical professor of psychiatry at the College of Physicians and Surgeons of Columbia University in New York City and president of the National Council on Problem Gambling, states:

The impulse to gamble has been attributed to several causes: the death instinct; a need to lose; a wish to repeat a big win; identification with adults the gambler knew as an adolescent; and a desire for

action and excitement. . . . He's defending himself against aliena-
tion, paralysis, boredom, smallness, and weakness. Through his
gambling, the gambler can pretend he's favored by "lady luck,"
specifically chosen, successful, able to beat the system and escape
from feelings of discontent . . .

There are many theories behind the causes of excessive gambling, and many psychological, sociological, and biological factors
make a person at risk for becoming a problem or compulsive
gambler. However, most professionals agree that multiple causes
can be found within each gambler.

• *Psychological theories*. Either "too much" or "too little" parenting and early nurturing, which didn't meet the potential gambler's earliest basic emotional needs, can lead to prolonged
frustration and continued reliance on omnipotence and magical
thinking. Some children grow up in an unpredictable, unstable,
or overcontrolled home in which they have little control over
anything or anyone. They become anxious and impotent and
struggle throughout life to try to feel masterful.

It has also been noted that a disproportionate number of problem or compulsive gamblers have a parent who is or was dependent on alcohol, drugs, or gambling, or who suffers or suffered
from emotional problems, and was therefore unable to furnish
appropriate or adequate care of the gambler as a child. Others
suffered the loss of a parent or other trusted figure by death or
abandonment.

Parents, especially fathers, may be exceedingly critical or demanding, or may reject the gambler during his childhood or
young adulthood. Others are passive and totally ineffectual. Both
types of parents are emotionally absent. As Alan B., a recovering
gambler, said, "My father never showed or told me that he loved
me." All of this makes healthy identification difficult.

A physical or developmental problem that leaves a child embarrassed, self-conscious, or humiliated can result in a diminished
sense of self-esteem.

When a person (particularly a male) feels lonely, empty, rejected, guilty, depressed, or anxious, or suffers from unresolved
mourning, low self-esteem, or sadistic feelings, he may see gambling as a chance to finally "prove himself."

In contrast, some gamblers have an unconscious desire to lose (masochistic feelings) as a response to guilt. Gambling losses may be a means of repeating, in an attempt to master, early unresolved feelings connected to the loss of someone or something of importance.

• *Learning and perception theories.* Gambling is learned behavior. Random reinforcement (winning sometimes, losing sometimes) insures continued interest in gambling. As a result of winning experiences, gamblers develop the expectation that by their skill they can effect these outcomes.

Lottery winners are given much media attention; even raffle winners are highlighted at local drawings. Gambling games emphasize the winners and amounts paid out instead of the losses and the sponsors' profits. This influences our perceptions, so we begin to think we're next to win. Because the gambler needs to believe his skill and specialness is greater than anyone else's, he is more likely to become captive to these perceptions. He mentally relabels losses as "near wins." As one recovered gambler said, "I always saw losing as a sign that I had almost won, and spent hours thinking of how close I came to winning."

Some gamblers have a history of winning in some gambling conditions, but they are psychologically blocked from recognizing that when they play under *other* conditions (stronger players, a different game, or against the house) they no longer have this edge.

Many gamblers apply to their gambling the kind of decision making that is socially approved and successful in school, sports, or careers. The old adage "If at first you don't succeed, try, try again" pays off in many areas of life, but it's a poor choice when gambling.

• *Cultural and sociological theories.* Gambling may be an accepted or even valued behavior in certain cultures, families, and social settings. It can help shape and define identity or it can become the means toward group acceptance. Gambling has its own language, can provide ready-made "friends," ensure a "social" activity, and afford status within the group. Generally these theories explain why someone begins to gamble, and may gamble more than is wise, but do not explain compulsive gambling.

• *Biological theories.* A theory that gamblers have a low level of serotonin (a substance found in the central nervous system) and increased responsiveness of the noradrenergic system, which is associated with poor control of impulses, is consistent with the official psychiatric classification of pathological (compulsive or addictive) gambling as an impulse disorder.

Some researchers believe that many risk takers and gamblers have low levels of a byproduct of the brain chemical norepinephrine, which regulates arousal, thrill, and excitement. This would explain why gambling and other risk-taking behavior is often pounced on by people who feel chronically bored and seek an *extraordinary* amount of excitement (almost like a shot of adrenaline) just to feel the way others feel normally. These are the people who seem to thrive on "living on the edge."

People whose untreated depressions are biologically determined may "medicate" themselves with alcohol, drugs, *or* an activity like gambling in an attempt to relieve their depression. Some experts believe that additional research may reveal that people with other psychological problems triggered by a biochemical disorder may also gamble excessively.

It has also been noted that many people with a history of attention deficit order, sometimes referred to as hyperactivity or high distractibility, turn to gambling when they are older.

Increasingly research shows that some people have a biological temperament that makes them more sensitive and reactive to their environment and requires that they develop stronger coping skills than others. This temperamental vulnerability is often associated with addictive disorders.

• *Addiction theory.* Compulsive gambling is an illness that takes a predictable, progressive course if left untreated. This theory proposes that all addictions are similar and that one substance or activity can be substituted for another. People who abuse alcohol or drugs, or who suffer from some other addiction, or who are in recovery, are considered "at risk" for other addictions. Indeed, many individuals are "cross-addicted" to more than one substance or activity.

• *Antisocial personality disorder.* Gambling may be just one of many symptoms of an antisocial personality disorder. People with this disorder have a history, going back to middle adolescence, of cruelty, truancy, destroying property, lying, and stealing. As adults they have inconsistent work habits, get into unprovoked fights, physically abuse spouses or children, don't live within the laws of society, and lack remorse.

• *Mental illness.* Gambling addiction may coexist with other mental illnesses, often because it offers the individual socialization or a way of defending against the pain of his or her problems.

The above theories are illuminated by the following stories as well as others you will read throughout the book.

Lou Anne had a rotten childhood. Her mother, Sallie, had been brought up in a series of foster homes. As soon as she was finished with high school Sallie had married a man who was a brutal, rigid alcoholic who regularly beat her up. From the time Lou Anne could remember, she felt protective of her mother.

Sometimes Lou Anne would look to her older brother for help, but he was usually out of the house with his friends, and, at eighteen, he joined the marines. One day when Lou Anne was fourteen, a male neighbor (one of her father's friends) raped her. Too scared to tell anyone, Lou Anne suffered continued sexual abuse for more than a year, until the neighbor suddenly moved away.

Later, a brief relationship with her brother's friend home on leave resulted in a pregnancy. Married at nineteen, Lou Anne was divorced shortly after her son was born. A year later she married an older, fatherly man who treated her kindly and loved her little boy.

Life seemed good at last, but Lou Anne's lack of trust and deep feelings of shame prevented her from making friends. When her son was killed by a hit-and-run driver at age sixteen, Lou Anne felt as if her life had lost all meaning. Depressed, she began to drink, which exacerbated her depression, and a doctor who didn't know she drank gave her a prescription for Valium. The combination of alcohol and Valium landed her in a hospital. She detoxed there, tossed out the Valium, and stopped drinking, but she didn't seek comfort from a twelve-step program or from a professional.

Lou Anne went through the motions of healing and got a job

as a bank teller and occasionally chatted with the other tellers but never socialized after work. One day she discovered a video poker machine in the back of her local laundromat. Lou Anne tried it. She became mesmerized, and every day after work or during her lunch hour she would take her bag full of quarters and sit, numbed, in front of the machine. Soon she was in deep debt.

Why was gambling such a lure for Lou Anne? It helped fill her overwhelming sense of emptiness, guilt, and depression. Lou Anne didn't seem to care if she won or lost. Perhaps because she felt such monumental responsibility for everything that had gone wrong in her life she wanted to punish herself. Or maybe she was just replicating, in a symbolic way, earlier losses, unconsciously trying to overcome them.

James is a hard-working man who takes great pride in his family, his life, and his country. His grandfather, the son of a slave, had been a sharecropper. James's father moved to Michigan during World War II to work in a factory. James joined the army, where he gambled a bit with the other guys. After the war, he got a job with the post office, married a young Detroit woman, and they raised a family. Their children eventually moved away and raised families of their own.

James's wife's health was always precarious. She suffered from diabetes and high blood pressure and eventually had a leg amputated. James took early retirement to take care of her. They were socially isolated, and her care became James's entire life. When she had a stroke and died he was grief stricken. His children, who came home for the funeral, urged him to join a local senior center. He did, and began to play cards and enjoy himself. It reminded him a bit of his army days. Many of the people at the center would regularly pool their few dollars to buy lottery tickets, but this "action" soon wasn't enough for James. He began buying more and more tickets himself.

When James took a trip to California to visit his married son, he stopped off at Las Vegas. This was action he had never experienced.

Two years after his wife died, James was in serious financial trouble. The grief he had felt at her death was too difficult for him to face; he needed an escape, and he found one in gambling.

Being involved with a gambler is like living on an emotional roller coaster that keeps on going. At times you feel as if you are crazy. It can also cause bankruptcy, a lifetime of debt, harassment from people who are owed money, threats from loan sharks, visits to jail, loss of friends, shame, humiliation, fear, homelessness, suicide. . . . The list is endless. But there are things you can do to prevent these disasters.

CHAPTER 2

The Tip-offs

Identifying the Problem

According to some observers, gambling has surpassed baseball as America's national pastime. And no wonder. It has gained unprecedented social acceptance through church sanctions and state promotions. Advancements in technology and the ever-present media have brought gambling into almost every neighborhood and home in the country.

Before too long, sophisticated telecommunication systems will enable anyone with access to a telephone to gamble by electronically transferring funds to and from their bank or credit cards.

Currently a $300 billion industry, legal gambling is growing at about 10 percent annually. Gaming revenue in Las Vegas rose 20 percent in the first quarter of 1990 compared with the same period the previous year. The state lotteries are ranked alongside America's largest corporations in terms of gross profits and represent upward of 5 percent of revenues in some state budgets. Illegal gambling is also thriving; it is estimated that four times as much money is wagered illegally as legally. The "numbers" games continue to have a large and loyal following, particularly in the inner cities. Games with traditionally low payouts, such as bingo, are now high-stakes games worth thousands of dollars.

Casino hotels now promote themselves as "family entertainment centers" and have begun providing child care services and elaborate sports facilities. Racetracks have become gambling emporiums by offering simulcasts of other races and coverage of sporting events.

The opportunities to gamble on televised sporting events are also growing rapidly. The three networks and cable systems aired 7,300 hours of sports programming in 1989, almost double the amount of hours in 1980. This averages out to 140 hours a week. Although some of the programming overlaps, new television sets permit the viewer to watch two shows at once—a real bonanza for sports enthusiasts or those addicted to sports gambling. Gambling is now readily available to everyone, rich and poor, young and old, male and female.

If you have picked up this book, it's probably because you have been worried about someone you care about. You suspect that gambling may be at the root of some of the problems that are affecting your life. But you're not sure. And no wonder. Gambling is frequently hidden from everyone, even the immediate family.

The number of people who have an emotional attachment to gambling is growing. They come from all social, economic, and age groups. Sixty-five percent are men. Most started when they were very young, but others don't discover gambling until much later in life.

Sales pitches like "all you need is a dollar and a dream" have lured many people to gamble for the first time, usually by buying a lottery ticket. These new gamblers frequently move on to other forms of legal and illegal gambling. On any day in almost every neighborhood across the country you can find some way to gamble.

The proliferation of state-supported lotteries and easier accessibility to gambling have contributed to an increase in the numbers of gamblers who gamble too much. There are four times as many problem gamblers in 1991 than there were in 1975, and the number continues to grow.

These numbers reflect two new significant categories of gamblers: *teens* and *senior citizens*. Recent studies indicate that approximately 7 million adolescents gamble, with one million experiencing significant problems. Many mature people who have only recently started gambling to excess are losing their Social Security or pension benefits to gambling. Some have even lost their life savings.

Maybe you've noticed that your husband, wife, friend, parent, adolescent, or adult child or coworker gambles, but you're not sure if it's becoming a problem. Everyone who gambles is not addicted, or even at risk of it becoming a problem. Trouble is brewing if someone is investing more *money, time,* or *emotional energy* into gambling than is acceptable within their community or culture. Trouble is already here if the gambling is causing negative consequences to the gambler, family, friends, or others.

What are these consequences? And how do you know whether gambling is merely a social, recreational activity or is a problem?

The problem gambler is someone who spends considerable time and emotional energy in planning to gamble and actually gambling, and plays for stakes that are higher than he or she can afford. Although they are often under stress, they continue gambling, trying to recoup losses. This is called "chasing," a strategy influenced by their inability to emotionally accept losses and their need for action to cope with their feelings.

The compulsive gambler seems unable to stop; he suffers from urges and needs similar to those of other addictions. Compulsive gambling is a progressive and chronic illness, intricately tied to the individual's self-esteem. Gambling raises the spirits and brings excitement to a life that for some reason seems boring and depressing, yet it also dulls the pain and anxiety brought on by losing and/or other concerns. Gambling is a stimulant to some, a sedative to others. Many people find it is both, and so they ride a roller coaster of emotions and experiences. One thing is certain: The compulsive gambler invests an excessive amount of money, time, and emotions in gambling.

Compulsive gambling often goes unrecognized because of its hidden nature. There are no track marks on the arm, no smell of alcohol on the breath, and often both the gambler and his spouse or family are unaware he is hooked. Then one day disastrous consequences in vocational, social, or family life jolt either you or the gambler into an awareness of the severity of the problem.

Susan and Jack L.'s children are grown. Several times a year they drive two hours to the track with some friends. They enjoy dinner in the lounge, then select horses according to past performance, or sometimes just on a hunch. Susan likes to make her decision based on what the jockey is wearing! They bet a predetermined amount and, whether they win or lose, have a good time.

The financial, emotional, and time cost of Susan and Jack's gambling: comparable to any special evening out on the town.

Susan and Jack are *social*, recreational gamblers.

Four women who live in a retirement apartment complex have a regular mah-jongg game, alternating as hostesses. Aside from the mah-jongg, there is some friendly competition about who serves the best salad and dessert.

The financial, emotional, and time cost of the games to each woman: about the same as lunch in a local coffee shop and an afternoon movie.

These women are *social*, recreational gamblers.

Jean and Len K. enjoy a winter vacation in the Caribbean and occasional trips to Las Vegas. They love tennis, golf, and swimming. In the evenings or on rainy days they try their luck in the casino.

The financial, emotional, and time cost of Jean and Len's gambling: about the same as any luxury vacation.

Jean and Len are *social*, recreational gamblers.

Norman R. regularly buys a lottery ticket where he buys his daily newspaper and looks forward to hearing the results announced on local television. He's thrilled when he wins and collects his few dollars, usually using it to buy something special. When he's been "close" to a big win, he chuckles and tells his friends about the near miss, comparing it to the fisherman's tales of the one that got away.

The financial cost of Norman's gambling: same as the cost of attending a football or baseball game. The emotional and time cost: same as a few frames of bowling.

Norman is a *social*, recreational gambler.

If Susan and Jack begin to go the track more often and spend considerable time thinking about it and planning their bets, or allow it to interfere with family, social, or work time, or decide to relocate to be nearer to the track, they may be heading for trouble.

If one of those retired women starts looking for a game that has higher stakes, or gets upset when the clock says it's time to wind down, she may be heading for trouble.

If Jean and Len find they won't consider any vacation that doesn't have gambling, or seek more and more getaways to places that have gambling, or forgo tennis for an extra hour or two in the casino, they may be heading for trouble.

If Norman starts to buy more and more lottery tickets, diverting household or lunch money for this purpose, or always uses his winnings to buy more tickets the next day, he may be heading for trouble.

Most of these people, however, will remain social, recreational gamblers.

Sally P.'s early shift in a cafeteria in her hometown of Kansas City offers her little stimulation, job satisfaction, or salary. Each day she hurries from work to one of the local bingo halls, plays several games, and then rushes back home to defrost a couple of frozen dinners. When her husband settles down in front of the television, she's off again to the bingo hall.

When her daughter's second child was born, Sally took time off from work to go to St. Louis to help her. Almost as soon as she got there she consulted the newspaper to determine if there were any bingo games in the vicinity.

The financial cost of Sally's gambling: debts so large she had borrowed to the limit on her pension fund. The emotional and time cost: so preoccupied with gambling and finding the finances to support it that she is constantly stressed, guilt-ridden, and frightened, with little time or energy left to enjoy her children and grandchildren, home, or life with her husband.

Sally is a *problem* gambler. When she was in St. Louis, her husband found the pension statement that she had carelessly left around. Upon her return he confronted her with her withdrawals. Relieved to have someone intervene, she agreed to stop playing bingo. She kept her word with just a few slips.

*   *   *

Carl D., a stocky, single twenty-nine-year-old man lives in the home where he grew up. A graduate of a local community college, he is now the manager of a small local supermarket that is part of a large chain. Always a sports enthusiast, he gambles on whatever sport is in season. He spends considerable time studying statistics and analyzing teams and calling the local bookmaker, whom he looks up to and considers a friend. Carl hangs out at a local sports bar with some of his drinking and pool-playing buddies, with whom he also bets. They are quick to order drinks for any new women that stop by the bar, but most of the time their eyes are riveted to the big television screen tuned into the sports channel. When they are not watching a game, they are playing pool.

Carl drives an eight-year-old car that probably won't pass its next inspection, but he rationalizes that it doesn't matter since he doesn't really need it anyway because he spends all his spare time (as well as extended lunch hours) playing pool or planning his next sports bet.

The financial cost of Carl's gambling: Carl has borrowed so heavily on his three credit cards that he can no longer use them, is unable to accumulate enough money to move out on his own, fix the old car, or buy a new car. The emotional and time cost: Carl has started to borrow from the guys with whom he plays pool and gambles, has no other friends, and hasn't applied himself to his career. He is beginning to worry about a lot of things: whether he will ever be able to pay his debts, earn more money, or move out on his own. He recognizes that he has no social life away from the bar and that gambling is no longer fun. Concealing gambling and its consequences from his mother is starting to trouble him.

Carl is a *problem* gambler. He may be able to stop gambling altogether, or he may remain a problem gambler, never getting into serious trouble, but never moving on with his life, or he may become a compulsive gambler.

Some gamblers don't *ever* try to stop, even when they recognize the damage their gambling does to themselves and others. Others try to stop unsuccessfully.

Tall, blond, and handsome, Adam T. was on the debating and tennis teams at his suburban high school, and was a member of the school's honor society. Life came easily to him. Despite his successes, he never showed much enthusiasm for anything. His stepfather (whom he called Dad), a stockbroker, and his mother, an interior decorator with a local furniture store, were proud of his talents, pleased that he wasn't a "show-off," and sure that he would be admitted to any college he chose.

In high school he was well known for his accurate sports predictions, and in his junior year he became interested in horse racing. His parents noticed that Adam's school grades were dropping, but they attributed it to extracurricular activities. They were right—up to a point—but what they didn't know was that Adam's major activity was betting heavily with bookmakers to whom he was in debt, and that their son had lost interest not only in school but in most things other than horse racing.

Adam told his parents that his stereo was at the repair shop, and it couldn't be fixed, but in reality he had pawned it to get money to gamble. His parents gave him money for a new one, which he never bought, using the money instead to try to win back some of his losses. When his parents finally confronted him, asking where the money had gone, Adam confessed that he had been gambling. His parents were surprised, but viewed it as a temporary problem and bailed him out by repaying all his loans.

Adam went away to college, and his parents thought that was the end of his gambling until one night when they heard Adam's desperate voice on the phone.

He was in jail. He had been caught breaking into the tennis coach's home. He had stolen all their valuables, not just to pay off large gambling debts but to remain in "action" because he could no longer resist the urge to gamble.

The financial cost of Adam's gambling: large but not insurmountable debts. Time cost: expulsion from college and possible jail sentence. Emotional cost: shame and humiliation, fear that the arrest record may stand in the way of future plans for college or employment.

Adam is a *compulsive* gambler who got caught, but with sufficient motivation (and family support) he can recover.

Stan F. is forty-two, and owns his own large plumbing supply business. He's married and has two children, ages nine and eleven. Stan has played cards since his adolescence, when he often won huge sums of money. When he was twenty-one he won ten thousand dollars in the Irish Sweepstakes. From that day on he was hooked.

For many years Stan has been in a weekly high-stakes poker game, with which he allows nothing to interfere. A few years ago he began going to casinos to play blackjack, and his betting increased by leaps and bounds.

Stan lies habitually. He lies to his wife about everything: how often he gambles, how much he loses, how much he wins, and how much money they have. He tells her that his poker games and trips to Atlantic City are to please his "big customers" who expect that extra attention from him. He lies to his employees who think he's out of the office trying to solicit new business, when in reality he is meeting with loan sharks and other moneylenders, trying to get more money with which to gamble.

His debts to individuals and casinos have become so great that they threaten the solvency of his business, and he is about to remortgage his home. Stan's gambling is totally out of control, but because he cannot imagine a life without gambling and the urge to gamble is so great, he continues. When his losses mount, he begins to "chase" after his money. One day Stan's wife, who had long suspected his gambling was getting out of hand, overhears a threatening phone call from a loan shark. Without any discussion, she informs Stan that she is taking the children to her parents' home, halfway across the country. Stan realizes that because of his gambling he might lose his family as well as everything else.

The financial cost of Stan's gambling: debts that will take many years to repay and the near loss of his business and all assets. Time cost: gambling took him away from his family and his business. Emotional cost: he has lost all trust and respect of family, friends, and employees. His marriage is at risk; he may become estranged from his children. He is frightened that loan sharks may physically harm him. And finally, he has lost all self-respect. Yet he cannot stay away from the action.

Stan is a *compulsive* gambler.

Unfortunately, family members and others may not even know that someone is gambling at all, or gambling too much, until a crisis occurs. At that point, you as well as the gambler may be in the kind of trouble that is hard to reverse.

You may find it difficult to believe that someone you care about has a gambling problem. He or she may not fit the gambling stereotype. The many myths that surround gambling stand in the way of your seeing the truth about someone's gambling.

• *Gamblers have flamboyant, carefree personalities.* That's how they are often portrayed in movies and books. But you can find gamblers of every different personality type. Some *are* flamboyant and carefree, but others are quiet, introverted, and serious-minded. In addition, they come from all walks of life. Every culture, ethnic group, and economic group is represented.

• *Gamblers enjoy risks in all areas of their life.* Actually, many gamblers are conservative in their personal habits and work life. But others (like some nongamblers) are big risk takers.

• *If you don't gamble daily, you're not a problem or compulsive gambler.* Some gamblers think constantly about gambling, and a day doesn't go by without their making some kind of bet. Others go on occasional "binges," then refrain from gambling again for months. For example, someone may go to Atlantic City or Las Vegas for a few days of nonstop gambling, or plan vacations around gambling.

• *You can't be addicted to an activity—only to a drug or alcohol.* An activity such as gambling can be as addictive as drugs or alcohol. Some experts believe it may be even more so. New evidence indicates that gambling changes the mood by affecting the biochemistry of the brain in much the same way as substances that are ingested.

• *All gamblers are thieves and criminals.* Some criminals like to gamble and some gamble too much. But many honest, law-abiding people who become problem or compulsive gamblers may in desperation resort to illegal activities. In the last and desperate stages of the illness, compulsive gamblers will stop at almost nothing to get gambling money.

• *A compulsive gambler will bet on anything.* Compulsive gamblers generally have preferences and identify themselves as cardplayers, sports bettors, casino players, or lottery or bingo players. They may not be tempted by every betting situation.

• *All compulsive gamblers want to lose.* This psychological theory has now been supplemented by new understanding. It has some validity, since many gamblers are dealing with guilt about their aggressive feelings, and that is why they may continue to play until they lose all their winnings. In addition, when compulsive gamblers are losing, they get desperate and begin to gamble foolishly, giving the impression that they want to lose. It should be noted, however, that most compulsive gamblers are addicted to the action, and even though they prefer to win, they would rather lose than be out of the action.

• *Compulsive gamblers are weak-willed; otherwise they would stop.* Like those addicted to drugs and alcohol, people addicted to gambling suffer from an overwhelming illness. It is not lack of character or willpower but the tremendous, unrelenting urge that accompanies the dependency on the action that keeps the gambler from stopping.

• *The gambler knows he has a problem, but just won't admit it or do something about it.* Gamblers, like other addicts, are often in denial and cannot admit even to themselves that they have a problem. Even when confronted with evidence that their gambling is out of control, they still may fail to recognize it. He may be rational in every other aspect of life but be irrational about gambling. Only when the gambler truly "hits bottom" does the reality seep in. The "bottom" differs among people.

There are many tip-offs that gambling is going on and may be getting out of control. By honestly answering the Gamblers Anonymous Questionnaire (see appendix 1) the gambler can learn if his gambling has become a serious problem.

It's not as easy for a family member or person associated with the gambler to know if gambling has become a problem. It's possible that you suspect this person is gambling, but are not certain, or you may know about the gambling but don't realize its extent. For instance, if the gambler lives near enough to a casino to go for a day or evening, you may not even know he has gone there. Many sports bettors hide their betting by appearing to be just sports enthusiasts who like to watch or go to games. Track bettors can sometimes get away from work for a few hours. And it only takes a minute or two to call a bookmaker.

Many gamblers hide all evidence of their gambling. Lottery tickets can be hidden almost anywhere, and stock confirmations or margin calls can be rerouted to a secret post office box. Many people keep their gambling "paraphernalia" (cards, betting tip-sheets, football sheets, even cash set aside for this purpose) in hidden places: the trunk of their car, at work, at a neighbor's home, or any place you are unlikely to look.

They are also adept at keeping a straight "poker face," and take great pride in appearing nonplussed even if they have just won or lost a fortune. You might notice a subtle intensity or mental preoccupation that seems to exclude everything in the background.

Gloria N. is a shy, soft-spoken, reserved thirty-five-year-old woman. She never suspected that her husband, Rick, gambled, or that his gambling was at the root of her problems. Her father was an alcoholic who died of liver disease, and Gloria was comforted by the fact that neither Rick nor anyone else in his family drank. She was content in her marriage to Rick and liked being home with their three young children. She began suffering from severe headaches. Her family physician could find no medical explanation and referred her to a local mental health agency. The agency had a sliding fee scale, but Gloria told her therapist that she preferred not to provide any income information, so she paid the full charge.

One day, after several sessions with her therapist, she blurted out her story.

> I never told you why I didn't give you any information on money. It was because Rick refused to tell me anything. He said to just tell him how much the sessions would cost, and he would give me the money. I know he's successful—he won salesman of the year three years in a row. But he simply wouldn't tell me anything. And it's been like that all along. He's just so damn secretive about anything to do with money. He keeps his checkbook at his office, and has everything to do with his stocks sent there too. He gives me cash each week for the household expenses, you know, food and little things for the kids. Everything else is charged, and he takes care of all the bills. He says I have enough to do to take care of the house and children, and he's right, I guess. I'm really rather glad I don't have to worry about bill paying and all that. But I can't stand all this secrecy, and lately his moodiness is driving me crazy. All evening he

sits and reads things about the stock market, and makes all kinds of notes. Once or twice I woke up at night and found him sitting in the kitchen reading all that stuff. Then sometimes he flies off the handle for no particular reason. Usually it's something to do with one of the kids. But then he got into this terrible argument with his cousin on the phone, and he hung up. And the cousin called back and I could hear them arguing about a loan. Then there was the time my engagement ring disappeared from its special place in my jewelry box. And then it mysteriously reappeared, and when I told him how scared I had been he began to laugh at me and then scream that I must be going crazy. Maybe this sounds insane, but I have the feeling that he took that ring and then brought it back. Oh, my God, maybe I *am* crazy.

A therapist's initial reaction to this might be to assume that Gloria suffers from depression, guilt, and anger about her recently deceased alcoholic father, and that she has so little confidence in herself that she's letting Rick dominate her. The therapist might recommend individual therapy for Gloria to help her resolve her feelings about her father, and marital therapy for Gloria and Rick to bring about a better balance in their relationship.

But Gloria's therapist was familiar with gambling and saw several red flags in Gloria's story. Secrecy about money, Rick's personality changes and arguments with other people, and what sounded like an obsession with the stock market might indicate that Rick was preoccupied with stock market gambling and was headed for serious problems.

As you might imagine, Gloria found it difficult to believe that gambling could be at the root of their problems. But when she learned how to recognize the signs that Rick was gambling too much she began to do something about getting her life together.

WHAT HAPPENS TO YOU?

When you care about someone who gambles too much, you may lose *your* self-respect, friends, and family. You may even discover that some friends blame *you* for the gambler's behavior. You may lose all *your* money, and every tangible thing you own. This may be a gradual process, or you may not have noticed warning signs until a sudden crisis takes you by complete surprise.

Every gambler has a direct impact on the lives of at *least* eight other people, sometimes for many years afterward, even if the gambler has stopped or the relationship has ended. The emotional effects can be as devastating as the financial losses. For anyone who ever loved a gambler, Adelaide's words in "Sue Me" from Frank Loesser's *Guys and Dolls* have a familiar ring.

> *You promise me this, you promise me that*
> *You promise me anything under the sun*
> *Then you give me a kiss and you're grabbing your hat*
> *And you're off to the races again.*
>
> *When I think of the time gone by*
> *And I think of the way I try*
> *I could honestly die.*

Why do people like Adelaide stay in this no-win situation? Perhaps they buy into the gambler's beliefs and dreams.

Or like so many others involved with a gambler, they may feel they can change the gambler *or* make everything turn out all right.

Or maybe they just don't know what to do.

If you are involved with a gambler, you need to recognize the subtle signs that signal there is a problem with gambling, fully understand the potential consequences, and learn how to protect yourself whether or not you remain in the relationship.

Perhaps you are the spouse, close friend, parent, grandparent, sibling, or adult child of a gambler. The relationship may be one you can't or don't wish to sever. The gambler may not be interested in getting help. Still, *you* can achieve your own recovery.

You *must* learn the facts and understand the consequences, even if they are truly frightening. If you are involved with a gambler, it is possible to prevent the consequences, or to survive them, and go on to lead a full and satisfying life.

CHAPTER **3**

Payoffs, Payouts, and Bailouts

You and the Gambler's Money

It is said that money makes the world go round, and indeed it does influence every aspect of our lives. It can symbolize love, power, status, self-worth, freedom, and security, or the lack of these things. We all have conscious and unconscious highly charged feelings, memories, fears, superstitions, and even passions that are connected with money. Some of this goes back to our childhood, to the way our parents related to each other and treated us in regard to money. We also learn about money from our cultures and society: the neighborhood and community in which we were raised, our religion, our politics, and even when we were born. For instance, people who lived through the Great Depression tend to be conservative with money. Their children may subscribe to the same beliefs and customs; or adopt a 1960s disdain for money, or rebel and become "big spenders." This can cause conflicts about money between the generations and among relatives.

When people with very different attitudes toward money come together—in marriage or by close association—there may be friction that spills over into all areas of family life. If spouses' attitudes toward money are similar and they both tend to be extravagant, they may get into financial trouble. If they are both ultraconservative, they may build up a big bank account but never have much fun. In-laws may praise or be critical, also causing antagonism. Children may transgress their parents' beliefs when they are able to handle or earn their own money.

Even the most reasonable of us—those who are neither extravagant nor miserly—sometimes have to juggle income, assets, and expenditures to remain solvent. But the gambler is *always* juggling money, "borrowing from Peter to pay Paul." Without this juggling act, he can't lead any kind of normal life *and* also be in on the gambling action! If the gambler doesn't earn enough or win enough to keep up this juggling act, he has to beg, borrow, or steal it.

The gambler's dilemma becomes *your* dilemma, and too often you are also called upon to juggle money. You may not even know why you feel as if you're always strapped financially, but it is becoming clear to you that money and its role in your life are taking their toll. This pursuit of money and the gambler's juggling act indicates that gambling is becoming or has already become a major problem.

At thirty-three, petite, brown-eyed Sandra looked like a college coed. But she didn't go to college, despite her dream of becoming a schoolteacher. Her husband, Gregory, a bus driver, encouraged her in the dream and agreed that when their children, now seven, ten, and twelve, were older she would go to college and get her degree. In the meantime, she worked as a paraprofessional in her local school. The money wasn't great, but the hours and vacations coincided with her children's and she was learning more and more about teaching.

Sandra and Greg had a budget. His salary was supposed to cover fixed expenses: rent, utilities, food, union dues, his uniforms, and their yearly one-week summer camping vacation at a nearby national park. Sandra's salary was used for clothes for all of them, car expenses, and other extras. Each payday Sandra put aside some of her money in their joint savings account to be used eventually for her college tuition.

One day when Sandra went to make her deposit at the bank, she discovered that Gregory had withdrawn a large amount from the account but had returned it a few days later. She was puzzled but had learned from experience that any questions about money made Gregory furious, so she never mentioned it. Several weeks later she overheard a telephone conversation between Greg and her sister's husband, Jordan. It was clear that Greg had borrowed money from Jordan and was late in returning it. Sandra became more puzzled when Gregory announced one night that the family couldn't afford their usual one-week camping trip. When Sandra asked why not, he began to scream about the "huge" utility bills. "Don't you people ever turn off lights around here?" he thundered.

Sandra hated to disappoint the kids, so she said, "Let's use our savings."

Accustomed to putting her own wishes and dreams on the back burner, she thought, "So I'll get back to college a little later."

It never occurred to Sandra that their shortage of money was due to Gregory's gambling. She knew that he liked to buy lottery tickets, but she never realized how much he was spending each week on them because she never saw them around the house. She also had no way of knowing that a thriving illegal "numbers" business was being conducted at the bus depot where he worked. If she had been alerted to the signs that gambling was becoming a problem, she would have realized that money disappearing and suddenly reappearing in their savings account was a clue, just like Greg's attempt to shift the blame to the family for his being short of money.

Gamblers leave clues, and, when you know them, you can recognize even the most subtle ones. For instance, both the absence and the presence of money can mean gambling is occurring. It can *also* mean other things, such as drug use or illegal activity instead of or in addition to gambling. The following signs of trouble mean that a crisis may be on the horizon.

- A discrepancy between income and assets
- Money or assets disappearing, or suddenly appearing
- Secrecy about money
- Vagueness or double-talk about assets, income, and expenses
- Unexplained bills, debts, or payments

- Loans from legal and illegal sources
- Urgent requests to family and friends for money
- Decline in savings
- Sale of stock (and no reinvestment)
- Reports that equipment and jewelry are being repaired or have been lost or stolen
- Mysterious and angry phone calls and messages

The consequences of gambling may or may not rock the family's financial boat until a crisis occurs. For example, the everyday lifestyle of those with ample income and resources may not be affected for a long time, even if the gambler is wagering large amounts. But a few dollars more "expense" each week or month may make a crucial difference to those earning "just enough," and may be attributed to rising food or utility costs.

For instance, you need to be concerned if a person who has been a high earner for many years and has some investments announces there is no money to pay for a daughter's wedding. If a retired civil servant suddenly is unable to afford his annual visit to children across the country, casinos, bingo games, or lottery tickets may be getting a big share of his fixed income. If a teenage boy with a part-time job is always broke, gambling may be the reason.

Angry discussions and even fights about money are common in most families. One member thinks some expenses are luxuries, another thinks they are necessities. Differences of opinions are natural, and can take much time and effort to reconcile.

But conflicts with gamblers are different. Gamblers misrepresent, deceive, and lie about money—how much and where it came from, and how much and where it went. To keep their betting hidden, gamblers "gaslight" people. They confuse and fault those around them, who soon begin to think *they* are dumb, inadequate, or even crazy. Soon they stop pointing an accusing finger at or even questioning the gambler for fear of having everything turned against them.

Bailing out a gambler becomes second nature to many people. Like Sandra, who took it upon herself to take over her husband's financial responsibility to pay for the family vacation, you may rise to the occasion and begin to solve *all* the gambler's financial problems. If you do this, you are an enabler (unwitting, perhaps). You do without something you wanted, or you borrow money from others, or you get someone else (like your parents) to pay for things.

The following questions may seem unrelated to gambling. That's because the clues to gambling are often subtle. Some gamblers may exhibit a number of these traits, and others only a few. These clues are often unrelated to the severity of the gambling or to how much the gambler is wagering. They will help you realize that you are involved with someone who gambles too much.

1. *Are you puzzled because you're always short of money?*
    If it seems that your income should be covering your expenses but it doesn't, it may mean that some money is being siphoned for gambling.

2. *Does this person sometimes borrow money to pay ordinary monthly bills even though there has been no known change of income or specific increased expenses?*
    A gambler may have increased his bets, be on a "losing streak," or be waiting to collect winnings from another gambler. To meet cash-flow problems, it may be necessary to borrow money.

3. *Has anything of personal or property value mysteriously disappeared?*
    You might "misplace" a piece of jewelry, but if this happens more than once, or if the stereo or lawn mower disappears, think pawnshops. Gamblers need money, and sometimes they need it immediately to pay off debts.

4. *Have you sold anything of personal or property value to pay debts?*
    Gamblers often convince others to sell something so they can pay "legitimate" bills. The reason: the gambler has gambled the money reserved for those bills. When you sell something under these circumstances, you are "bailing out" the gambler.

5. *Is this person secretive about money?*
Some cultures reinforce secrecy about money, even among family members. But gamblers are especially secretive. Some may boast about winnings or carry inordinate amounts of cash with them at all times, but more often they are uncommunicative about money.

6. *Does this person seem to be more reckless about money than other people and not really weigh his chances?*
Although all gamblers aren't reckless with money (except for gambling purposes), many are reckless in *all* financial aspects of their lives. Others are quite the opposite.

7. *Have you accidentally discovered secret loans?*
Gamblers don't want to be "found out," so if they need money to pay off gambling debts or to remain in action, they borrow money secretly from either legitimate sources or illegitimate ones such as loan sharks.

8. *Does this person continue to acquire different credit cards?*
The more credit cards a person has, the more money he can borrow. Having extra credit cards means more legitimate expenses can be charged, freeing up salary and income for gambling.

9. *Has this person ever urgently requested you to cosign a loan?*
What was the loan for? And why was it urgent? When you sign such a loan you may be providing a bailout.

10. *Do you have any reason to question whether this person has filed an accurate or, for that matter, any IRS return?*
Gamblers frequently file false IRS returns, not just to hide winnings but to hide their other income. This avoids using money for taxes that they have "budgeted" for gambling. Some don't file at all.

11. *Has there been a change in the way this person handles money? (Example: bills paid late, paid in part, or not paid at all.)*
When a person needs money for gambling, there isn't always enough to pay bills, so they are paid late, in part, or not at all.

12. *Has this person reordered spending priorities?* (*Example: giving up his car and taking public transportation, not buying needed new clothes, neglecting basic home maintenance.*) Money only goes so far, even for an expert juggler. So gamblers often reorder priorities. They would rather walk a mile than give up a bingo game; wear old clothes than stay home from the track; live with peeling paint than spend money that could be used to buy lottery tickets.

13. *Has this person let health or life insurance lapse?* This is another way to save "gambling money." It also fits the gambler's risk-taking behavior.

14. *Do you have to resort to subterfuge to get money you need from this person?* (*Example: overestimating some expenses, underreporting your own income, stealing from this person.*) You've been locked in a power struggle over money for a long time, and you know from experience how difficult it is to get money you genuinely need. So rather than make a scene (knowing you'll never get the money anyway) it's easier to be clever and get it the only way you can.

15. *Has this person ever been in trouble with the law because of money?* This person may be basically honest, but when money is needed to support a dependency, breaking the law frequently follows.

16. *Does this person sometimes pay bills far in advance for no apparent reason?* The gambler does this as a means of controlling his gambling. Aware that his gambling is getting out of control, he pays bills in advance to help avoid the very real temptation of using that money for betting.

17. *Have you noticed that this person is avoiding certain friends, acquaintances, or family members?* He may owe these people money, so it's best for him to avoid them. Or they may be fellow gamblers who will "spill the beans."

18. *Do you suspect this person took money from you?*
Trust your instincts. This person may take money from you to pay debts or to remain in action.

19. *Does this person use double-talk when you try to discuss spending, income, or assets?*
Gamblers "gaslight" by using double-talk to explain where money came from, where it went, and how much is left. You become totally confused and feel inadequate. Eventually you stop asking.

20. *Has this person dipped into savings, pensions, or other assets, or cut back or stopped contributions?*
To avoid changing their life-style and to keep gambling hidden, many gamblers stop building up their assets and then utilize their savings.

21. *Is this person seeking new ways to earn extra money? Does he already have a second job or work overtime, although there are no known additional expenses and you see no evidence of additional earnings?*
Gamblers usually aren't lazy, and they may work harder than ever to be sure they have money for gambling action.

The following questions relate more directly to a *known* gambler.

22. *Do you often hear this person on the phone buying and selling stock or commodities? Do statements regarding purchases and sales come regularly in the mail?*
Many people are active in the financial markets, but those who constantly buy and sell may be motivated more by the activity than the actual wisdom of careful investment strategy.

23. *Have you ever lied to someone to hide the financial consequences of the gambling?*
Why should you lie if gambling isn't a problem? When you lie for the gambler regarding money, it's just as much of a bailout as providing the money itself.

24. *Are you aware that the wagers have increased?*
People with addictions (whether to alcohol, drugs, or gambling) have to increase their use to get the same effect: stimulation or sedation. Gamblers who increase their bets may do so to get more excitement or to alleviate their anxiety. In addition, they may be chasing their losses.

25. *Is this person gambling with greater frequency?*
The gambler may be betting on more sporting events; going to the casinos, racetrack, or card games more often; or trading stocks, options, or commodities with greater frequency. This usually signals that he is betting more money—a sign of increasing dependency on gambling.

26. *Does this person disguise how much is at stake when gambling?*
Gamblers often disguise their bets from nongamblers for fear that they will be questioned, criticized, or pressured to stop.

27. *Have you ever received lavish gifts—the results of the gambler's winnings?*
Gamblers who win a lot don't *always* lose it immediately or put it away for future gambling. Sometimes they buy lavish gifts just to be nice, to appease family members who may have criticized them, or to look like a "big shot."

If you answered more than seven of the first twenty-one questions with a firm *yes*, then something is going on, and it may very well be gambling. In *addition*, if you answered two of the last six questions with a firm or even tentative *yes*, gambling has become a problem.

YOUNGSTERS AND GAMBLING

Youngsters gamble too. It is not unusual for teens, especially boys, to gamble. Gambling is sometimes viewed as a normal "rite of passage" that is usually outgrown as their social, academic, and other interests strengthen. But some youngsters become very drawn to gambling and can get "hooked" even faster than adults. Youngsters often hide all signs of gambling for fear that they will be stopped by the adults in their lives. Financial problems or unexplained wealth may be the first clues.

1. *Has the youngster been asking you for more money than you think he needs?*
   A youngster who gambles is often in need of money.

2. *Do you have reason to think the youngster has borrowed money from other family members, friends, or even strangers?*
   A youngster who has to borrow money usually needs it for some secret purpose other than buying a birthday or Christmas gift for a family member.

3. *Has the youngster displayed unexplained "wealth"?*
   If the youngster is on a winning streak, unexplained wealth may result.

4. *Has the youngster been stealing?*
   Youngsters steal for many reasons, sometimes to sell items for money to finance gambling.

5. *Has the child had problems with the law that relate to a need for money?*
   Gambling may be the cause.

6. *Have you come across gambling paraphernalia such as racing forms, lottery tickets, betting sheets, betting advice literature, or souvenirs from gambling places?*
   A youngster who acquires or collects these things is probably gambling.

   If you can answer two of these six questions with a *yes*, trouble is afoot. It may be gambling or drugs.
   The way an adult or youngster handles money—how it is spent—and the way others are enlisted to help juggle money are clues that gambling is becoming a problem, is already a problem, or is an addiction.

CHAPTER 4

Post Time

You and the Gambler's Timetable

The gambler's internal and external clocks tick louder than yours and mine. The twenty-four-hour day is never long enough for the gambler to place bets, earn money, meet payments, and fulfill all the expectations of everyday life. The gambler needs a lot of time to balance this complex existence.

Most of us have a single clock, in which we divide our time in a somewhat organized fashion. Our clocks tick at the same rate. But the gambler's clocks sound like clocks in a clock repair store. They're all ticking at different rates, chiming at different intervals. You may wonder why the dissonance doesn't drive the clock repairer crazy, but you know the answer. He's used to it and doesn't even consciously hear it anymore. If all the clocks would stop, the sounds of silence might really get to him.

The gambler gets used to his clocks ticking. He always has at least five clocks going: the gambling clock, the social/family clock, the career clock, the debt clock, and the biological/internal clock. The clocks turn, tick, and flash, and if one speeds up, it can throw the others out of whack.

The gambler's time isn't his own. He's at the mercy of his gambling clock. He's got to get his bets in, wait for results, collect if he wins in time to have money for the next bet, find the money to pay out if he loses, get more money, and meet the loan shark, banker, or bookie. And all the while he needs to find time for his legitimate job to make the money to gamble, to meet family responsibilities, and to cover up the gambling activities. Is it any wonder that gamblers are often exhausted, smoke or drink too much, and suffer from stress-related problems?

The gambler keeps an eye on his gambling clock so that he won't be "shut out." Each kind of gambling has a different schedule. For instance, East Coast sports bettors must be available to place their phone bets for evening games between 6:30 and 7 P.M.; illegal numbers players may have to choose their numbers before 11 A.M.; horse players have to pick up their racing forms on time and then get to the track or off-track betting parlor before post time.

The gambler may spend hours in a casino or bingo hall or at the track, or he may take only a few minutes to place a sports bet or talk to a stockbroker. Even when the gambler isn't "in action," he is obsessed with gambling, either thinking about it or preparing to do it.

All too often the gambler's timetable becomes *your* timetable. Without your knowing how or when it got started, your family's routine soon revolves around the gambler's schedule. You may feel neglected, hurt, angry, and rejected, often assuming there is something wrong with you because the gambler prefers to spend time elsewhere.

Kim met Wayne when he was visiting Japan during his tour of duty in Vietnam. For the last twenty years they have been living in the Philadelphia suburb where he grew up. She works as a real-estate broker, and her husband is part owner of a popular local restaurant. Their twenty-two-year old son Drew is in the air force, and seventeen-year-old Laird is in high school.

While vacationing in the Caribbean, Kim discovered the casinos and after winning a few small jackpots in the quarter slots moved up to the two-dollar slots. She won so much that they were able to put the money aside for their next vacation.

Buoyed by her success she decided to try her luck in Atlantic City. Soon she had moved on to blackjack and the five-dollar slots. Kim could hide her trips to Atlantic City easily; as a real-estate broker she was often "out of touch" (except by phone) with her local office.

Spending so much time in Atlantic City, in addition to working and maintaining her home, began to take its toll. She started to neglect her usual homemaking chores: Laundry piled up, she didn't get to the supermarket, and sometimes she wasn't home at the usual dinner hour. She suddenly stopped the redecorating project she had begun for the family room.

Work began to suffer. She didn't follow through on some good leads, and was late for an important closing. The boss began to question her dedication.

Uncharacteristically, she missed a few of Laird's high school wrestling matches. She began to skip her regular visits to her aging mother-in-law. When her husband suggested they visit their son at the air force base, she resisted, instead suggesting that they would get a better rest if they took an island vacation.

One day Wayne got a call from Laird's school. Laird had broken his collar bone during wrestling practice. Wayne tried to reach Kim at her office, but they didn't know where she was. They thought she was "out with a client." Kim didn't call in all day. Laird kept saying, "Don't worry. I'm OK. I don't need Mom. She's busy."

Something doesn't seem right, thought Wayne. The office doesn't know where she is. My son is acting mysteriously. He began to mull over all the changes in Kim's recent behavior. Where is she? he wondered. Things just didn't make sense.

When Kim got home about 7:30 that evening, Wayne confronted her. As Laird had known all along, Kim had been in Atlantic City.

Wayne soon learned that this was just the tip of the iceberg. Kim was in tremendous debt and at risk of losing her job because of all her absences and lack of attention to details.

There are time clues that indicate gambling is becoming a serious problem. The gambler begins to schedule his life around gambling, increases the time spent gambling, and establishes new ways and places in which to gamble. There are frequent excuses or unexplained absences from home or work. There is an intense interest in information useful for gambling, and the gambler uses the telephone more often. Many gamblers seek additional ways to earn money and also start to avoid and then withdraw from social, family, and community activities.

As gambling becomes more of a problem, the gambler's time becomes less available to others. The sales rep may schedule appointments early in the day to make the two o'clock post time, but miss an important afternoon sales meeting. The nine-to-five office worker uses personal days and vacation and sick time to visit casinos, leaving no time to attend to family needs or desires.

The gambler makes less time available for nongambling activities. A Sunday afternoon at the zoo interferes with watching professional sporting events. There are no leisurely family dinners; gamblers need that time to call their bookies and listen to the radio or watch TV for results. Bingo players often get home too late to start cooking dinner or rush off too early to finish eating it.

The following questions will help you identify the gambler's timetable.

1. *Does this person claim to be too busy to do ordinary things like renewing his driver's license, making a dentist appointment, or sitting around relaxing with friends?*
   As gambling becomes the primary focus, important things necessary for maintaining quality of life become less valued. Also, gamblers don't like to play by the rules and balk at waiting on line. They are impulsive and like to do everything "their way."

2. *Is this person sometimes late, absent, or leave early when expected at home, work, or some other event or obligation? Are the excuses sometimes outright lies?*
   A person who is irresistibly attracted to gambling action often feels no responsibility to be where they ought to be or promised to be.
   Gamblers have obligations more important than the ones we set for them. They must prepare for gambling, get into the action, and wait for results. This not only takes time but sometimes conflicts with other activities. They lie so that you won't find out about their gambling. Other gamblers are meticulous about their obligations and are never late and never miss any event they have agreed to attend.

3. *Does your life seem to revolve around this person's personal timetable?*

When someone gambles too much, everything else becomes secondary to their "action." If the gambler is a sports bettor, for example, your dinner hour may have to revolve around evening phone calls to his bookmaker. Televised games may dictate your life. The gambler is not an ordinary Sunday sports fanatic. If you or someone else interrupts, especially when results are being announced, the gambler may become enraged and verbally or physically abusive.

4. *Does this person use sick days and personal days for reasons unknown to you?*
Sick days and personal days give the gambler extra opportunities to play cards and go to nearby casinos, the track, or other gambling attractions. The gambler uses this time to meet with loan sharks, bookmakers, or others to arrange loans or to pay debts.

5. *Does this person tend to use vacation days one at a time rather than in weeks?*
If the gambler wants to go to a resort where there is action, he needs blocks of vacation time. But if he favors card games, the track, or a nearby casino, taking one vacation day at a time, like using personal days and sick days, fits his schedule well.

6. *Does this person take responsibility for the office pool?*
Gamblers often create opportunities to gamble. The office pool offers them a chance to show off gambling knowledge and skill. To disguise their urge to bet, gamblers make use of socially acceptable occasions to gamble. Profits from office pools can also be easily siphoned for the gambler's own use.

7. *Is your life often disrupted by "mysterious" visitors at home or work?*
These visitors are often loan sharks, people he owes money to, those paying him off, and others who share gambling activities.

8. *Does this person seem to constantly tune in to sports stations or news? Does he use earphones or have a small transistor*

radio with him even at inappropriate times like weddings or meetings?
The gambler feels compelled to follow his action. If he is a sports bettor or a stock, commodities, or options trader, the radio may be his source of information.

9. *Does this person tend to begin projects that are never completed?*
Gamblers make promises to themselves and to others. But too often the "action" gets in the way of those promises. Procrastination and deferment become a way of life.

10. *Is this person often ready to quit or cut short activities or social events that you and others wish to continue?*
Gamblers have a low stress and frustration tolerance and get bored easily. They are often "chomping at the bit" to move on to some gambling-related activity.

11. *Do you find that you are often arguing with this person or criticizing how he spends his time?*
Families of gamblers often feel neglected or ignored, and are irritated by the gambler's absence and attention elsewhere.

12. *Is this person only willing to take jobs with a flexible time schedule, such as outside sales?*
Many people like flexibility in their work life, but the gambler has a particular need and desire to create an environment that permits him opportunities to gamble during the day.

13. *Does this person seem to live at the end of the phone?*
Calls to place bets, trade stocks, or deal with loans may be brief or long, depending on their purpose, but there are usually a great number of these calls.

14. *Does this person refuse to accept invitations or procrastinate when planning social events?*
Until the gambler has consulted his schedule and knows whether an event will conflict with gambling, he is unlikely to commit himself to attending.

15. *Does this person seem to be watching the clock?*
The gambler may be waiting to make or receive a phone call, or to check radio or television for scores or stock results. Or he may be planning to go somewhere to gamble or to meet someone to collect or pay off a bet.

16. *Does this person seem unable to account for blocks of time?*
This time may be used to gamble, to prepare for gambling, or to arrange loans or repay debts.

17. *Has this person begun to neglect regular responsibilities such as home and car maintenance, household chores, or care of children or elderly relatives?*
Gambling can be so time-consuming that there is little energy left over for everyday responsibilities. But it should be noted that some gamblers are so careful to "cover their tracks" that they meet all their responsibilities despite hours spent gambling.

18. *Is this person constantly calling stockbrokers and other financial managers? Does he spend a great deal of time following the market in the newspapers, on cable television, or at the stockbroker's office?*
Many people who invest in the stock market are careful investors who do their homework thoroughly, but those who gamble in the market spend an inordinate amount of time checking out leads.

The following questions relate more directly to a *known* gambler.

19. *Have you noticed that even when the gambler is not gambling, he spends a lot of time on preparations like studying gambling books or racing forms or checking sports statistics?*
Many gamblers pride themselves on being smart, skilled, and knowledgeable about gambling. To this end, they spend a great deal of time preparing themselves for gambling. The preparation may become ritualized and be as exciting as the actual wagering.

20. *Has the gambler sought new ways and places in which to gamble?*
    As the gambling obsession intensifies, gamblers often spend time seeking new ways to satisfy their cravings. They may also get caught up in chasing lost money.

21. *Does the gambler insist that every vacation be in a place where gambling is available?*
    Many gamblers become restless, uncomfortable, and irritable away from gambling. A vacation without gambling holds no pleasure for them.

22. *Is the gambler spending more and more time gambling?*
    Compulsive gambling is a progressive disease. Spending more time gambling, like spending more money, is a tip-off that the gambling is out of control.

If you have answered *yes* to six or more of the first eighteen questions, and *yes* to two or more of questions nineteen through twenty-two, it is clear that the gambler in your life is investing a great deal of time in wagering. In all likelihood gambling is about to become, or has already become, a serious problem.

TEENS AND GAMBLING

Youngsters from preteens through young adults frequently gamble. Often their gambling gets out of control quickly.
Ask yourself the following questions.

1. *Does the youngster receive calls from strangers?*
   These calls may be from bookmakers or others with whom he gambles or to whom he owes money.

2. *Has the youngster been using the telephone more often or become extremely secretive about his calls?*
   The youngster may be calling betting or sports results services, or placing bets with friends, acquaintances, or professional gamblers.

3. *Is there a pattern to the youngster's phone calls?*
A call to a friend just to chat is seldom dictated by schedule. But the youngster who makes calls on a specific schedule may be placing bets.

4. *Have there been unexplained absences from school, less time spent studying, or withdrawal from afterschool activities?*
The youngster may be spending time on gambling activities or be worried about losses.

5. *Has the youngster withdrawn from family and old friends?*
If gambling is becoming an important part of the youngster's life, old friends and family members hold little interest for him. Withdrawal may also occur if the youngster owes money to some of these people.

6. *Does the youngster have new friends who you think have little in common with him?*
The new friends may be gambling friends.

7. *Does the youngster show intense interest in waiting for the final score of a sporting event even if it is clearly one-sided?*
The youngster may be betting on the "point spread"; thus, the score itself is of vital interest.

If you answered *yes* to any of these questions, something is going on in the youngster's life that warrants your attention. It may be gambling, although some of the warning signs of drug use and depression are similar.

CHAPTER 5

Win, Place, or Show

You and the Gambler's Emotional Life

Trust your feelings. You know more than you think you do. You may have felt for a long time that no matter how much time the gambler spends with you, no matter what he gives you, you can't totally win his heart. Sometimes you wonder if you even place or show. Spouses, children, and other family members and friends may all share these feelings.

Unless you are sure that gambling is the cause, you may think there's something or someone else. And even if you do know that gambling is the problem, you may feel as if there's something wrong with you that keeps the person from experiencing and showing real pleasure, excitement, and relaxation when he is with you. You may even like it when the gambler is gambling because that's the only time he really comes alive and seems happy. When not in action, the gambler may seem to just be going through the motions of life, causing others to say, "His body is here, but his mind seems far away."

This consuming interest in gambling and the stress associated with it lead the gambler to slowly withdraw from emotional connection and attachment to family and friends. Employers and colleagues note that the gambler isn't giving his "all." This makes the family feel angry and hurt, unloved and unlovable, and fosters resentment in the workplace.

Maureen D.'s childhood was marked by one sad event after another. Her father died in a boating accident, and her mother, prone to depressive episodes in which she would verbally and even physically attack her children, was so overwhelmed with her husband's death that she sent Maureen and her older sister to live with her parents temporarily but never returned to claim them. Later Maureen learned that her mother was hospitalized briefly for severe depression and later committed suicide. Maureen's sister became involved in the sixties drug scene and died of an overdose. Before Maureen finished high school her grandfather, who suffered from Alzheimer's disease, had to go into a nursing home when his care became too much for Maureen and her grandmother.

It's no wonder that Maureen thought she was the luckiest girl in New England when Kevin asked her to marry him. Tall, red-headed, and freckle-faced, with a grin guaranteed to melt the heart of any woman, Kevin was a real charmer. Maureen met him at the local library where she worked, when he came in to borrow some books on sports. Maureen recognized Kevin; he had been a high school baseball star when she was just a freshman. She knew his two younger brothers and his sister, who had been in her class.

Kevin didn't go to college; instead, he worked for an uncle who ran a local outdoor driving range and miniature golf course. When his uncle retired, Kevin took over. Within a short time he increased business by adding some popular touches; then he bought a franchise of a national family indoor sports center that included baseball batting ranges, billiards, video games, and miniature golf. In the next five years, Kevin's two younger brothers (both of whom looked up to him) came into the business. They added a pro shop selling sports equipment and clothes, and began to market the center to families and business groups. The center was open seven days a week from mid-morning until 2 A.M.

Kevin treasured his role as a local sports figure; it was as close as he could get to realizing his dream of playing pro ball. Kevin's patient instruction could make even the most uncoordinated child feel masterful. Maureen sometimes helped out when there was a birthday party scheduled at the center, but she was essentially a stay-at-home mother who kept busy by rearing their five children. She loved being a mother, raising a big family, and being part of Kevin's family, all of whom lived close by. She felt as if she was giving herself what she had missed in her own childhood.

Needless to say, Kevin was one of the most popular guys in town. He was generous with his kids, his friends' kids, and his nieces and nephews and *their* friends. They knew they could always practice their batting and even get some free instruction at the center.

Maureen had "no complaints." There was enough money, and although Kevin worked long hours, she and the children saw plenty of him because they could always go to the sports center.

When Kevin installed a large-screen television in the center, even nonplayers liked to hang out there to watch the games. Instead of leaving employees in charge, Kevin began staying at work many evenings.

Maureen soon felt something was wrong. She was aware that Kevin liked to gamble, but since everyone else she knew did too, she told herself she shouldn't worry.

But Maureen worried anyway. If she said anything about the gambling Kevin would remind her he bet only on sports (about which he was an expert) and pool, about which he would say, "You know I'm a better player than anyone else who comes into the center." And he would add, "Don't you always have enough money?"

Maureen kept quiet because she still couldn't believe her luck at being married to Kevin. And with five kids and no confidence in her ability to earn a living, she wasn't about to make any waves. Suppose he left her?

But after a while she began to admit to herself that she was no longer lucky. Life with Kevin was becoming miserable. His personality was changing; he became irritable, moody, and sometimes sarcastic and hostile. His verbal explosions seemed to come out of nowhere. If she or the kids talked when he was listening to the scores, he would scream at them to shut up. He was drinking a lot more beer than ever before.

Sometimes Maureen would wake up at night and hear him

pacing in another room. He became very withdrawn and seemed to have less interest in hearing about or noticing what she and the kids were doing.

Maureen tried to avoid Kevin when he was home. If she attempted any conversation, he would cut it off immediately. When she suggested he help one of the kids with homework, he would make her feel as if she were "nagging." She suspected he might be having an affair. He was so preoccupied and showed little interest in sex.

Maureen began to change too. She would lose her temper and have crying jags. The only thing that seemed to make her feel good was eating. Always proud that she had kept her figure after having five children, she gained twenty-five pounds in six months.

Kevin's impatience with the kids kept getting worse. One night he heaved a dinner plate across the table because the kids were noisy. Then eleven-year-old Shawn said, "You're just mad because the Celtics lost the play-offs." Kevin screamed "shut up," bolted out of his chair, picked up Shawn, and threw him down.

Silence came over the room. Shawn's forehead was bleeding and a tooth had been knocked out.

The emergency room physician who examined Shawn asked him what happened. Shawn said he and his brother were wrestling and he fell near a table. Kevin had already told the doctor another story: Reaching for a box of crackers, Shawn had fallen off the kitchen stool. The medical evidence and conflicting stories alerted the hospital's child abuse team.

What he had done horrified Kevin. Shawn had unwittingly identified just what was upsetting Kevin; he had lost three thousand dollars on the Celtics that day. Kevin could no longer avoid facing the fact that he was in trouble because of gambling. Maureen had been stifling her feelings for too long. She was ready to walk out. Kevin's brothers had not known the extent of the gambling. They felt as if their brother had toppled from his pedestal, betraying all of them. Kevin's children were frightened and confused.

Maureen could have recognized signs that Kevin's gambling was getting out of control before the crisis if she had known what to look for.

EMOTIONAL TIP-OFFS

1. *Has this person recently withdrawn from old friends or family members?*
   Gamblers are often embarrassed to face people who may know about their problems with gambling, especially if they owe them money.

2. *Does this person act nervous and jittery when he has nothing to do?*
   Gamblers like to keep busy with some activity so they won't have to deal with their feelings.

3. *Is this person becoming deceitful?*
   Most people who lie do so to avoid consequences. If a person's gambling is causing problems, he may do everything possible to avoid having the truth emerge. Compulsive gamblers often become habitual liars; they will lie about anything and everything whether or not it is related to gambling.

4. *Has this person's debts ever embarrassed you?*
   Bank loans and credit cards are acceptable in our society, and most people are not embarrassed by them. But gamblers are often in debt to local merchants or have borrowed heavily from family members, friends, coworkers, or acquaintances. This can embarrass family members.

5. *Are you surprised that you're constantly on edge?*
   Whether or not you are aware of the gambling, you are aware that this person's behavior is making you miserable. You don't know what will happen next. In addition, this person may be hypercritical—frequently criticizing you, your family, and your friends.

6. *Are you trying to control or change this person's behavior?*
   People who are involved with someone whose behavior is unacceptable often believe that they are responsible for the behavior and can "fix" the person. This is referred to as co-dependency.

7. *Have you noticed that this person has changed his behavior, perhaps becoming moody, tired, indecisive, less interested and involved in family, work, social activities, and hobbies? Has there been a change in this person's sleeping or eating patterns?*

The behaviors identified above are often symptoms of depression. Gamblers are often depressed as a result of gambling losses or because they are chronically or acutely depressed. They find that gambling helps them to feel *less* depressed.

8. *Do you sometimes feel that this person is a "thousand miles away"?*

Gamblers may be ruminating over past losses, wins, and debts, or daydreaming about a change of fortune. Some gamblers play an all-consuming mental game known as "mind-betting" when they don't have money to wager. This also keeps them from focusing on what's going on around them.

9. *Has your sexual relationship with this person changed?*

Many people obsessed with gambling begin to lose all interest in sex. Others begin to link sex with gambling. "If I have good sex, then I'll win; if I win then I'll 'give her a good time.'" If the gambler loses, sex may be used to bolster self-esteem, or it may be perceived as too threatening.

Other gamblers find that sex is just another way of having some excitement, reducing stress, and avoiding real feelings, so their interest in sex never wanes. Some people become *more* interested in, or even compulsive about, sex.

10. *Do you find yourself wondering why your life is out of control?*

Because gamblers are often secretive about much of their lives, families have little or no inkling about what's happening. Little by little your whole life may revolve around this person, making you feel like *your* life is out of control. If you initiate a confrontation about your feelings, he may tune out or "gaslight" you, turning the discussion around so that you feel *you're* the one who's got everything all mixed up. That makes it hard for you to trust your own feelings and perceptions.

11. *Does this person change the subject or become "edgy" every time you or anyone else mentions debts?*
    Embarrassed, guilt-ridden, and uncomfortable about having been "found out," the gambler is also worried that he will be put out of action.

12. *Do you feel as if this person's investments have a personal or emotional meaning to him that seems to go beyond the actual profits and losses?*
    It is quite natural to be pleased to make a profit in the financial market and to be disappointed at losses, but the person who gambles on the market sees things differently. The market takes on a persona, as if it's a symbol of his own sense of self that goes beyond the basic ability to choose a good stock. Trust yourself: If the person's interest in the market irritates or upsets you, it may be because this interest goes beyond what is normal and is happening at the cost of other emotional attachments.

13. *Has this person cut down on or given up nicotine, alcohol, or other substances and begun to gamble?*
    People who have given up other dependencies or addictions frequently turn to gambling to satisfy the same or similar needs. It is not unusual for gambling to then become a problem or compulsion.

14. *Does this person seem upset after a day or evening of gambling, but return the next day to gamble more?*
    When gamblers lose they are naturally upset, but instead of quitting they often return to the action to "chase" their losses.

15. *Do you worry about this person's gambling?*
    Trust yourself. If you are worried, there's probably a good reason. Maybe you have stopped worrying because you feel so helpless. Maybe you never let yourself become upset because the gambler was so reassuring, or you convinced yourself not to worry because you didn't want to deal with the fear.

16. *Are almost all of this person's friends or acquaintances gamblers?*
    Gamblers often feel most comfortable around other gamblers, whom they know will understand them and not be critical.

17. *Does this person's household become especially tense and anxious when he is involved in preparing to gamble (rushing to go out, reading racing forms or the sports pages, studying lottery tickets, etc.) or listening to a sporting event or the results of one?*
    The family unconsciously or consciously recognizes the gambler's tension and intensity and experiences it themselves. They have learned that the gambler is likely to meet any of their needs or requests with a range of emotions from disinterest to fury.

18. *Does this person change the subject, become upset, or lose his temper (verbally or physically) when you bring up gambling?*
    The gambler may feel uneasy, guilty, or furious that you are trying to interfere with his pleasure, or making him confront his denial that his gambling is out of control. The gambler also may fear having to make a choice between you and gambling.

19. *Has someone else mentioned this person's gambling behavior to you or to others?*
    Someone may be trying to warn you or to raise the issue of loans.

20. *Does this person sometimes apologize and act remorseful after gambling, perhaps promising "never again"?*
    At some level, the gambler wants to stop because the gambling is harming himself or his family. But if the gambling persists, it may be that he never intended to keep his promise, or the urge is simply greater than any resolutions.

21. *Have you given up social, family, or recreational activities, or had them ruined because of gambling?*

As difficult as it may be to believe, gambling can take precedence over just about anything.

22. *Have you often heard this person boast about his skills at gambling or about big wins?*
Gambling becomes the foundation of the person's self-esteem and identity, so he exaggerates winnings and minimizes losses.

23. *Do you feel that you are somehow responsible for this person's urge to gamble?*
It's not unusual for someone to feel that she causes another's unacceptable behavior (such as drinking too much) or has the power to somehow control or stop this behavior. This is part of the codependent behavior that we will discuss in part 2.

24. *Do you sometimes lie to cover up this person's gambling?*
Family members or friends frequently provide excuses or even outright lies to others to hide the person's gambling. This is done to protect the gambler or themselves from embarrassment, shame, or censure. When you offer this kind of bailout, you enable the gambler to continue his gambling activities.

25. *Have you ever lied to someone to hide the financial consequences of the gambling?*
Gambling causes financial problems; it keeps you from meeting obligations or necessitates a change in your standard of living. Instead of admitting that gambling is the cause of this change, you may fabricate a story to explain it. Often referred to as enabling, this approach is common among those involved with people who have a variety of dysfunctional or addictive disorders.

26. *Does this person use gambling to celebrate a special event like a birthday, anniversary, or new job?*
Many people like to celebrate with a night or weekend on the town. Gambling may be part of the scene. But people with gambling problems use every possible opportunity to gamble. Because a special event may make them feel particularly

lucky and elated, they seek out still more excitement by getting into action.

27. *Does this person use gambling to relax after a particularly stressful period of time?*
People gamble for excitement and to "relax." Gambling can dull the pain as reality fades into oblivion, and the mind is relieved of stress and other troubles.

28. *Does this person seem to "relive" gambling experiences, talking about wins or ruminating on losses?*
People obsessed with gambling often keep the gambling alive by talking about it, even when they're not in action. They also think about it a lot.

If you answered *yes* to five of the first thirteen questions, and *yes* to eight of the last fifteen questions, gambling has become a serious problem.

If you have a total of thirty yes answers to all of the questions in chapters 3, 4, and 5, gambling already has thrown your life into crisis, or is about to do so.

YOU AND THE YOUNGSTER'S GAMBLING

Many youngsters, especially teenage boys, gamble. Gambling may be a rite of passage for these young people that will be outgrown as their social, academic, and other interests become more prominent. To find out if your youngster is gambling and if it is causing problems, ask yourself these questions.

1. Has the youngster's behavior changed at home?
2. Has the youngster changed friends or lost friends?
3. Has the youngster's interest in school or hobbies declined?
4. Has the youngster become preoccupied, distant, and worried for reasons not understood by other family members?
5. Has the youngster's lying, cheating, or stealing become a problem for the family? Have these behaviors caused friction or conflict within the family or community?
6. Does the youngster gamble alone?

If you answered *yes* to any of the first five questions, your youngster has some kind of problem. If you answered *yes* to question six, you should be concerned. A youngster who gambles alone may be becoming dependent on the activity and you may need to intervene.

PART TWO

RIDING THE ROLLER COASTER

Consequences of Gambling Too Much

CHAPTER 6

Second Place

The Family's Emotional Toll

Years later Megan S. said she never dreamed Al's gambling was so out of hand. "I was standing in my friend Jane's living room, in shock, saying over and over, 'How could I have been such a fool?' "

SENSE OF BETRAYAL

Feeling as if the wool has been pulled over your eyes can be a total affront to your personal sense of worth. It can make you question or doubt all that you once deemed important: your own sense of right or wrong, faith in others, your own strengths and abilities. When someone you care about gambles too much, the very foundation of this faith and trust may be shaken. It is not unusual to wonder who or what you can ever trust again.

Living with someone who gambles too much can cause these feelings. The gambler lies, blames, and rationalizes as a means of escape, giving rise to so many deceptions that you may have either been kept totally in the dark or, like Megan, know only *part* of the story.

I knew Al gambled, but I thought it was just a casual thing, his weekly poker game, a bet on a football game, a little money riding on a basketball game. We never had any real money problems. Bills were paid, we had even redecorated the living room the year before. Although he didn't complain when I did that, I always knew that my needs and even the kids' needs had to take a backseat to everything he wanted. Al liked vacations, and we went on some nice ones. We went to the Caribbean a few times, where Al often spent time in the casinos while I relaxed around the pool.

Al's moodiness used to bother me sometimes, but I would attribute it to his stresses at work. Often he would get these mysterious phone calls from people I didn't know, and if I tried to overhear his part of the conversation he would get furious, saying it was about work and that I should mind my own business.

Like my father, he was always complaining about money— screaming at me to turn off the lights, questioning little expenses like groceries, and asking why the children needed so many toys. But then he would go out for no reason at all and buy me or the kids some really expensive gift.

I had given up trying to get him to account for his whereabouts on business trips. When I would question him he would go on the offensive, saying I was acting like a detective. Who did I think I was, his mother? Besides, he said, it's impossible to reach him in some of those places.

Friends would tell me he boasted about how the physician I worked for could never get along without me, how beautifully I ran our home, and how attractive I was. But that's not how he talked to me. When we were alone, he would often put me down, criticizing meals, making my part-time job as a lab technician sound like nothing, and even suggesting I take his sister shopping with me for clothes. From the beginning of our marriage, Al handled all the bills and money; I simply deposited my paycheck and took out enough for spending money and groceries.

I guess I put up with all of this because in some ways I was used to it. My father always took care of the money in our family, and he always belittled my mother. He had treated my brother as the "smart one" and even encouraged him to go away to college. But he made it clear that college would be a waste of time and money for me, so I went to work when I finished high school, attended the local two-year community college for a while at night, and lived at home, which wasn't so bad, because that's when I met Al.

My father was a telephone installer and to help pay the mortgage we used to rent a room to students from the University of Pennsylvania. Al was getting his MBA there, and he rented a room from us. After he got his degree, his parents gave us this fancy wedding at their country club, and he went into his father's large sportswear manufacturing business. Al opened up a whole new world to me, and I grew to like it. But socially and in every other way, I never felt I measured up to his family.

One day Al was off playing golf; the children were in nursery school, and I was cleaning out his closet when I spotted a piece of paper on the floor. It was a carbon of a bank check made out to one of Al's poker friends for seven thousand dollars, and signed by Al. My heart began to race—I was terrified. I had never looked through his things before but suddenly decided to look in the drawer where he kept all the bank statements and canceled checks. There I found checks made out to his golfing buddies, cardplayers, and a lot of other people I had never even met. Some months they added up to thousands. And I discovered that every Wednesday, the night of his poker game, Al had taken five hundred dollars out of his checking account. Obviously, that was the cash he brought with him to gamble.

But that wasn't all. I looked in the file where he had neatly placed all the credit card charges. I discovered charges for round-trip airline tickets and a hotel in Las Vegas on three occasions in the last year when he had told me he was in Honduras looking for factories to produce their sportswear.

Suddenly it all came together. Al had never given me a straight answer about his income; his eagerness to handle all our money and all that secretiveness about business trips and how he spent his free time were related to his attempts to keep me from finding out about the gambling.

When I called my friend Jane and asked if I could come over, she heard the panic in my voice. How could I have not known what was going on? When Al used to say he worked hard all day and needed to relax and watch a game on television or play golf on the weekends, I didn't object. I figured he was entitled to time for himself, and anyway it just seemed easier than arguing. And I knew that he was used to having his own way—his parents had spoiled him. Thinking I was being a supportive wife, I spent evening after evening and weekend after weekend without him so he could "relax." And all the time he was gambling.

I think it was both fear and anger that made me gather up all the checks and statements and bring them over to Jane's, where we added up all the withdrawals and checks he had made out for the last three years. When I realized the extent of all the gambling, I stood there in shock. I think that for the rest of my life I will remember the sight of her living room floor covered with all the checks as I tried to make sense out of what had happened. I alternated between shock, sobs, and anger. Trying to calm me down, Jane said, "There *are* a lot of deposits too. And you're not broke, are you?"

"I don't think so," I said, "But that's not the point. I feel abused."

It was a few more years before I got up enough courage to really *do* anything about my life.

Later we will learn how Megan managed to muster up enough strength to begin on the road to survival and recovery. Her story is not unusual. She knew Al gambled. She knew something was wrong with her life. But she didn't know Al's gambling was a major cause of her unhappiness.

DENYING THE PROBLEM

Like many other people, Megan simply didn't see that Al's gambling was out of control. Gambling and its related problems are easily hidden, so it is not easy to recognize them. Even when faced with what seems obvious, many of us may *mis*understand because we don't comprehend the implications.

We may also deny a problem exists.

Denial is far more complex than just putting your head in the sand. It is a variety of unconscious defenses that distorts perception of reality and helps to protect us from facing something that might be too painful if we were to acknowledge it to ourselves. We tend to deny something when it:

- Threatens our beliefs in ourselves or others
- Challenges our sense of emotional or physical safety and security
- Constitutes a blow to our personal pride, sense of worth, and self-esteem
- Stirs up early childhood fears of rejection and abandonment
- Conflicts with the self-deceptions we have come to believe

When we're confronted with someone we care about who gambles too much, denial can take many forms. Despite clear-cut evidence to the contrary, we insist that gambling isn't occurring. Sometimes we deny to a lesser degree by merely minimizing the problem, admitting the person gambles, but believing he doesn't lose too much or too often, and playing down any consequences of the gambling. We say things like "she only plays the slots" or "he always pays his bills."

We rationalize the behavior, perhaps by explaining it away in any number of ways that seem quite credible. We say "everyone gambles" or "at least he stopped drinking" or "she doesn't spend money on clothes or vacations like a lot of other women."

Sometimes, instead of expecting the gambler to take responsibility for his own behavior we blame it on others or on particular situations. Parents of an adult son say "if his home life was happier"; parents of a teen say "it's that crowd at school"; a spouse says "if his job weren't so boring." And we hurl anger and blame at the system that encourages the sale of lottery tickets or at the bookie who takes the gambler's bets.

Sometimes we find justifications or excuses, saying things like "with her husband traveling so much, she's lonely, so going to the track or playing bingo is an easy way to fill her days."

Another form of denial is repressing all your feelings and treating the gambling problem intellectually, as if it were an interesting social phenomenon affecting everyone but yourself.

To avoid "hearing" when someone attempts to call the gambling to your attention, you change the subject, get angry or hostile, or feel personally attacked. This reaction usually keeps people from discussing it again in your presence.

Paradoxically, as the consequences of excessive gambling worsen and become *more* obvious, the denial of those around the gambler may also intensify, leading to a greater distortion of reality. Over time, an elaborate system of defenses develops within both the gambler and his family or friends. Sometimes it takes a crisis to pierce this denial. Or, as Megan learned, it takes concrete evidence to make someone recognize the extent of the gambling and stop the denial.

FEELING LIKE SECOND PLACE

Like Megan, you may feel that if only you had known about the gambling you could have done something to avoid the consequences.

Why didn't someone tell you? Perhaps they did, but you defended against hearing what they had to say. Or they may also have misunderstood, denied, and saw only what the gambler revealed to them. Perhaps they knew, but in an attempt to be kind or considerate conspired to protect you from the knowledge. And in all likelihood, they minimized the emotional impact of the gambling on you.

Even if you don't know the person is gambling too much, you feel cheated if he is spending considerable time or emotional energy elsewhere, as if you are "second place" to something else.

You may accept this "second-class" citizenship because you have always been treated that way, and so it meets your expectations. Perhaps you feel that you don't deserve any more than being "second place." Perhaps you struggle, sometimes for years, but the gambler simply wears you down with rationalizations, explanations, and other "gaslighting" techniques, so you simply give up and live under stressful conditions.

STRESSFUL CONSEQUENCES

The financial, social, and emotional consequences of living with a gambler can be overwhelmingly stressful. You live from crisis to crisis or in a constant state of unpredictability. You don't know how much money you will have, how others will treat you, and when or where you will be threatened. You wonder when the gambler will be available to the family or be at home, and what kind of mood he will be in when he does get home. Children as well as adults experience these consequences of gambling. Dad will come to the Little League game if there's no heavy action on television; you'll get the washing machine fixed unless he loses; he'll notice your new hairdo if he's feeling good, but ignore you if he's preoccupied with his gambling.

You may feel responsible for the gambler's behavior. If you scream, plead, cajole, lie, or manipulate in an attempt to control the gambler and/or the situation, you may be angry and ashamed that you're unsuccessful, or be mortified by your own behavior. If the gambler reassures you or acts remorseful, you may step back and then feel foolish and lose confidence in your own perceptions. Often the gambler's arguments are so persuasive, the "gaslighting" so effective, that eventually you become so exhausted, bitter, detached, and defeated that you are ready to give up on trying to have any control over your own life. Regardless of the scenario, you are likely to feel powerless, frustrated, fearful, ashamed, humiliated, and misunderstood. All of this can lead to your becoming secretive, holding your feelings inside, perhaps not even acknowledging them to yourself.

As the stress from the consequences of gambling builds up, you may feel sick and suffer from problems such as backaches, stomach disorders, headaches, or sleeping too much or not enough. Existing conditions like asthma, ulcers, hypertension, or skin rashes may worsen.

In an attempt to numb yourself, you may develop compulsive disorders: overeating, drinking, using drugs, working too hard, and helping others to the exclusion of caring for yourself.

You may become depressed and lack energy; sleep or eat too much or not enough; feel inadequate or worthless; have poor concentration or difficulty in making decisions; feel hopeless, full of despair, or empty; and feel a general and pervasive sense of sadness.

Or perhaps you worry, but keep your concerns to yourself, thinking no one will understand. Consequently, you may feel lonely and hide or deny your feelings, avoiding having to deal with them.

You may displace your frustrations on other family members. Many wives of gamblers are often verbally and physically abusive to children; parents and siblings of gamblers find their own relationships and marriages shaken.

Day after day you feel as if you have bought a perpetual ticket to ride the emotional roller coaster, with no chance of getting off.

EFFECTS ON CHILDREN IN A GAMBLER'S HOUSEHOLD

Children may be affected directly by the gambler's behavior, or indirectly because of your reaction to it. The impact of the gambling depends on how disorganized or dysfunctional the family was to begin with, and how much the gambling disrupts family routines. Sometimes parents are pulled away from their roles as caretakers, and they are unable to successfully cope and communicate with their children or recognize their feelings. This lack of involvement usually results in more problems. The age of the children, their underlying personalities and characters, and the amount of marital discord all contribute to the total picture of how children will react.

If the gambling is well hidden, or if the nongambler tries to conceal it from them, children may feel confused and worried, and sense that something isn't right. To avoid upsetting their parents, they often keep their feelings locked up inside. They may feel responsible for things they don't understand and become anxious and guilt-ridden. They begin to develop a sense of shame, feeling as though they are bad, even though they can't figure out why. If these feelings are neither recognized nor acknowledged, children may cope with them by becoming very competent and responsible to feel good about themselves, or by "acting out" in an attempt to have their bad feelings noticed and punished.

When someone is addicted to drugs or alcohol or gambling, family systems become burdened by prolonged stress, frustration, fear, and marital discord. Unpredictability plays a significant role in the family's patterns, and even after they become adults, these children feel as if the rug is always ready to be pulled out from under them. Children in such families sometimes take on specific roles; one child becomes overly responsible for others in the family; another regularly misbehaves to deflect attention from the real problem in the family; another becomes a mediator who always tries to make peace; and another becomes the invisible child who never attracts attention to himself. These roles are often carried over into adulthood.

Marital arguments ensue when the gambling is apparent or is singled out by the nongambling parent. The children become highly critical of and angry at the nongambling parent, who they blame for making all the trouble or for not stopping the gambling. Indeed, the nongambling parent often creates most of the disturbance in the household by shouting and nagging. Some children exploit this division by playing one parent against the other.

The gambler may enlist the children as coconspirators, asking them to lie to the other parent. He "borrows" money from the children, takes them to the track, or simply tells them that the other parent just doesn't care about having fun. To deflect attention from gambling, the gambler spoils the children and buys them off with inappropriately extravagant gifts. This helps to assuage the gambler's own guilt and to win the children over to his side in disputes. The nongambling parent tries to enlist the children's sympathy and punish the gambler by telling the children that "if it weren't for the gambling we could go to Disneyland."

The martyred parent contributes to the children's confusion, making them feel as if they are the rope in a game of tug-of-war. Exposure to a gambling atmosphere often shapes children's values about money. Their values are distorted; they may become extremely materialistic spendthrifts, or perhaps become exceedingly thrifty, even stingy.

To avoid conflicts with parents whom they perceive as stressed and inconsistent, children may vent their anger by fighting constantly with siblings. Sometimes they vie with one another for attention from their parents through a variety of attention-seeking behaviors.

Some children behave well at school but not at home; others are good at home but create problems at school. A girl behaves well but doesn't attend to her schoolwork; a boy buries himself in his studies to avoid dealing with the stress at home. Like adults, children can become depressed. They may seem sad and withdrawn, but their depression can be masked by behavioral problems such as aggression toward themselves or others.

It is important to note that many children are virtually unaffected by gambling within a family. Innate resiliency, early good parenting and a continued sense of being loved by both the gambling and nongambling parent, or outside stabilizing resources can serve to form a strong foundation that protects them from the emotional consequences of gambling.

Each person in the family may react and feel differently, but many are or become codependent or have some codependent traits. As they attempt to control and solve the problems caused by the gambling, their solutions result in something called "codependency."

ARE YOU A CODEPENDENT?

Healthy people help others constructively and appropriately and are sensitive to the moods and needs of those around them. They help because they are considerate, compassionate, empathetic human beings. They understand that being responsive to others is the hallmark of a mature individual, and their identity is based on more than just the performance of "good works."

Codependents, however, are *driven* to come to the rescue of others for the purpose of shoring up their own identity and raising their sense of pride and worth. They have developed an unhealthy pattern of relating to others *and* have an extreme emotional, social, and perhaps overall dependence on someone else. Their self-esteem and emotional life depend on how the other person is doing emotionally and in other ways. In addition, codependents believe they are helping to avoid family disruption. Some experts in the field of addictions describe codependency as a progressive disease.

Codependents have trouble with boundaries: They're not sure where they end and the other person begins. They become obsessed with controlling and changing the other person's behavior and are willing to suffer to do so.

Codependents help to protect people from the consequences of their behavior because they are terrified of being abandoned and left alone. Fearful of facing an uncertain future, codependents prefer to keep things the way they are, even when the situation they find themselves in becomes increasingly intolerable.

Gamblers often have a codependent in their lives. With their illusion of power, these codependents believe that if they try hard enough they will eventually control others and gain inner peace. Some codependents grew up in dysfunctional homes where someone suffered from an addiction, or they were abused or emotionally neglected or deprived. They may have experienced a pervasive sense of shame and believe they don't deserve a better life.

Many re-create feelings they experienced in early childhood, unconsciously hoping to master the feelings. This makes it easy to understand why so many children of alcoholics, gamblers, or abusers establish relationships with people who exhibit the same behavioral patterns as the dysfunctional parent. It seems as though they are looking for a second chance to make things turn out right. Unfortunately, the odds for rescuing this new person and changing the story's ending are poor.

Some people gradually become codependent by living with someone whose gambling interferes with normal family life. Megan, for example, showed many codependent traits, some of which she had before she met Al. Her life with him was a constant erosion of her self-esteem, and it reinforced her codependent thinking and behavior.

CODEPENDENCY AND ENABLING

Paradoxically, codependents often encourage the progressive development of the very behavior that they wish to control or stop. This unintended encouragement is called enabling, and it is a frequent response to the emotional consequences of living with someone who gambles too much.

All codependents tend to enable, but even people who are *not* codependents and who are psychologically independent of the gambler may unwittingly enable, thus bailing out the gambler.

Here are some of the ways you might enable gambling.

• *Protection.* If you cover up the gambling, others won't find out about it, and the gambler won't have to face criticism or pressures.

• *Control.* If you attempt to control the gambler either by manipulating, coercing, pleading, or threatening, you only further increase his frustrations and diminish his self-esteem, which lead to further gambling. The gambler now seizes the opportunity to blame the gambling on you, and so the behavior continues, unabated.

• *Assuming responsibilities.* If you bail out the gambler by taking over responsibilities for which he has neither time, emotional energy, nor money, you enable him to have more of these resources available for gambling.

• *Rationalization.* If you buy into the gambler's excuses and explanations for the gambling, you support the self-deception.

• *Cooperation.* If you knowingly join the gambler at a casino, track, or bingo hall; take messages regarding the activities; cosign loans necessitated by gambling; assume gambling debts; or assist in illegal schemes to finance gambling, you are enabling the gambling process.

• *Rescuing.* When the gambler faces severe losses and you try to cheer him up, find a way to bail him out of jail, comfort his wounded ego, nurse him back to health when he has been beaten up for welshing on debts, or let him return home after he has disappeared for days on end, you enable the gambling to continue.

For instance, Megan unwittingly enabled Al's gambling by freeing up his time and rationalizing the reasons for it. If after learning about the gambling, she had tried to control it, protected him from the consequences of it, or cooperated with it, she would have been an enabler.

SHOCK OF DISCOVERY

Sometimes the gambling is totally hidden. You would have to be a detective to discover it. You may suspect something is wrong because of the tension in the home, or have a vague sense of being left out of part of the person's life, but you may not know that the person gambles. A spouse may suspect an affair. Parents may think that a teenager's problems are related to school, friends, or even drugs. Young or adult children may think their parent just doesn't care about them.

Or maybe everything was okay until one day your whole world collapsed. A phone call, a letter from a collection agency, or a suicide attempt jolted you into the reality that the person was gambling, or that the gambling you thought was just social and recreational was totally out of control.

There are several emotions that emerge as a reaction to this revelation. Anger. How could he do this to me? To all of us? Fear. What will happen? Will bills be paid? Will we lose our house, our car, our self-respect? Will he go to jail? Will I be left alone to face it all? Will "they" break his legs? Would they hurt us? Ambivalence. How can I feel such anger and hatred toward someone I love?

Coexisting with these thoughts are increasingly frightening feelings of abandonment, betrayal, guilt, and inadequacy. Like Megan, you may wonder, "How could I have been such a fool?"

There is shame. How could I be married to such a person? How could I have brought up such a child? Some people think: How could I have such a parent?

Self-pity and sadness are pervasive. The grief and mourning for what you had (or thought you had) and what may never be can be devastating. At first you may believe that the problems will be easily solved, or you may be willing to change or revise your social, emotional, or financial expectations, denying and avoiding the major issue. You may be overwhelmed with a sense of panic, rage, exhaustion, and stress that can immobilize you or make you ill. You may even doubt your sanity.

The family system is impacted and severely strained. A sudden discovery or a crisis can jolt the family into facing problems that were hidden or avoided. Once gambling is acknowledged, other family issues come out from under the rug, and other things get shoved under it. The anger and hurt on the surface cause people to say things they withheld either out of politeness or repression. Those issues that were minimized may come into clearer focus and suddenly everyone has to deal with them. Each member will cope in his or her own way and this can magnify old conflicts or create new ones.

Searching for a reason or explanation for what has happened, everyone seeks out confirmation of their ideas from other family members. Some place blame strictly on the gambler; others assume guilt themselves; others place it on other family members. This leads to further conflicts and misunderstandings among the members. Relationships seesaw. It is not unusual for some family members to see the gambler as a fallen hero, especially if they have admired his bravado and bought into his grandiosity.

Perhaps the most common placement of blame by children, parents, and in-laws is on the nongambling spouse. Megan said:

> My father, who never thought I was too bright, said, "You must have been stupid not to have known." My children, even when they became adults, sometimes suggested I was somehow responsible for their father becoming a gambler. And I *know* Al's father thought that if Al hadn't married "beneath himself" none of this would have happened. Often I wondered about it myself.

THE SOCIAL TOLL

The social toll exacted by gambling can be high too. Lost friendships, withdrawal from others, social ostracism, erratic relationships, lost status, and rejection by others who are uncomfortable with family friction are all consequences of gambling by a family member.

Often these consequences are so gradual, occurring over a

period of years, that you don't even notice them. Megan, for example, didn't notice that Al had pulled away from many of their friends and neighbors because he preferred to be friendly with people who would gamble with him.

Whether the news of the gambling comes like a bolt of lightning, is known but the family is unaware of its extent, or is a chronic problem or addiction within the family, and regardless of the amount of money involved, there are profound emotional consequences of caring about someone who gambles too much.

Most people in their Minneapolis suburb envied Karen and Skip A. Their life seemed to have a storybook quality. Tall, blond, and effortlessly attractive, Karen balanced a career as an associate dean at a community college and management of a busy household with three teenage children, still finding time to entertain Skip's business associates and hosting large gatherings that included their parents, friends, and neighbors. Skip, a stockbroker with a national firm, had a number of large accounts as well as many small but growing ones. Skip worked hard, often sitting up late at night poring over reports. Karen knew he occasionally used cocaine to help him "keep going," but didn't know the extent of his use. Once or twice she had even tried it with him, and their sex was better than ever! Life was good, and they were looking forward to celebrating their twenty-fifth anniversary with a trip to Hawaii.

And then the call came.

Skip was called in by the legal and compliance department of his firm. A personal check of his had bounced and it triggered a review of his own accounts. It appeared that his losses with the firm during the last months were excessive, and he was unable to cover them. Unless, of course, we took a second mortgage on our house. But then there was a further investigation and review of all his clients' accounts. It seemed that Skip had been churning, that is, making excessive trades for his clients to generate commission. Some of the trades were done without proper authorization, although Skip claimed he had been given verbal permission. It soon became clear that Skip had done all of this to support buying and selling of his private holdings and lost all control as he got deeper and deeper into debt. Skip had gone from being a skilled trader to becoming a compulsive gambler.

At first I simply didn't believe it. I was sure there was some mistake. But it was true. I couldn't imagine how this could have happened without my knowing. Could I have closed my eyes to what was going on? But there didn't seem to have been any clues.

Later, in retrospect, I could see that Skip's double-talk about assets and income was to throw me off the track, and his eagerness to pay bills far in advance was an attempt to control his gambling. Then I remembered his numerous phone calls to the office even when we were on vacation. I had thought it was just his sense of responsibility to his clients, but now I realize it was because he couldn't stay away from his own daily trading.

Sometimes I used to think that the market had taken on a personal and emotional meaning that went beyond the actual profits and losses. But I figured that's how stockbrokers are.

"Hindsight is always easier than foresight," said Karen's friend and colleague Julia. But everyone else seemed to think Karen should have known.

So, in addition to the shock of finding out what had been going on, Karen now had to contend with people's sarcastic and critical comments. Their storybook lives had deteriorated into a tabloid feature. Embarrassed and ashamed, Karen was completely humiliated.

"Here I was, with a graduate degree in psychology, and I didn't even know what was happening in my own family. How could I advise others?"

Initially, Karen was flooded with information and almost immobilized, but she soon began to react with characteristic forthrightness and vigor. She discussed the situation with the children, her parents, and her in-laws. An attorney gave her advice on how to protect her own interests.

Karen kept so busy she didn't have time to feel or think about anything else other than the details of surviving the financial crisis.

And then her emotional walls came crashing down.

I became furious at those who had known what Skip was up to and hadn't warned me. I began to feel betrayed. How could Skip have done this to me and the family? If he could have done such a thing and kept it from me, how could I believe *anything* he had done or told me for twenty-five years? Why did he need money? If this was just for excitement, what other kinds of excitement did he seek? Were there other women? Was he using more cocaine than I knew about? Could I believe anything *anyone* told me anymore?

Karen's whole life suddenly seemed like a sham. Formerly composed and restrained, Karen almost overnight became accusing and critical of everything and everyone.

Two of the children, fourteen-year-old Ted and sixteen-year-old Libby, felt sorry for their father and were fiercely defensive of him. They were furious with their mother for making such a scene. Underneath their acceptance of their father was a need for reassurance that life would go on—reassurance that their mother couldn't give them. They feared but wouldn't acknowledge that their father couldn't be trusted to keep any promises. Gwen, a seventeen-year-old senior, feigned disinterest, but in truth, she was frightened that her college plans would be scuttled. She experienced a sense of impending doom that would follow her into adulthood.

Karen's parents tried to be supportive of her and the children, but their anger with Skip was so overwhelming that it spilled over into their relationships with their grandchildren. Karen's father, who had been battling prostate cancer for three years, suddenly became worse, as the disease spread to his bones. He could barely walk, but radiation therapy held promise for a remission of his symptoms. Karen's mother postponed cataract surgery, but she couldn't see well enough to drive him for his daily treatments. This responsibility fell on Karen for the next six weeks.

Ted and Libby, hurt that their grandparents had turned against their father, refused to see them. Gwen felt guilty about her anger at her father. Karen found her parents' support to be a double-edged sword: It was comforting but it made her feel as if they thought she couldn't take care of herself, and their criticism of Skip was a message that they thought Karen had made a poor choice in a marriage partner.

Skip's parents blamed everything on Karen and her expensive tastes. Why did she need such a large home? Had the children really needed ice-skating and tennis lessons? Why did she entertain so lavishly? One day they would say, "If Karen had stayed home and hadn't worked, she would have given Skip more attention and he wouldn't have looked around for 'excitement.' " Then the next day they would say, "Why couldn't she have had a job that paid more? Then he wouldn't have needed more money."

The two sets of parents, who had always laughingly said, "We'd be the best of friends even if our children weren't married to each other," were no longer talking, and Skip's parents were totally unsupportive of Karen's parents' health crises.

Karen's sister, with whom she had never been close, suddenly began calling daily from Chicago, conveying that she had never liked Skip, adding to Karen's feelings of failure.

Skip's older sister sarcastically said that it all sounded like a rerun of a bad movie. The secret was out: Skip's father, a thirty-year recovering alcoholic, had embarrassed her many times during her adolescent years. Skip, who had blocked out much of those early days, felt he never pleased his father. One of his early recollections that he had never shared with Karen was his father criticizing a B on an otherwise straight A fifth-grade report card, then spilling a drink over it. Skip had to wave it dry before his father could sign it. Skip still remembers his teacher sniffing and looking up at him quizzically when he returned it.

Skip's mother secretly blamed her husband for Skip's problem, and their relationship became increasingly strained. She was worried that he would begin to drink again.

Friends began to pull away, although a few were there for Karen through thick and thin. Life would never be the same again for this family.

Initially, Roy G. was pleased to learn that his mother, Rose, was going to Atlantic City with other people from her neighborhood. He felt that it would add a little diversion to her life; so many of her friends had died or moved away, and she no longer had companions with whom she could play cards, shop, or go to an occasional concert or to the theater.

Roy never dreamed his attractive, outspoken mother could get "hooked" on gambling.

When my dad died, Mom was only sixty-three and she pulled herself together, keeping busy. She lived in Queens, New York, and she had plenty of friends. Then a neighbor who had been widowed around the same time took an interest in her, and they got married and he moved into Mom's apartment. My brothers and I were pleased; we had known that man all our lives. But when he died eight years later Mom was devastated. By now, her old "network" was gone, and so she joined a neighborhood leisure group. When trips to Atlantic City were scheduled, she was usually first in line.

We lived only fifteen minutes away on Long Island, and spoke to her often, but we were busy with our own activities and saw her only occasionally. One of my brothers lives in Washington, D.C., and another in Cleveland. Those trips to Atlantic City were filling a void for Mom, and so we actually encouraged it. My children were somewhat amused—the thought of a gambling grandma seemed rather charming and unconventional!

One time when I was leaving Mom's I ran into Ella, the busybody who has lived next door to her since I can remember. Out of the blue she said, "Do you know your mother goes to Atlantic City three and four times a week? I think she's gambling too much."

I told my brothers but they dismissed it as foolish gossip. Then about a month later my cousin mentioned that my mother hadn't been to see her mother (Mom's older sister) for quite a while.

My wife usually has a good handle on these things, but she was unconcerned. Still, I was worried. I felt that my mother wasn't herself. The last year she had forgotten the kids' birthdays, and when she saw them she seemed impatient. I figured she was getting older and I put it out of my mind. That is, until the day we asked her to come to our son's graduation from junior high school. Mom asked us to pick her up. I was surprised because she had driven here hundreds of times.

Mom explained that she had gotten rid of her car. "It wasn't working right, and I just didn't see the sense in getting it fixed."

Now I was really puzzled. Mom always asked my advice about cars or anything mechanical, so why hadn't she consulted me this time? She could have traded it in or sold it, then bought another. So I decided to take a ride over there and see what was going on. When I came into the apartment the first thing that struck me was that the silver candlesticks that had been on the dining room table since I could remember were gone. Then I noticed an empty spot on the wall where the antique clock had been.

"What's going on?" I asked. That's when Mom broke into tears and admitted she had sold things and that the car had been repossessed because she hadn't made payments.

I couldn't believe it. Ella had been right. Mom *was* gambling too much. The tip-offs had all been there, but had been casually dismissed by the family. And now, it certainly looked like it had gotten out of control.

When I got to the bottom of the financial mess, it turned out that Mom had wiped out her savings and had given up her supplemental insurance that paid the Medicare deductible and other extras, but she *did* have her monthly Social Security checks to pay basic expenses.

The emotional consequences seriously shook the family. The brother from Cleveland was laying the guilt on Roy because he hadn't noticed what was going on. The brother from Washington, who had never gotten along too well with either of them, took a "so what—it's not our problem" attitude, which increased the strained relationships among all of them.

Roy was annoyed with his wife, because she had minimized the problem when he first presented it to her. They both felt tremendous guilt because they hadn't spent enough time with Rose, perceiving this as the reason she was gambling too much. At the same time they were angry and resentful. And scared. What would happen now if she got sick? She no longer had any savings to pay for her care. And in the meantime, what will they do about the gambling?

Roy got into terrible arguments with his mother. "What's the matter with you? How could you gamble like that?" All his shame, humiliation, self-blame, and helplessness was subsumed under anger.

Rose's sister and niece finally learned what had happened, and they vacillated between feeling sorry for her and being furious and mortified.

The grandchildren knew Grandma gambled, but had no idea that things had gotten out of control. Roy and his wife tried to keep it a secret, but the children were confused and bewildered by the whispering and secrecy in the household, and imagined that their parents were about to get divorced or something else terrible was going to happen.

One widowed grandmother living alone had become a problem gambler. Three sons, their wives and children, and a sister and niece all felt the impact of the gambling. And it would be a long time before the tension and distrust abated.

* * *

Cynthia B. was not unfamiliar with gambling:

For as long as I can remember, gambling has played a role in my life. My father was a gambler, and life at home had been continuous lies, secrecy, fights, and never enough money. I always felt ashamed and guilty, as if it were up to me to make my mother's life better. When I met William I saw him as my savior. I was shy and never very popular, and he was good-looking and had a lot of friends. He seemed so different from my father or my mother or me. He was fun-loving and at ease in a crowd. He made me feel happy and alive when I was with him.

William and I used to sometimes gamble at illegal gambling clubs in St. Louis. One time William had this really big win, and we went to the Caribbean, where we gambled still more. It was the first vacation I had ever had, except of course for the honeymoon weekend we had in New Orleans.

After a few years it seemed to me as if William were gambling far more than we could afford. He mostly bet on sports, but he also liked poker. Sometimes he stayed out almost all night playing. But I always knew where he was.

Truthfully, I didn't really care after a while because when he was home he was moody and critical or else he didn't pay any attention to me at all. And our sex life was almost nonexistent. When we did have sex, William was finished in a minute or two, then he would get out of bed and go into the living room to watch television and smoke a cigarette. It made me feel so degraded and inadequate.

But you know, I loved him anyway for he still had this boyish quality that made me laugh and feel young. I was scared that he would leave me and I would be alone. No matter how awful things were, it still seemed better than being without him. Often I would threaten to leave him, but I don't think he ever believed I would do it.

And of course we had Bill and Anna. So I would try everything I could to please William, but nothing worked. I guess that's when I put on all that weight. I was just always eating. Except when I was smoking.

I would pester him to stop gambling. Then he would explode and walk out of the house. Later, he would come back but say he gambled to get away from me because I was such a nervous wreck and had gotten so fat and become such a nag.

Every time the phone rang I wondered if it was a collection agency, loan shark, bookmaker, friends, or relatives asking for money. We didn't have credit anywhere. The local supermarket, the cleaner, and the gas station had a "cash only" policy for us. I was embarrassed to even take the kids to the doctor because we had bounced checks there. I lived in dread of being evicted from my apartment and having no place to live.

Sometimes I would really hate William and then the next thing I would be catering to all his desires. Then he would show remorse and I would feel so guilty for how much I had nagged him. I would feel very loving and sort of maternal toward him. I just couldn't bear to see him worried about anything, even bills, and I would even try to reassure him that it would all work out.

One of the few pleasures I had was my kids. I liked doing things for them, and would put myself out to think of fun things to do. But then there were the times I would be at the end of my rope with all I had to think about, and I would start hitting. I was always sorry later.

I figured that if I could just keep the kids out of the way while William relaxed at night, made special favorite meals for him, was a good housekeeper, and thought of more ways to please him he would stay home happily and not want to gamble. When that didn't work I felt like a failure. Sometimes I would yell at him and call him names.

As the years went by, I was always tired, sometimes to the point of exhaustion. The house was a mess and I couldn't even seem to make minor decisions. It might be two o'clock before I even thought of making the beds, and the laundry would pile up until William and the kids didn't have any socks left. Sometimes I would stand staring at my closet deciding what to wear; I couldn't decide what to watch on television and would walk around the supermarket in a daze, not knowing what cereal to buy.

Then I began to develop lower back pain, probably because I would tense up my muscles and then they would go into spasms. It seemed I was always tense.

I began to lie a lot. For instance, I would tell William people said things they didn't. And I would do things to get even. Like forgetting to do errands I had promised, and not buying his favorite foods. Once I disconnected the cable on the television and threw away a part so he couldn't watch the big game that night. Often I "stole" money from the place I knew he kept it hidden.

I never let on to my mother about William's gambling. I told myself I didn't want to worry her, but I was probably mostly ashamed that I had done the one thing she had warned me about: never marry a gambler. And then there was my sister, who had married "well." She and her kids were such a source of pride to everyone.

Most of the time I was juggling so many excuses to everyone I had trouble keeping all my stories straight. On open school nights, I would tell the teachers William had to work even though I knew he was out gambling. And I would make up excuses when my sister invited us to her house. And of course I had a million excuses why we didn't pay our bills. And at times I tended to agree with him; a big gambling win would solve all our problems. That's when I began waitressing two nights a week at the restaurant down the block.

The children seemed to feel the tension in the house. When Bill was fifteen he got into trouble with gambling at school. Later I learned that when the principal said he would call his parents, Bill begged him to just call his father, saying, "My Mom's not been well lately. Her back and all, and she just can't take the stress." So the principal called William, who came in and "smoothed things over" and never told me. I found out about it a year later when Bill was expelled for selling pot at school.

Anna was like my best friend instead of a daughter. It used to kill me the way William would dote on her one minute, and then later ignore her. But Anna seemed to take it all in stride. At least I thought so. Then when she was about nine things changed. She began to get into trouble at school for pushing other kids, and, later, for stealing a pencil case from another child. I was constantly being called by the school, but I couldn't believe she did all those things at school because at home she was so good.

Anna's sixteen now and she's as good at school as she is at home. But then she's practically never home. She's always at a friend's house—Faith's or Brenda's. But when she's home she helps me, and is always trying to smooth things out between William, Bill, and me. But sometimes she says that if I was more understanding of William, lost some weight, and got some interests of my own he wouldn't gamble so much.

Bill is really hard to take lately. He's twenty-one and he works for a printer in St. Louis. He's got a good job, but he gambles and drinks too much. I don't seem to have much luck with the men in my life.

It was now twenty-five years since Cynthia had married William, and for all of these years she struggled to control his gambling. Initially she thought the gambling was fun, then when she saw it getting out of hand, she was confrontational, but eventually she learned to keep a lid on her feelings and went through the motions of life, never really having any pleasures or showing much anger. Cynthia became a classic example of a codependent and enabler, roles she had learned as the child of a gambler. Anna may be headed in the same direction. Bill appears to be following in his father's footsteps.

One Friday night, Anna was visiting a friend, Bill was out, and William was at his poker game. Cynthia's back was bothering her more than ever. She had never felt so alone. She stared at the bottle of pain relievers on the table next to her and decided to call William at his poker game to tell him that if he didn't come home immediately she would swallow everything in the bottle. He said he would come home as soon as the game was finished.

Two hours later he walked into the house. Cynthia was passed out on the living room couch, the empty bottle of pills next to her. The medics got her to the hospital in time, where her stomach was pumped. On Monday morning she told her story to a social worker.

The following Friday William went back to his poker game.

When gambling is a problem or an addiction, each family member will react in his or her own way.

Spouses are humiliated, betrayed, helpless, and immobilized. Children are neglected, confused, and worried. They may grow up feeling shame, believing there is something wrong with them. Many never learn to trust. Some marry gamblers or other addicts; some become addicted to gambling, alcohol, or drugs; some seem not to have been affected.

Parents and grandparents stand by helplessly, feeling responsible or guilty. Siblings are often angry and jealous of the way the gambler gets all the attention, and resent the sacrifices they make. Friends become divided in loyalties and feel confused, exploited, and betrayed.

Almost everyone hurts, some more than others, even if there's no financial crisis. It tends to get worse, and even if a financial crisis hasn't occurred yet, it probably will; then the damage may be irreparable.

CHAPTER 7

Against All Odds

Financial and Legal Consequences of Gambling

There are financial and legal consequences for the spouses, parents, grandparents, children, siblings, friends, and coworkers of compulsive and problem gamblers. Whether the gambler is young or old, working class, middle class, or wealthy, a loss of savings can mean immediate hardship or translate into a shattered life goal or lost economic security.

When Vernon T. retired as a public utilities inspector, he thought he would realize his life's dream. He certainly never believed that his wife's gambling could change all of that.

> I had figured that my wife and I would buy a small place in the country where we could get away from our city apartment, and I could fish, relax, and do some gardening. From the day we married forty-two years ago, my wife, Hattie, had managed our money. When I suggested it was time to start looking for a place, she just kept stalling and making excuses not to go to look.
>
> I couldn't figure out why she had lost interest. Hattie had retired when the auto parts store where she worked closed a few years ago, so I thought she would be ready for a change of scenery. I had noticed she hadn't been herself lately and thought it was because she missed her sister, who had moved to North Carolina.

Then one day a friend told me about a perfect place for us. It was only a two-hour drive from our apartment, and it had good fishing and a lake for swimming. The price sounded fair and I thought it would be good to know exactly how much we could put down. I asked Hattie to show me the bank accounts and that's when I learned that we had nothing left except one small certificate of deposit.

It seemed that Hattie's day trips to the casinos in Atlantic City and her fascination with the slots had just about wiped us out.

What could I do? I loved Hattie and in every way she had been a good wife. We never had any children and she had devoted her life to me, our godchildren, and our nieces and nephews. I guess she was lonely, and when she saw her friends and her sisters enjoying their grandchildren she missed not having kids more than ever. How could I be angry with her? She was my whole life.

So I went back to work. Our minister, bless him, put Hattie in touch with someone who could help her with the gambling problem, and she got a job in a local beauty parlor. She really enjoys that.

I know we'll never have enough money to buy that place in the country or to protect us from financial emergencies. But I do have a pension and Social Security, so I guess we're better off than some people. And I do have Hattie.

In one quick moment Vernon experienced the loss of savings and a dream. But, as he said, he's better off than some people.

ADULT CHILDREN AND THE GAMBLER

Gambling debts sometimes make it necessary for adult children to offer financial help to parents even before they are firmly established in their careers. The children of Roger L., a fifty-one-year-old dentist, were hit hard.

Roger's twenty-one-year-old twin sons, Jason and Gary, had just graduated from college and were about to get their first jobs. Susan, his twenty-five-year-old daughter, was a computer programmer. "The Accident," as they would forever refer to it, happened on a rainy June evening. Roger's wife was killed, and he suffered head injuries when their car was hit by a truck.

Susan tells the story.

We were heartbroken to lose our mother. She was the sweetest, most lovable woman you ever knew. She was a nursery school teacher and every child and parent loved her.

We were grateful that Dad survived, although for quite a while it looked as if he might not make it. But slowly he began to improve, and we learned that although he might always have seizures, medications could help control them. His vision was blurred, his speech was slow, and he had problems with coordination and memory. He needed help with most everyday activities like dressing and eating, but he could go home *if* someone was with him all the time.

My brothers and I had to do some fast growing up—suddenly we had all these responsibilities. We went through Mom and Dad's papers, checking for savings and insurance information. We were floored. Dad had only the most basic medical insurance from his dental association and had no life or disability insurance, and no retirement plan. Despite a busy and thriving dental practice, he had only a little over three thousand dollars in his checking account, no savings of any sort, and he owed more than fifty thousand dollars on a number of credit cards. We couldn't find his tax returns. The big, beautiful house in which we had grown up was mortgaged to the hilt. It looked like foreclosure was imminent. Later, we salvaged some of the equity to pay off six years of back taxes and the credit cards.

The social worker at the hospital suggested that if we couldn't pay a home health aide to care for him, Dad could go to the county residential health care facility where he wouldn't have to pay anything. That was the same place where Dad used to donate his dental services. He would sometimes tell us about the place—and say it was clean but depressing. And he once said, "No relative of mine will ever go there."

How could we send *him* there? And besides, Dad kept saying, "I want to go home." So we decided that Dad would move into my apartment. I would sleep in the living room and give Dad my bedroom. Jason would temporarily live with our aunt, and Gary with his friend's family. We each agreed to chip in to pay for a home health aide to be with Dad while I was working. My aunt said she would give us some money toward it.

We couldn't understand why there was no money. But we soon learned that everyone else knew, because they were aware of Dad's gambling habits. We had always known he was a sports fan, and we knew he bet, but it never occurred to us that he gambled heavily. My aunt told us she had occasionally lent Mother money, but Mother chose to keep it from us, so we had never known.

We really loved our Dad. He was such a good father in every way. How could we let him down now?

Eventually Dad got Social Security disability benefits, but this still didn't completely cover the cost of someone to be with him during the week while we all worked.

Sometimes I'm just furious with Dad. If he hadn't gambled everything away, it would have been so much easier. He could have gone back to his own home with help, or we could have sold the house and bought something suitable where I might have lived comfortably with him. And then maybe we could have afforded help for evenings and weekends, too, so that we wouldn't have had to take turns caring for him.

For the next ten years, until their father had a fatal heart attack, at a time when they should have been building their own economic future and making other plans for their lives, Susan, Jason, and Gary took on the financial responsibility of supporting their father. His sister-in-law, a woman of moderate means, also helped in order to ease the burden for her late sister's children.

THE GAMBLER AND THE BUSINESS WORLD

One compulsive gambler can affect the financial well-being of coworkers and others in the business community as well as that of members of his own family.

When Sam Y. died at thirty-five, his wife became the owner of a wholesale food business in San Francisco. When her three sons, Michael, Ken, and Henry, were old enough, they worked for her. Michael and Ken each married and began to raise families. Henry, always a loner, remained single. In addition to her sons, Mrs. Y. employed some nephews and nieces and other members of the Chinese-American community.

Michael began to notice that Henry gambled far more than other people he knew, and it seemed to him that it was out of control. He tried to tell his mother, but she just didn't want to hear about it.

I tried to tell her that Henry didn't gamble the way our family and friends did. Gambling was much more than a pastime for Henry. I told Mother that Henry just couldn't stay away from those downtown clubs and casinos in Lake Tahoe. But she believed he would keep his promise to stop "when the time was right." Sometimes he would be away for days on end and she would worry, then he would come to work, broke and hungry. I would hear my mother get angry, but then she would feel sorry for him, and give him an advance on his salary, and make excuses to everybody for his absences.

I didn't find out until much later that she was constantly giving him money. My mother was a good businesswoman who ran the company well and even took care of some of the accounting. My brothers and I were on salary and made a good living. We knew that after our mother retired, the business would be ours.

One day when Henry wasn't there, my mother called Ken and me and our three cousins into her office. She was closing the business, she said. There were not enough funds to pay the rent or our suppliers.

We were shocked. Business had been better than ever. But then I began to think about Henry, and how Mother was always loaning him money.

Mother explained that her accountant and banker had warned her that this might happen, because they knew she had been taking large amounts of capital from the business to cover Henry's debts. She didn't listen to their advice to stop because loan sharks had been threatening Henry, and she was afraid of what might happen if she didn't give him money. She told us that she had given Henry close to a million dollars in the last few years. "What could I do?" she asked. At this point she broke down, sobbing.

There would be salaries that week for everyone, but no money left for severance pay. We would all have to look for new jobs.

I thought if I saw Henry I would kill him. He had hurt so many people. Not just Ken and me, but our cousins and the other workers and all our families.

I looked at my mother, and I saw a broken woman, who was shattered by having to close the business that she and my father had worked so hard to build. She felt deeply ashamed for having caused so many problems for so many people who depended on the business.

I wasn't sure how I would tell my wife and children what had happened. And I had no idea how I would continue to provide for them.

THE GAMBLER'S NEED FOR MONEY

Loss of money is the consequence most commonly associated with gambling too much. To remain in action *and* pay off debts, the gambler needs a constant flow of money, and this drain of funds impacts all those with whom he has any economic connection.

Sometimes the gambler has occasional or even chronic problems relating to money, but some or even all family members, friends, or business associates may remain unaware of the extent of the problem until losses cause *them* to suffer a financial crisis.

Usually, though, there are ongoing recognizable problems with money; bills don't get paid, savings or equity is not built, and assets (and accompanying life-style) are less than what would be expected from the gambler's known or assumed income.

The need of problem or compulsive gamblers for more and more money eventually depletes their own savings or assets and forces them to borrow from relatives, friends, coworkers, credit cards, or banks.

TURNING TO CRIME

As losses continue to mount and these sources "dry up," the gambler often turns to illegal sources, such as loan sharks. They do this despite the high interest rates and their knowledge that defaulting on repayments may result in threatened or actual violence.

As a last resort, the gambler may turn to criminal activity to obtain a cash fix, to remain in action, to repay loans, and/or to prevent "tipping his hand" to his family or others. The gambler dreads letting anyone know his gambling is causing financial trouble because this threatens his self-esteem and challenges his denial. Exposure also may cause others to try to put a stop to his gambling. In the end, the gambler, like other addicts, will lose all self-respect or integrity and go so far as to steal or even physically threaten those closest to him.

Usually the crimes committed by gamblers are nonviolent. The gambler, especially a compulsive one, is a master at exploiting the business community and his family and friends. Because so much of our business and personal lives revolve around paper transactions, it is easy for gamblers to obtain money from others. They commit forgery, siphon money from business to personal accounts, or "con" the public with financial get-rich-quick schemes. Many turn to insurance fraud by creating or staging accidents, committing arson, or faking business, home, or personal burglaries. The lists of ways gamblers can illegally obtain money are endless.

Those closely involved with the gambler, especially spouses, are most often the victims. The gambler lies about investments or earnings in an attempt to convince you that money is legitimately needed. Or, using indirect approaches, the gambler forges your signature on checks, loans, credit cards, or charge accounts, or "borrows" your bank cards to get money from cash machines. Without your knowledge, the gambler sells off jewelry, cars, electronic equipment, even furniture. Whether your money is being held in a bank or a brokerage house, the gambler uses his charm and cunning, exploiting his relationship to you to make use of these funds. The gambler may truly *believe* he will put the money back before you notice and bets on the likelihood that you won't bring legal charges against him.

WHAT HAPPENS TO YOU?

Since your economic and legal well-being may depend on the gambler in any number of ways, you may suffer dire consequences from the gambler's behavior. For instance, in addition to losing your money, you become vulnerable to financial disaster when he doesn't pay premiums or cashes in life, home, business, or medical insurance policies. You may find that *your* credit rating has been seriously damaged, and it may become impossible for you to get legitimate loans or credit cards.

You may be placed in a great deal of jeopardy if you cosign loans for the gambler or your name is used for business transactions such as trading stocks and commodities. If you have filed tax returns jointly with the gambler, you may later learn that the return was either fraudulent *or* it was never even filed.

Are you responsible for what the gambler has done? Generally when people can prove they did not *knowingly* participate in any of these illegitimate activities, they are not held *criminally* libel, but they may be *financially* libel. In the next section, we will talk about what you can do to avoid some of these consequences.

Even if you don't lose money or get directly involved in the gambler's criminality, there is an impact on you. For instance, gamblers often associate with criminal elements of society when gambling or obtaining loans. This may lead to threats and further involvement with the underworld and its dangers. Gamblers become entangled in the criminal justice system by being subpoenaed as witnesses or being arrested or jailed themselves. This can be frightening and can affect your career and relationships with others.

The family is a system: One member's emotional and economic changes affect the others. Therefore, the gambler's job loss, revocation of professional licenses, diminished or eliminated income, mounting debts (greatly increased because of interest and penalty payments), and dissipation of assets affect the entire family. Your family's basic needs may not be met presently or in the future. You may lose all financial security against catastrophic or even ordinary but unexpected expenses. Bankruptcy may be on the horizon, and although this seems like a solution, it has its consequences: It is difficult to obtain credit for many years.

FROM LUXURY TO BASICS

It is easy to see how the out-of-control gambler can render even a wealthy or middle class family impoverished and homeless. Lorraine H. thought it could never happen to her.

We had just returned from a cruise around the Hawaiian Islands aboard a yacht belonging to one of Neil's clients. When Neil returned to his office the next morning he was greeted at the door by officers from the district attorney's office. His partners had already changed the lock to his office and prepared their announcement for the press: "Following a pattern of questionable financial transactions, we have asked Mr. Neil H. to resign. Simultaneously we have reported our findings to the bar association and the fraud unit of the district attorney's office."

Up until then, we had enjoyed a life that most people would envy. We had beautiful homes, luxurious cars, went to the best restaurants and film openings, entertained at home and the club, vacationed in Europe, Hawaii, and the Orient. Neil loved to gamble, so we often spent weekends in Las Vegas, and always had the best tables at the shows. I never dreamed Neil had become addicted to gambling and was playing beyond his means.

As a partner in the law firm begun by his father back in the 1940s, Neil had a large income. The firm specialized in trusts and estates and had a variety of clients: Hollywood luminaries, physicians, other attorneys, as well as many wealthy widows.

I couldn't imagine that Neil would ever do anything illegal. But apparently his partners had reason to believe otherwise. They

accused him of falsifying records, forging executors' checks, cashing
an estate check intended for taxes, and misappropriating money that
was in escrow.

I had absolutely no idea that he was being investigated until we
returned from vacation. It was dreadful. They brought him down to
the police station where they booked and fingerprinted him. They
let him call a lawyer. And another lawyer, and still another. No one
would take the case when he told them he didn't know how he could
pay them.

When Neil was finally able to call me I already knew what had
happened. At the same time that he was being arrested at his office,
detectives were at the door to our home. Armed with search warrants and carrying badges and guns, they went through the entire
house, opening every drawer, closet, and cabinet, looking for in-
criminating documents. Everything was a mess. When I couldn't
find the key to the safe in the den, they took the whole thing. Then
they broke open the drawers to Neil's beautiful antique desk, because I didn't have that key either.

I think those officers thought that I knew something. But I didn't.
Why should I have known? Bills had always been paid and our life-
style was never disrupted.

I had so much to think about. I knew he would need bail. And he
certainly needed a lawyer. I called my friend Elyse, whose brother
was a lawyer. He agreed to help and warned me that the judge might
set bail at almost the same amount that Neil was accused of stealing.
I wasn't sure how I could raise it, but I figured I could pawn my
jewelry. I raced down to the bank where we have a safe deposit box.
When I opened it I almost fainted. My big diamond ring, bracelets,
pins, and earrings were all gone. Instead, I found pawn tickets. I
started sobbing. How could Neil have done this to me? When I put
the box away, I was waving the tickets and blurted out my story to
the security guard. He took pity on me and told me that I could
sell the pawn tickets.

Between Elyse and her brother I managed to get myself together
and show up at court the next morning. I was terrified when I saw
Neil marched in with the dregs of society: a child molester, drug
dealers, a male prostitute, and a man who was accused of murdering
his neighbor. I panicked when I realized Neil must have shared a
cell with one or more of these people.

Somehow Elyse's brother got Neil out of there and home that day. I
needed a sedative to calm me down. Neil just sat in the den, staring.

The whole thing had been on the local news the night before. Neil had seen it at the police station, and I'm sure all our friends had too. A few called, but most didn't.

Things began to settle in after a few days. Elyse's brother agreed to start working on the case, but said we would have to get a public defender if we couldn't drum up enough money.

I knew we had no income from the law firm, but I figured things were not that bad—we still had some assets. But no. It seemed that our personal holdings were either nonexistent or worthless. Neil had withdrawn, borrowed against, or sold all our stocks, bonds, real estate, and some business partnerships. He had even taken out second mortgages on our Beverly Hills home and the beach house, and had taken on other huge loans. We were actually millions of dollars in debt, and I had never suspected it.

Then I learned that the IRS was also investigating our joint tax returns for fraud. This was especially frightening because I knew I might be held liable. I had never even looked at the return after giving Neil information on my earnings and expenses. I just signed it, never suspecting that Neil might be lying about his income.

With no income at all, we had to turn to family and friends for day-to-day living expenses. I felt I was living in a nightmare. Realizing we were nearly destitute brought back old memories of my childhood when I had to wear the cast-off clothes of my rich cousins.

The children really suffered. Our oldest boy was at Stanford University, our daughter was at Princeton, and our younger boy was in the ninth grade at a prep school right here in L.A. He had heard the whole thing on television, and so had his friends.

The tuitions were paid only through that semester, so the two children in college had to transfer to the state university and look for work. Our younger boy had to switch to the local public school. Not that there was anything wrong with these schools—I had gone to public schools—but it meant the kids would be leaving friends and having to adjust to a whole new way of life.

The thing that bothered me most was that Neil had totally wiped out the younger boy's savings account. He had opened it himself with the cash gifts he had received for his bar mitzvah just two years ago. That seemed like the worse betrayal of all.

The consequences of Neil's out-of-control gambling were far-reaching: embarrassment and major financial losses to his firm and to its clients and the ruin of his family's wealth and security. He faced disbarment and a jail sentence. While awaiting trial, he took a job with a telemarketing firm.

It was all more than Neil could face. Six months after he was arrested, and before the trial was to begin, he went down to the basement where he kept his service revolver from his Korean tour of duty, and put a bullet through his head.

Lorraine had to borrow money to pay for the funeral.

FROM MIDDLE CLASS TO POVERTY

In one quick step, a middle-class family can go from financial solvency to poverty. Growing up, Theresa A. never dreamed she would end up on welfare.

My parents were hard-working, no-nonsense people who never expected to get rich, but enjoyed a lot of good things in life. When Frank and I decided to get married they were really happy about it, although they thought he still needed to do some settling down. They figured, and so did I, that after we started a family he would stop hanging out with his friends so much and be more of a homebody. I was working in an office, and Frank was working for an alarm system and security company near Tampa. We both wanted to have our own business, and after we were married a few years we decided to "go for it." We didn't have any savings, but my parents gave us some money, and that together with some business loans gave us enough to open our own small company. Some of the customers that Frank had serviced came over to us for their repairs, and it wasn't long before we had a lot of new customers and were installing central alarm systems in their homes and businesses.

I handled the phones and billing, and Frank took care of the rest of the business and hired two assistants to help him with installations and repairs. Things were going well and I wanted to get pregnant. Frank kept saying, "Let's wait a while."

In the next few years I began to see a lot of changes in Frank. He was drinking a lot and going out with his friends more than ever. He also used cocaine, saying he needed it to keep up with all the hours he was putting into work. And I knew he and his friends bet on sports, jai alai, horses, and the dogs.

Frank was a hard worker, but he was careless about time and money. Customers would call to complain that he hadn't shown up when he promised. I would make excuses to the customers, but later I would fight with Frank about it. I tried to keep the billing straight, but I never could figure out what he had charged a customer because he didn't always give receipts or bring back the paid bills. I realized he often gave people a break if they paid cash. Only much later did I discover he had lied to me about a lot of things, like how much he was making on installations and repairs.

One day two police detectives came in to the office looking for Frank. They said there had been a series of robberies in homes and businesses where we had installed alarm systems. I figured it was a coincidence and their questions were just routine, until Frank walked in and looked scared to death. They asked—no, told—Frank to come to the precinct to talk with them.

Well, to make a long story short, it seemed that Frank had a lot to do with the robberies. Although he hadn't participated in the actual break-ins, he had "sold" information (about the alarm systems, the individual security codes, and what was on the premises) to the guys who did the jobs.

Why? Frank explained that he did it to cover gambling debts. He admitted that for the last few years he had been secretly borrowing on credit cards in his own name as well as on a few of our joint cards.

But that's not all. The business was in both of our names, and I had cosigned a lot of bank loans. Because I was an owner *and* worked there, I was also a suspect in the robberies, and it looked as if I was responsible for loans too. I seemed to be in as big a mess as Frank, although I had not known anything about all of this.

We needed money for a lawyer and some money to cover our regular expenses. I thought I could solve that because I had my own money market account, which I had opened when I inherited ten thousand dollars from my grandfather two years ago. But it was gone. Between my last statement and the day I went over to see the broker, I discovered that Frank had withdrawn it. He had forged my signature on the withdrawal request. I was too devastated to be angry.

My parents paid for a lawyer for me, and she was great. She managed to get criminal charges against me dropped, but she couldn't do anything about all the loans I had cosigned or debts incurred on the joint credit cards. Ignorance just wasn't a defense.

People from the bank and collection agencies were constantly calling, and I didn't know where I would get money to get through the day, no less pay them. And as luck would have it, I found out I was pregnant.

It seemed definite that Frank would go to jail. With the help of his family, we paid some of the loans, and while Frank was away I tried hard to pay off the credit cards, but I didn't even make a dent in them.

When Frank Jr. was born, I moved into my parents' small apartment. When Frank got out, we declared bankruptcy. Even though we couldn't get credit again for years, I figured it would give us a fresh start.

Things were OK for a few months, but after I became pregnant with Marie, Frank must have started gambling again. He disappeared after bouncing checks in my name and borrowing all over town.

I haven't heard from him since he left, but I hear from his family that he is living out of his car near New Orleans.

THE GAMBLER'S FAMILY TAKES ON NEW ROLES

When one person gets into trouble with gambling, other family members often have to take on new or additional roles. It seemed to Martha and Victor S. that they would never get a chance to have some time to just relax and enjoy life.

Victor and I brought up our four children to be good students, to go to church, and to do the right things. And they were, until they became teenagers in the late 1960s. That's when they started using drugs. The two younger kids straightened out soon enough, but our oldest dropped out of school and got into a lot of trouble. Eventually he joined the army, and now he's a staff sergeant. He's doing fine.

But Laurie, our next oldest, was never able to get things together. She was wild in high school, got arrested twice for shoplifting, dropped out, and then married some bastard. They drank and used drugs together and he hit her a lot, but she never told us. They had a beautiful little boy, and that seemed to bring Laurie to her senses. She came to us asking for help, and we took care of the baby while she went into a rehabilitation center. But when she got out she took the baby and went back with her husband. The next thing we knew she was pregnant again, and he was still drinking and using drugs and abusing her. She stayed clean, thank goodness, and after the baby was born, she finally left her husband. This time for good, she said.

She moved near us and got a part-time job. We helped her a bit. Victor and I were still working, so we couldn't baby-sit much during the week, but we would help her on weekends so she could go out with her friends. I was so pleased she was sober, and we hoped and prayed that she would meet a decent man who would be good to her and the boys. I wished she had gone to AA or one of those other programs for alcoholics and drug users, but she didn't.

When the children were old enough for preschool, Laurie got a good full-time job with an office supply firm.

Everything seemed to be going just fine until the day Laurie was arrested. She was caught with hundreds of thousands of dollars' worth of drugs near the airport. It seemed that Laurie was a courier for a big-time organization that sold drugs.

Laurie told us that it wasn't drugs that made her do it. She needed money to repay gambling debts and to be able to keep on gambling. Laurie had gotten hooked on the lottery and numbers.

The lawyer we hired for Laurie argued in court that her addiction to gambling developed as a substitution for her former addictions to alcohol and drugs. Unfortunately, the judge didn't accept this as a defense. Now Laurie is in jail and her two boys are living with us. We adore them, but at our age raising two little hell-raisers isn't easy.

When Laurie's ex-husband learned she was in jail he tried to get custody of the boys even though he hadn't seen them in a few years. We hired a lawyer and have been back and forth in family court several times. So far we still have custody, but he did get visitation rights. Now every time we see him drive away with the boys, our hearts sink. Will he hurt them? Will he bring them back?

Victor and I never thought that at our ages we would be taking care of little ones. Their care and the legal fees have placed a tremendous financial responsibility on us. It's eaten right into our retirement money and takes up so much energy that we don't even feel like going anywhere ourselves. Besides, we can barely afford these luxuries now.

Alcohol, drugs, and gambling. I just don't know how this could have happened to us.

WHEN WILL IT END?

The financial and legal consequences of being involved with someone whose gambling is out of control may threaten or destroy your life. Long after the gambler abstains from gambling, your financial problems may continue or worsen because the clock doesn't stop ticking as interest and penalties on debts increase. Legal problems are costly and take time to resolve. The stress and strain seem to go on forever.

Most people know someone who has been financially devastated by someone else's gambling. For instance, fifteen-year-old Dwight C.'s gambling losses one football season were so large that his parents had to sell their house to get the money to pay his bookie.

Stuart B.'s lover, Howard, was addicted to gambling. Because of this he had no savings and had let his medical insurance lapse. When Howard developed AIDS, Stuart jeopardized his own financial future by using all of *his* savings to pay for his lover's care.

Gus P., the owner of a small but successful neighborhood restaurant in a Tacoma suburb, made the mistake of running a bookmaking establishment in the back, not just to support his own gambling but to be surrounded constantly by action. When the city marshals closed him down, everyone who worked for him lost their jobs, and his grandfather ended up using his life's savings to bail out Gus.

Helen R., a young widow, became so addicted to bingo that she depleted first her own savings and then her widowed mother's. Eventually her two sisters had to support Helen's two children and their mother.

When Robert K.'s income and earnings from his men's clothing manufacturing business no longer covered his gambling debts, he stopped paying his employees' medical insurance premiums and figured out a way to use money from their pension fund. Robert planned to return all the funds after he won back all he had lost. But the more he chased his losses, the more he lost, and eventually the business went into bankruptcy. Then the employees found out they had no medical insurance, and those approaching retirement age were devastated to learn they no longer had a pension.

You may have already suffered many of these consequences, or you may be concerned that these losses can still happen to you. You probably did not realize how financially and legally damaging it is to be involved with someone who gambles too much.

You can cope—even if you have already experienced some of these consequences—and you can protect yourself in the future.

PART THREE

A SURE THING

Survival Techniques

CHAPTER 8

Moving Ahead

You may recently have recognized gambling is a problem or that continued gambling will further erode your life.

Problem gamblers are sometimes (but not always) compulsive gamblers in the making, and the addictive spiral will continue unless arrested.

You may be worried that your life is destined to be caught up in one crisis after another. There are steps to take to prevent further crisis, but first you need to look at your feelings.

LOOKING AT BLAME AND SHAME

Perhaps you are ashamed of the gambler and ashamed of what you and your life have become. Try to remember that the problem gambler is struggling with his emotions and the compulsive gambler is suffering from a disease. Gambling too much is not a moral weakness or sin. And *you* haven't sinned because of your association.

In time you will be able to stop the blame and shame cycle. Millions of people have come out of their shame-filled closets.

FEELING POWERLESS

No matter what your personal scenario is, you feel powerless to control the gambler's behavior and the present circumstances. It's hard to give up the idea that you can "do something" to stop the gambling that is ruining your life or those close to you.

Accept this powerlessness. It is the first step toward surviving and reclaiming your life. Millions of people who have attended twelve-step anonymous groups for families of alcoholics, drug users, and gamblers have done just this. They will tell you that you didn't cause it, you can't control it, and you can't cure it. Accepting your powerlessness doesn't mean you have to accept your lot.

Recognize what you have accomplished so far. You have already recognized there is a problem. You have decided that you will no longer accept things as they are. You've decided to no longer deny that a problem exists. No more illusions. No more excuses. No more pretending that everything is fine. No more saying it doesn't matter.

With this knowledge and new perspective, you can now begin to move on.

MOVING ON

Fear may prevent you from initiating change. If the gambler in your life hasn't already plunged you into financial or emotional ruin, you wonder if change might make your life worse. Perhaps you are thinking that things aren't so bad. The gambler isn't being threatened or about to be arrested. Your bills are still being paid, and the cost to yourself and other family members has not been that great. And besides, almost everyone you know gambles. Remember that the gambler in your life *isn't* like those millions of people who quit while they're ahead or before they lose too much.

His gambling may remain at a plateau. Or it may progress slowly or rapidly as addictions do. The gambler may financially "bottom out" so badly that he has no choice: He stops gambling even though he doesn't really change attitudes and values. Most of the time, though, the gambling will just get worse. So you are going to have to make changes.

But first you must trust yourself to be able to make changes in your life. It's hard to do this because trust is a word you no longer have in your vocabulary. Each time you have doubts about your judgment and convictions (and you will from time to time), remind yourself that as the gambler loses more control your situation will worsen.

You have used various coping strategies in the past. Chances are you haven't just sat around while the gambling continued.

Even if you *didn't* know about the gambling, you probably intervened in other ways, because some of the gambler's behavior was causing you discomfort or unhappiness. This probably wasn't effective, but you still may have persisted. You may have recognized that you were enabling the gambler and yet you found yourself unable to change your reactions.

Knowing that the outcome of your efforts would be unsatisfactory or even harmful probably left you feeling angry with yourself. You may have felt like a failure because you didn't recognize what was going on, or if you did you were unable to do anything about it. You may have also begun to see yourself as "dysfunctional" or even "sick."

Stop judging yourself. Be kind to yourself.

HEALTHY VERSUS UNHEALTHY RISKING

A normal reaction to being involved with a gambler is fear of risks. It may seem easier to continue living your life the way you have rather than trying something new.

Risk taking is part of life. If we didn't take risks, we would barely survive; we would never grow, achieve, or thrive. The secret of risk taking is knowing the difference between healthy and unhealthy risking.

Healthy risking involves trust in yourself and others. It involves loss and letting go of something that has been comfortable, familiar, and reliable, even if it is unsatisfactory. It means facing uncertainty. It's knowing *what* you are giving up and realizing that there are no guarantees you can get it back. It is undertaken with the understanding that risk is necessary to grow to your full potential. Still, it is frightening because the losses bring up those earliest normal anxieties about being alone in the world.

Many people have trouble with healthy risking because it involves taking responsibility for themselves. Sometimes it seems easier to sit back and let the world happen around you rather than make choices and take charge.

Unhealthy risking is either acting impulsively or taking chances without recognizing or measuring the consequences. This kind of risking is risk for risk's sake alone, with no specific or realistic goals in mind. It is often undertaken to mask or change feelings. Gambling too much is unhealthy risking.

There are so many risks that are worthwhile—like taking a chance on yourself. Take a chance that you can make changes that will make a difference in your life.

GETTING STARTED

Picking up this book and educating yourself about the impact of gambling on you and others was a healthy risk. You saw yourself as well as the gambler in some of the stories you have read. You are better able to understand the gambler and yourself and this may have brought your rage, bitterness, and fear into focus. You now realize that your life became difficult or even intolerable because you were standing in the gambler's destructive path. Now that you know *how* and *why* the gambling got out of control you want to avoid the fallout and debris.

What can you do?

It will take courage to honestly look at yourself as well as your shrinking finances. When you first look, you may see yourself as a timid fool. You don't have to spend the rest of your life beating yourself up because you hid your head in the sand and were too scared to face reality. Look with new and deeper understanding and forgive yourself.

FINDING COURAGE

The frightened child in you says, "Be careful—it's scary out there."

Perhaps you can't ever remember trusting or feeling courageous. Reach back and welcome that child who may have suffered emotional or physical hurts. The child needs encouragement. Give it. Take that child by the hand, and say: Remember how brave you were. You climbed up and went down the slide when you were still so small. Later you rode a bicycle, stood up in class, and still later you learned to drive a car, and once upon a time you invited someone to the senior prom. Remember that this took courage.

Now, comforting each other, you and that little child you were can go forward.

You can be courageous again. Reread this book. Reach out. Take that risk we talked about. Seek a friend who understands.

Join a support group. Talk to a spiritual leader. Find a mental
health counselor or therapist. Look in the mirror. And see someone who matters. Someone who is worthy of your love. Someone
who just needs the confidence to face something frightening.
Someone with courage.

REACHING OUT

You may need help to move on. In many cases, the gambler has
entangled you in financial and illegal situations. You need to
protect yourself in these aspects of your life. The next chapter will
guide you through this process.

The emotional aspects are just as difficult to face. Although
getting help makes good sense, it may still feel like an enormous
risk. It may mean facing those old feelings of fear and shame.
Perhaps you have felt, and continue to feel, alone, misunderstood, and overlooked. Reaching out to someone who will
listen takes courage. But try it. Remember some other time in
your life when you reached out and someone was there for you.

Reaching out is a test of trust and faith in the goodwill of others.
Hurts and disappointments may have eroded that faith, but you
can find it again. Don't let other situations color your perceptions
or lock you into rejecting help. Don't assume you will be humiliated or repelled. Just *one* understanding, caring, knowledgeable
person can help you with your goal of moving ahead. It is extremely important that you find that person (friend or professional) or group of others who have been where you are now. Trust
that you will find this person or group, and it will happen.

In the past, you may have sought some advice from friends or
others to get the gambler to stop. They may have misunderstood
or minimized the problems of having a gambler in your life.
Perhaps the advice you heard was useless: It consisted of the same
strategies you had already tried. Or maybe someone suggested
that *you* also needed help. If you took this as an accusation that
you did not do enough or were inadequate, you may have turned
away, feeling angry, humiliated, and even more alone. You were
looking for someone or something to "fix" the gambler, so being
told you needed help might have felt like a devaluation of your
efforts and a blow to your self-esteem.

People often resist asking for help because of the fear of the unknown that accompanies the anticipation of change. You may also be fearful that others will criticize and disapprove of you. It is not unusual to feel that you will be seen as the villain and the gambler as the victim. You may be afraid of the intensity of your feelings, that the hurts will never leave, or you may be frightened that your anger at the gambler will become out of control. Old fears of abandonment often emerge.

You may feel ashamed that you married a gambler, have such a child or parent, or are in any way related to or associated with such a person. Thinking that the family secrets will come out or that you will have to keep them can fill you with shame. Self-disgust and self-contempt can overcome you; admitting your ignorance about the gambling may increase those feelings. Seeking help may make you ashamed because you feel that it means you are weak-willed, have been disgraced, and are different than others. In addition, you may feel guilty and ashamed that you are betraying the gambler by telling others about him.

You may refrain from seeking help because you worry that it will confirm your worst fear: that you are the one who is "sick." Or you may view seeking help as an admission that you were foolish because the tip-offs were there, or other people knew about the gambling and tried to tell you but you didn't listen. Admitting you need help may make you feel that everything you believed in is a sham.

You may hesitate to seek help because it is uncomfortable for you to be dependent on others. You may believe that you should be able to solve your own problems. Reaching out to others makes you feel that you are an incompetent and helpless child. At the same time, you may wonder if your expectations of other people are realistic, and you may reject the idea of needing someone because you feel that no one will be there for you anyway.

SEEKING THERAPY

It's easy to see why you may resist going for help. Perhaps your family believed that only "crazy" people sought counseling, that only criminals needed lawyers, and that people shouldn't "air their dirty laundry in public." Why in the world would you talk to others about your problems?

Just remember that many people faced with problems in life

overcome their initial resistance and then benefit from a therapeutic relationship with a mental health professional.

Having realistic expectations of this professional and the experience is extremely important. Don't expect this therapist to fix things. He or she acts as a sounding board and helps you explore your problems more fully and find your own answers and solutions to them.

The therapist should not be judgmental and should have an understanding of your experiences. Don't expect a therapist to read your mind. They can't understand everything about you, nor can they see right through you. This is a frequent fantasy and belief of people who are seeking therapy or counseling for the first time. Therapy arouses many of the feelings left over from childhood, when we felt that adults were omnipotent and knew everything about us.

The initial meeting with a therapist may evoke various feelings of anxiety within you. This is not necessarily bad, but it may be a warning that you are about to have new, old, or more intense feelings. Just thinking of something that is on your mind, even before you say it, can provoke anxiety. Trust that these feelings will pass as you become more comfortable in the therapeutic relationship.

It's important for you to trust your own instincts and feelings when you meet a therapist. If you're not comfortable with this person and continually feel misunderstood or judged, this may be the wrong therapist for you. Some therapists, qualified in other areas of the helping profession, really may not understand gambling or its consequences. Find someone who does. Or perhaps you started seeing a therapist before you began reading this book. Did you ever discuss the gambling? If not, be sure to bring it up in your sessions. The therapist you are already seeing should either understand gambling or be willing to learn more about it.

A good counseling experience will help you ventilate all that you have held back. This, in turn, will lead to repairing your own self-esteem, mitigating your anger, realistically redefining your expectations, and setting goals for your own life. And, you should feel assured that an ethical therapist will respect your confidentiality.

Therapy neither competes with nor replaces a good self-help or support program. Each can enhance the other. That is why we strongly urge you to go to a Gam-Anon meeting if there is one near you. Gam-Anon is a twelve-step anonymous and confidential program composed of family and friends involved with a gambler. You will be welcomed there if the gambler in your life is still gambling or has stopped. It is a place where you will gain hope and support as you move on with your life.

Gam-Anon is closely allied with, but not a part of, Gamblers Anonymous (GA), a fellowship in which people with gambling problems share their experiences and through mutual support can stop gambling and build better lives. Begun in 1957, it is modeled after Alcoholics Anonymous. It shares with that organization the commitment to mutual support, anonymity, and confidentiality, and the concept of taking things "one day at a time." GA has adapted the twelve steps of AA for their own program of recovery from gambling.

In the appendix you will find information on contacting a Gam-Anon group, but if there is no group in your area, then go to an Al-Anon or another recovery group for friends and family of people with addictions. One of the wonderful things about these groups is that you will be able to identify with others and find you are not alone, even if they haven't had your specific problems.

These twelve-step programs are based on trust and belief in a Higher Power. Many people define a Higher Power as God, but others consider it the group or some other belief system. People of every religion are part of these fellowships, and many have no particular religious affiliation or are nonbelievers. The programs can help you gain serenity and reclaim what you may have lost— your ethical standards and your spirituality.

SPIRITUALITY: LOST AND FOUND

The frequent loss of the gambler's ethics, morality, and religion can have a profound influence on you. It can make you lose your faith. Perhaps you feel you have changed in a way that compromises your basic values. You may have become deceitful, either because you have been attempting to control the gambler or punish him because you feel he has treated you unfairly. You may have become consumed by anger, hurt, and helplessness. Fear may have overtaken your faith. You may find yourself far more materialistic than you ever were before, and the mall may have become your house of worship. You may have become self-destructive: eating, smoking, or drinking more than you intend or feel is right. You may have sought "comfort" by taking drugs. You may have felt that without the gambler in your life, life was empty and meaningless. To keep the gambler in your life you may have sacrificed much of what you know in your heart is right and true. You may feel disgusted by who you have become. You may be without hope.

Whether a sudden acute crisis brought you to the awareness that the gambler was out of control, or you have been struggling with it for years, your recovery will require you to repair your spiritual damage.

What is spirituality? It has been defined in many ways and by many people, all of whom see it as necessary for a rich and meaningful life. It represents faith, trust, and honesty. It recognizes that we are all human and have our frailties and shortcomings. Spirituality encourages healthy humility, love of self and others, trust and commitment. When it governs our values, beliefs, and goals our lives become freer of bitterness, regrets, and unhappiness.

A spiritual core counteracts our childhood feelings of grandiosity and allows us to be comfortable even when we're not in the "driver's seat." Unfortunately, many people's spiritual focus is an attempt to control others, and that, as we have learned, leads to codependency. Others' spiritual focus is both self-destructive and hurtful to others. Liquor is the focus of the alcoholic's spirituality. Dice may be the focus of the gambler's.

To experience spiritual renewal and rejuvenation bring back or find faith, honesty, and trust. Belief in something greater than yourself or others, such as a Higher Power, can be of great comfort.

STARTING THE JOURNEY

You may have already begun your journey. You have recognized the problem and you have realized there is hope. Next will come the search for the resources, ideas, and beliefs that will help you change. Someday soon you will find yourself integrating these things into your life, and you will be able to stop personalizing your problems and feeling so down on yourself. Give yourself time. Don't try to rush things.

Worrying about the future only blinds you to what can be done today. Dwelling on the past, as opposed to learning from it, will not help you protect yourself. Surviving and growing is what you want to achieve. Right now you still may be giving lip service to the fact that gambling is an emotional problem. Someday you will fully believe it. There may be no quick financial or emotional solutions to the problems you face, but solutions *do* exist. Trust and believe this. Have faith.

NO MORE BAILOUTS

From now on, the creed you will live by is NO MORE BAILOUTS. You will no longer turn over the grocery money to the gambler. You will not make excuses to the boss for why the gambler didn't come in to work. You will not tell your cousin that the gambler isn't coming to her wedding because he has to work. Instead, you will tell your cousin (and let the gambler know you're doing it) that he doesn't want to come because he would rather stay home to watch the football game. You will not tell your children that Grandma isn't coming to Grandparents' Day at school because she doesn't feel well. Instead, you will tell the children (and let Grandma know you're doing it) that she's going to the casino or that it's her bingo day. You will not take a second job to help pay for his car; he can take a bus. You will not beg, borrow, or steal money to pay the gambler's bookie, no matter how many threats there are.

Say it over and over: NO MORE BAILOUTS.

You'll make mistakes sometimes. Perfection isn't your goal, progress is.

WILL THE GAMBLER EVER STOP GAMBLING?

Gamblers have been known to stop when the harsh realities of the consequences break down their illusions and self-deceptions. They may stop when the act of juggling time, money, and emotions wears them down. At this point, the gambler may say, "I'm sick and tired of being sick and tired," and just stop.

Unfortunately, this is not the end of their problems. If the underlying emotional depression, loneliness, anxiety, or other problems (as described in chapter 5) that led to gambling are not addressed, the gambler may turn to and become addicted to alcohol, drugs, food, sex, shopping, or become a workaholic, so family life and health suffer. Or the gambler may just retreat into depression or manifest other behaviors that the gambling had defended against.

It is not unusual for family members to say, "I liked him better when he was gambling."

This underscores the importance of the help and support from professionals and/or a twelve-step program like Gamblers Anonymous even for those gamblers who stopped on their own.

You too need the help and support from professionals and/or a twelve-step program like Gam-Anon. This will allow you to detach from the gambler with love and understanding, helping you find peace. It can aid in the process toward getting the gambler to stop, if he hasn't yet, and then to continue to abstain.

In the meantime, while the gambler is still active, it is very difficult to stand by and watch as he or she digs into a deeper financial, legal, and emotional hole. It can be extremely painful and frightening for you to deal with creditors, the underworld, or the criminal justice system. But it is vital that you stand strong, because your refusal to enable the gambling can play a major role in bringing the gambler's "bottom" up, so that he seeks help or accepts it when it is offered.

A formal "intervention" (like the ones used with alcoholics and chemical dependents) to get a gambler to agree to getting help will be discussed in chapter 10.

ONE DAY AT A TIME

For now, take it one day at a time. Think about change. Find a group. Inquire about a therapist. Look to your Higher Power. And just for today, no more bailouts.

Faith, like trust, will help you. Prayer can be a comfort. Belief in your Higher Power, however you define it, can help you. Find the courage to do what you must. To continue to go on living and to be the best you can as you face the stresses caused by the gambling.

And when you feel discouraged, remember the Serenity Prayer that has helped so many of those involved with addicts or other dysfunctional people get through the day.

> *God grant me the serenity*
> *to accept the things I cannot change,*
> *courage to change the things I can,*
> *and wisdom to know the difference.*

CHAPTER 9

Guide to Financial Survival

It is difficult to separate money issues from the emotional trauma brought on by the gambler's loss of control. Yet your very financial survival depends on your being able to do just this.

Your attitudes, beliefs, and past history in handling money may get in the way of seeing these issues clearly. Legal and financial ties to the gambler make this task even more complicated. Emotional dependency and fears of upsetting the existing delicate balance as well as input from family or friends contribute toward preventing you from focusing objectively on gambling-related problems.

You know there are many ways to bail out a gambler. Some bailouts are based on emotions or involve time, and you are learning to stop those. You know that you should stop the financial bailouts for many reasons, one of which is that no matter how much money you give or make available to the gambler, it will never be enough. Sooner or later the gambler's need for the money will exceed your willingness or ability to provide it.

If you refuse to bail out the gambler, he may turn elsewhere. You can't control that, but you *can* detach yourself financially and avoid becoming part of the problem. This is crucial for your own financial survival.

Refusing bailouts can have another equally important effect on the situation. As it becomes harder and harder to obtain funds, the pain and stress of mounting debt forces the gambler to confront or question his denial and self-deception systems. Financial losses challenge the gambler's sense of omnipotence and illusion of control. Experiencing his relationship with "Lady Luck" as destructive, painful, and fruitless makes him more likely to seek or agree to accept help to stop gambling.

IT'S NOT SO EASY

How easy it is for friends, neighbors, and even family to tell you "just say no." Sometimes the dilemmas you must face are overwhelming. For instance, when the gambler has spent the food money, what do you do if it means that your nieces and nephews go hungry?

There are times when you may feel you have to "help out" because someone else will suffer. Sometimes you may choose to bail out someone, but only on the condition they seek help. And if the situation arises again, the next time you say *no*.

Try to imagine what *you* would do in the following situations, all of which focus on different relationships to the gambler. You will see that the choices are not easy ones, and although you may initially feel that the bailout should be refused, when you think it through you will see how difficult it can be to say no, regardless of your relationship to the gambler.

• Your husband, a gambler, has been contributing less and less each month to your household expenses and now you are about to be evicted for nonpayment of rent. Your friends tell you to leave him, but you know there is no way you can afford your own apartment and meet other expenses on your salary. The little your husband gives you each month helps keep you afloat.

Do you take out a personal loan and then get a second job or work overtime to pay it back so that you can remain in your apartment?

• Your son, a gambler, is a law school student who has embezzled money from the business where he is employed part-time. The employer agrees to drop the charges if the money is repaid.

Do you repay the money so that your son's future career is not threatened?

• Your divorced sister, a gambler, is always borrowing money from you and everyone else. She hasn't paid her utility bill in three months and she is threatened with loss of service.

Do you pay the bill so that she and her young children aren't in the dark?

• Your stepfather, a gambler, hasn't met mortgage payments on his and your mother's trailer home.

Do you and your brother assume the payments so Mom doesn't lose her home?

• Your daughter's husband, a gambler, refuses to agree to the cost of summer camp for their eight-year-old son even though all the children in their neighborhood go to camp.

Do you take over this expense so that your grandson won't have to play alone all summer?

• Your brother, a gambler, doesn't pay his share of the money he, your sister, and you agreed to give your elderly parents to enable them to remain in the home they have lived in for more than fifty years. Without your help they would go to a nursing home.

Do you and your sister assume your brother's share of this commitment?

• Your business partner, a gambler, is a great salesman and a major asset to the business. He has taken huge cash advances on the company credit card, and this month's bill is so large that even a minimum payment will drain the cash needed to run the business. But if it isn't paid, the business's credit will be ruined.

Do you pay the bill out of your own personal savings?

• Your wife, a gambler, owes money on her salary advance. If she doesn't pay it back soon, she will be terminated, and you will lose the needed second income.

Do you borrow the money from your rich uncle to give to her?

• Your boyfriend, a gambler, and you own a condo together. Wheelchair-bound since a motorcycle accident left him paralyzed, he works full time but has been unable to pay his share of the payments for several months, and you will lose the down payment if you don't pay.

Do you continue to assume his share?

• Your childhood buddy, a gambler, has missed the last few months' payments on his health insurance. He asks you to pay the bill for him directly so he, his wife, and children will not be without medical insurance.

Do you pay the bill?

• Your sixteen-year-old grandson is a gambler, like his father. Your daughter has just been diagnosed with breast cancer, and you know she is under great emotional stress. The boy tells you his father has refused to pay his debts to a local bookie and expresses fear that the underworld will "get him."

Do you refrain from telling your daughter and pay off the boy's debts?

• Your ex-husband, a gambler, has suddenly informed you and your daughter, a college student, that he can't afford his share of her tuition this semester.

Do you dip further into your savings to assume the entire cost yourself so that she can remain in school?

These dilemmas demonstrate the various ways that people may enable a gambler, or enable someone else to enable the gambler.

THE ENABLING SYSTEM: PRIMARY, SECONDARY, AND AUXILIARY ENABLERS

Someone, usually the spouse and/or parent, plays the central role in the enabling system of the gambler. This person continually bails him out financially, emotionally, or by assuming his various obligations that require time. Others, usually someone close to this *primary enabler*, perhaps a sibling, parent, adult child, or even a friend or coworker, become what we call a *secondary enabler*, someone who "helps out" the primary enabler. Well-meaning, they usually don't recognize themselves as enablers. They nonetheless perpetuate the conditions that keep everyone (gambler and enabling system alike) from experiencing the consequences of the gambling. This can create either a false hope or sense of relief to both the gambler and those who surround him.

Auxiliary enablers are people who occasionally bail out the gambler. She may be the cousin who lends him money, aware that she will never be repaid. He may be the friend at work who tells the gambler's wife he is working late, knowing full well he is at the track. An auxiliary enabler is anyone in the gambler's circle who helps clean up his messes.

Until this enabling stops, the gambler is unlikely to feel enough pain, stress, or discomfort to stop gambling.

Are you one of these enablers? Can you stop the enabling?

Accept the fact that a bailout may sometimes be needed for the sake of others, as may have been the case in some of the dilemmas posed earlier. Find the courage to refuse when you should and try to find the wisdom to know the difference.

Do you have that wisdom?

Trust that with introspection and the willingness to consider all the ramifications of any situation, you will gain this wisdom.

IT'S ONLY MONEY

You may be thinking, "It's only money."

Nothing could be further from the truth. Money represents different things to different people. Although some people may see it simply as a means of exchange for necessities, most of us attach a particular significance to money. These meanings may mirror the message we learned from our parents, or they may be in sharp contrast to those values. Our feelings can also be influenced by adult experiences.

What does money mean to you? It may represent trust, love, self-esteem, success, power, care or lack of it, happiness, security, or specialness. It may be something you crave or it may be something you disdain. Money may reflect a general attitude of optimism or pessimism about life. You may look at earned money as different from inherited money and other people's money as different from yours. You may see gambling winnings as wondrously magical or distasteful.

Your perception of and willingness to participate in a bailout may be influenced by these underlying emotional meanings. For instance, a woman with a laissez-faire attitude toward money and a tendency to be extravagant may not be fazed by her adult son's gambling behavior and doesn't find his frequent requests for money objectionable. It is only when things reach crisis proportions that she questions his behavior or her own.

A fiscally conservative and thrifty grandfather may adore his only grandson and be planning to pay for his higher education, yet resist pleas for even a small financial bailout related to gambling.

In the above examples we see people whose behavior is consistent with their attitudes. But sometimes people surprise us. For instance, their beliefs and behavior may indicate that they are uncomfortable parting with money, and have always been cautious spenders. Yet they are attracted to or have married someone who gambles too much, whom they have bailed out many times. They may have an unconscious wish to spend and live recklessly. The gambler's behavior allows them to vicariously act out their own unconscious desires without acting irresponsibly themselves.

MONEY "TALKS"

Instead of or in addition to talking about it, many people use money to manipulate the gambler or to express their feelings about his behavior and the circumstances he creates for them. They may spend money to "get even," to feel better about themselves, or to try to control the gambler.

Do you do any of the following?

• Recklessly spend money to demonstrate your feelings of sheer frustration, impotence, and hopelessness. You may be saying, "If you don't care, I won't care."
• Secretly, alone or in collusion with others, hide or even steal money from the gambler. This may be in an attempt to control his

gambling or to avoid confrontation out of fear of losing the gambler's affection.

• Shop excessively in an attempt to fill the emptiness or heal the pain inside or to express your anger at the gambler.

• Deprive yourself of any necessities or pleasures that might cost money because of a fear of the future, or as a way of martyring yourself, or as an attempt to make the gambler feel guilty or ashamed.

If you have let money do your talking in these or other ways, you're not alone. The longer you are associated with a gambler, the more likely it is that your ideas about and use of money will take on more emotional meanings.

ENOUGH'S ENOUGH

You've tried everything to stop the gambling or to feel better about it and now you're thinking "enough's enough." You now understand that unless you look at the financial impact of the gambling on your life, you cannot help the gambler or anyone else.

Maybe the gambler has reached financial bottom and taken you along. Or maybe you're still financially sound. But you know that even if it's not on the immediate horizon, someday you may find yourself and those you care about debt-ridden, destitute, or even homeless.

Sometimes it appears impossible to stop the gambler who seems able to reach into your pockets at will, even without your knowledge. You may find that legally you are so entangled with the gambler that *you* could end up responsible for debts he incurred and share the obligation for his illegal activities.

AM I VULNERABLE?

Joint ownership or community property laws make a spouse or business partner extremely vulnerable. The gambler is likely to have easy access to common resources and financial holdings. Sources of credit are typically misused by the gambler to obtain funds. You may be shocked to discover that credit cards, loans, and other accounts that you thought were in his name, or knew nothing about, are jointly owned. Even if you have never used the credit, you may be responsible for such debts.

Anyone who cosigns a loan, lease, or contract requiring payments becomes financially and legally connected to the gambler. Family members like siblings, adult children, and parents who do not have any legal responsibility for the gambler's debts will often cosign for several reasons. They may be trying to help or protect the gambler or those who are directly impacted by the gambling, or they may be trying to help the family achieve financial or emotional stability.

Unwilling family members are also vulnerable. Cash, jewelry, safe deposit keys, bank books, checkbooks, car keys, cash machine cards, financial statements, and information about assets are often left around the house in easy reach of the gambler. A gambler may know a family member's cash machine access number and secretly make use of it. To obtain additional credit cards, the gambler may make use of the common family name.

FINANCIAL DETACHMENT

If you are financially connected or vulnerable to the gambler, you must financially separate and detach yourself from him. Refusing financial bailouts is essential. Separating *existing* financial resources is also important, but may create an ethical, cultural, and family predicament for you. For instance, if you and your spouse have always had joint checking and savings accounts, your attempt to have an individual account in your own name will be threatening to the gambler. It is difficult to predict his reaction, so be careful how you approach this. Still, you *must* do it.

By now you have developed a healthy mistrust of the gambler's use of money for *any* purpose. Begin to think about ways in which you can separate all finances, making sure that as little as possible is commingled. Consider how you can secure anything that the gambler might be tempted to use without your permission. No more divulging the access number to your cash machine. No more leaving things like jewelry around that the gambler might turn into cash. Consider getting a safety deposit box at a bank. Explore alternate ways of getting mail, such as obtaining a post office box. Detach everything that you can from the gambler.

TAKING CHARGE OF YOUR FINANCIAL LIFE

Even if you have enough money right now, you're probably getting frightened. What will happen? What will you find out? You may also feel as powerless over your financial situation as you do over the gambler.

You may be powerless over the gambler's actions, but you are *not* powerless over your own life. To deal with the stresses or crises in your life, you must aim to live one day at a time, but you also need to look ahead to begin to restructure your life.

If you are a spouse, someone who lives with a gambler, or a business partner, or your money is commingled in any way with the gambler's, read the remainder of this chapter very carefully. If you are a woman married to a gambler, you will find it especially relevant, but anyone connected to the gambler will benefit.

Money management has traditionally been part of men's "provider role," so many women are often not intellectually or emotionally prepared to make financial plans or arrangements that go beyond household or personal budgeting. Many expect the men in their lives to show their concern and affection by performing this role. They may assume that he will pay for a dinner out or take care of other expenses. The idea of taking charge of finances can be overwhelming even for women who have been raised to expect to work, and who handle money in their business lives. They often do not feel comfortable assuming the same level of independence and responsibility as their brothers, fathers, or husbands. But take comfort in the fact that millions of people who have never been in charge of their own finances (the recently widowed, divorced, or those starting out on their own after leaving the family nest) have done it.

Think. Don't act impulsively. Don't do anything you may regret. You don't want to discover later that you have lost certain rights or by taking certain actions you have precipitated reactions from the gambler or creditors that can make your situation more vulnerable or even volatile.

Don't panic because you feel as if you are in a financial crunch from which you will never recover. You will not be locked into the situation forever. Do what you need to do and try to let go of your worries. Turn these thoughts over to your Higher Power. Have faith that things will work out.

Remember you are *you*—a worthy person, not the sum total of the gambler's or your debts. Think of yourself as a deserving individual.

There is one thing you must do now. Make yourself one promise: Don't assume any financial responsibilities that rightfully belong to the gambler, who must alone become answerable and responsible for all debts and obligations. As you read the rest of this chapter, keep in mind that any legal and financial advice we include is for informational purposes only, and that you should get the advice and counsel of an attorney, accountant, or financial planner who is directly involved with your situation and knows the specific laws of your state.

These professionals often charge hourly fees, so do your homework. The eight steps we outline below can save you a great deal of time and money.

STEP ONE: TAKING INVENTORY

Taking inventory and assessing all sources of income and expenses will lead you to a better understanding of the financial and legal impact of the gambling on you. It will also aid you, if necessary, in setting up a sensible budget. It is essential for achieving financial detachment. This process can make all the difference between being solvent and being in crushing debt.

If you are married to a gambler, you should know as fully as possible the whole story, but you may find that the gambler's and your financial picture is hidden, just as the gambling had been.

If you are a business associate or another family member you won't need to know everything, but you certainly will need to know the extent of *your* involvement. Thus, the amount of information you need to know and the amount available to you will depend on your particular relationship to the gambler.

Before you begin this assessment, you should know where all important records of finances, investments, insurance, and other important documents and belongings can be found. Use this list as a reference.

- Bank books, bank statements, and canceled checks
- Safe deposit box location and key
- Automobile title card

- Property deeds
- Lease agreements
- Stocks, bonds, securities, mutual funds and trust funds, and any other brokerage statements
- Insurance policies (life, health and disability, vehicle, property, personal liability)
- Wills
- Marriage certificates
- Birth certificates
- Social Security cards (or at least the numbers)
- Military records and discharge papers
- Adoption papers
- Naturalization papers
- Divorce papers
- Tax records, including copies of all IRS returns
- Business records, including information about employment contracts or agreements
- Outstanding and paid loans
- Credit cards
- Retirement or pension plan

STEP TWO: SETTING GOALS AND OBJECTIVES

Your chief goals are to protect yourself, survive, and one day thrive.

You may have other goals or objectives as well. Perhaps you only want to know where you stand financially. Or maybe your objective is to protect someone else from the gambler's manipulations.

Or maybe you are considering becoming totally independent of the gambler, either by getting a divorce or by ending a partnership or a relationship.

STEP THREE: ASSESSMENT

Determining your financial worth is a simple concept that means assessing the monetary value of your assets and income less your expenses and debt liabilities. It's like taking your financial pulse and is essential to determining the impact the gambler has had or is having on you.

This assessment will enable you to see:

- How much you have now
- How much you can expect to have in the future
- How much you need to live on
- How much you should allocate to debt reduction
- How you have set past financial priorities
- How you can shift priorities now and in the future
- How you can identify significant gaps of information you may need now or in the future

FINDING OUT ABOUT ASSETS

Be sure to look carefully at all investment and banking statements. Assets usually include all of the following:

- *Cash.* Money may be in your wallet, purse, or stashed away in the house or in a safe deposit box at home or in a bank.
- *Checking account.* This includes other check-writing accounts such as a money market or money fund account.
- *Savings account.* They may be held at a bank, credit union, or brokerage firm.
- *Stocks and bonds.* To find the value, look in the *Wall Street Journal* or *The New York Times* or in the business section of your daily newspaper to see the price per share. Then multiply the number of shares by the current price to get the value. If it's not listed, call the broker at the firm where the stocks or bonds are held.
- *Mutual funds.* To establish the value, follow the instructions above. The net asset value (NAV) is the price per share.
- *U.S. savings bonds.* Their value is the face value of the bonds if held until maturity. If held past maturity they will increase in value; they can be cashed in before maturity, but not at face value. Further information is available from any bank that sells them.
- *Certificates of deposit.* Their value is the face value of the certificate at maturity. If withdrawn before maturity, there is an interest penalty. Many banks or brokerage firms automatically renew CDs at maturity at prevailing interest rates if you don't withdraw them or reinvest.

• *Life insurance cash values.* There is a guaranteed cash value on policies. Information is printed on the policy itself, but you can call the agent who sold the policy or the main office of the insurance company for further explanation.

• *Retirement funds.* IRA, Keogh, company savings plans, retirement programs, pensions, or annuities may have cash-in values.

• *Your residence and other property.* By checking ads or talking with a realtor, you can find out the realistic value of your residence, second home, or commercial property. Written appraisals are available for a fee. A realtor, accountant, or attorney can help you understand how much you would realize if the house was sold, taking into consideration any remaining mortgage.

• *Vehicles.* Most libraries have books that list the market value of your automobile, motorcycle, tractor, or boat. You can also compare your vehicle to others advertised in classified sections of your local paper or note what dealers are charging for similar vehicles.

• *Personal assets.* Electronic, camera, or sports equipment, valuable books including encyclopedias, and furniture usually have resale value. Furs and other clothing depreciate quickly. Jewelry, precious stones, silver, china, coin, stamp collections, antiques, and art objects are more likely to have increased in value since purchase. You may wish to have the latter appraised.

All of these assets are vulnerable, even if they are in trust for minors or elderly parents, in joint names, or in one spouse's name in a community property state. To stay in action or to buy time, gamblers will sell whatever assets they can get their hands on, even for a fraction of their worth. Anything bought on time or used as collateral is subject to repossession; homes may be foreclosed, and it is possible for creditors to get liens on other possessions.

LEARNING ABOUT INCOME

Do you know what your family income is? It is possible that you know only a portion of it. Despite boastfulness and grandiosity, the gambler may underreport income, or work off the books so it's not reported to everyone—the IRS, spouse, and other family members—to set aside funds for gambling. Minimizing income provides the gambler with an excuse and explains why there's never enough money.

It may take some ingenuity to find out about income if the gambler doesn't want to divulge information or if income exceeds a regular paycheck. Because many people get overtime or commissions, or are self-employed, their income fluctuates. Look for IRS W-2 forms (reflecting salaries) or 1099 forms (reflecting miscellaneous income for which a Social Security number is given). These forms will show you money that was earned for per diem or contract work. Banks and brokerage firms also send statements and various forms at the end of each year, listing the entire portfolio (holdings in their financial institution). This may also reveal overlooked assets.

Some assets yield taxable income, others are tax-free. Determine how much income you are receiving from the assets.

Look at the income tax returns from the last year or two to determine reported income, although as previously stated, it is not uncommon for gamblers to underreport income.

Attached to a paycheck may be pertinent information such as yearly income to date. A regularly deposited amount may represent salary. The bookkeeper or controller at the gambler's workplace may be willing to give you the total figure for the past year.

When evaluating income also include your own employment income, rental income, alimony or child support, Social Security benefits, Supplemental Security Income (SSI), Department of Social Service benefits, unemployment benefits, food stamps, gifts from family, and income tax refunds.

Knowing how much income you have will help you to find out where the money has gone and to plan a budget for the future.

CALCULATING YOUR EXPENSES

List your fixed expenses and others that occur on a regular basis, as relevant.

- Rent or mortgage payments
- Telephone
- Utilities (gas, electricity, water)
- Federal, state, and local income taxes

- Property taxes
- Fuel costs
- Insurance (life, health, property, auto)
- Car payments and expenses
- Other transportation
- Food costs (including school lunch money)
- Laundry/cleaning
- Spouse or child support
- Tuition and/or lessons for children

Other expenses include newspapers, magazines, books, barber, hairdresser, pet care, entertainment and recreation, clothing, shoes, dry cleaning, toiletries, medical expenses (including eyeglasses and prescriptions that are not reimbursed by insurance), home furnishings and repairs, contributions to charity or religious groups, holiday or birthday gifts for family and others.

It's easy to forget some daily expenses that can mount up quickly, so keep a daily log. Be sure to note in-between meal snacks, extra transportation, telephone calls, and odds and ends that you buy at convenience stores.

FINDING OUT WHAT YOU OWE

Finding out the extent of liabilities may be challenging, because the gambler is likely to have credit cards and bank and other loans you don't know about, and may also owe money to friends, bookies, or loan sharks.

Try to determine if the gambler has:

- Bank or brokerage accounts
- Outstanding loans from banks, credit unions, or any other money lender
- Credit cards held jointly or in his own name
- Taken out an additional mortgage on the house
- Cash advances on credit cards
- Failed to file or falsely reported income or other taxes

You can request a credit report in your name from a credit bureau. Your local bank or a merchant in the area can tell you which ones serve your area. When you get your report, you will learn if the gambler has taken out loans or has credit cards in your name from any institution that subscribes to the credit bureau.

Because this report does not include all financial institutions and doesn't include debts to unofficial sources (friends, loan sharks, etc.), you may never be able to get all the answers to your questions. You may have to accept the fact that there are some things you will never know and some things that will take courage to find out.

CHECKING OUT YOUR INSURANCE

It's important that you check out the extent of your insurance and obtain what you need. Being underinsured can lead to financial devastation. Many gamblers either drop insurance or skimp on it.

You may need some of the following:

- Basic medical insurance
- Major medical insurance
- Medicare and Medicare supplementary insurance
- Life insurance
- Mortgage insurance
- Home and personal liability
- Auto insurance
- Fire and burglary insurance

STEP FOUR: FIGURING IT ALL OUT

Following these steps will help you see your financial situation with greater clarity. There may still be a number of missing pieces, but in time you will be able to fill in most of the blank spaces.

You may find your financial net worth surprising. It could be more than you expected or much, much lower.

Let's say you are married to a gambler who tells you he just bets a little and usually breaks even or is ahead. You each work at salaried jobs. His income for the last two years is thirty thousand dollars after taxes; yours is twenty-six thousand dollars. You have figured out all expenses—including some of those easy-to-forget ones—and according to your figures there should be a surplus of five thousand dollars each year. You would like to start to put that away so that you when you have a baby you can move to a bigger place and stay home from work for a few months.

But you owe thirty thousand dollars on an assortment of cash advances on credit cards.

Until now you weren't sure the gambling was causing a financial impact. Your husband has been "gaslighting" you, doing a lot of fast talking: "How do you expect a net income of fifty-six thousand dollars could be enough for the way you like to live?" He reminds you of the expensive baby shower gift you gave your best friend, the bridesmaid dress you bought for another friend's wedding, and the living room sofa you insisted on buying. And how you eat lunch out every day instead of brown-bagging it like he does. And so on.

But now you've done your homework and the impact of the gambling is no longer hidden. You know that some of your hard-earned money is going to pay off gambling debts. And you realize that you may know only the tip of the iceberg. There may be a lot more debts you don't know about, and never will.

So what will you do?

If you're like a lot of people, first you'll feel waves of anger at yourself and the gambler. You will feel betrayed. You may feel your life is out of control, start to worry, then panic. You wonder if you will ever have a normal life.

You will also feel hurt and sad, remembering perhaps the times the gambler knowingly let you go without something you could have easily afforded if his gambling wasn't out of control.

You may also feel sorry for the gambler. You realize, perhaps more than ever, that he too is a victim—a victim of his misguided thinking or addictive illness. But that doesn't mean you should assume emotional responsibility for him or promise to handle or resolve his problems. That kind of thinking will only prolong his plight *and* yours.

Think. You know much more about your financial worth than you did before, and so you can plan realistically for the future. The gambler will no longer be able to successfully "gaslight" you into thinking that everything *but* the gambling is the cause of financial problems.

Try not to let your emotions take over, but use your anger as an energizer, your panic as a call for action, and your sadness and hurt as reminders that you won't let it continue happening.

If you are in great financial straits, a friend or the gambler may suggest bankruptcy. Gamblers Anonymous doesn't normally recommend bankruptcy because assuming debt repayment is a significant aspect of the recovery plan for the gambler.

But what about you? You may feel it's not your debt, so why not start with a clean slate? Keep in mind that bankruptcy isn't as simple as it sounds. It may be years before you can get credit again, and that can make your future life very difficult. Before jumping into such a solution, read one or more of the relevant books recommended in the appendix and consult a bankruptcy lawyer. Discuss it with some of the experienced members of Gam-Anon.

STEP FIVE: BUILDING AN ADVISORY TEAM

Presidents have advisers. Real estate magnates have them. Movie stars do too. You also need an advisory team.

Your advisory team should include those whose experience and expertise make them capable of giving you objective and professional counsel as you strive to protect yourself financially and legally, and work toward your own financial identity and independence. The team's composition depends on your needs, but might include an attorney, accountant, or financial planner, insurance agent or broker, and, if possible, members of Gam-Anon who have "walked in your shoes."

Evaluating and choosing these professionals should be done carefully. Select advisers who work full time in their fields, have passed relevant proficiency exams, and have attained the title that represents a level of competency. They should belong to professional organizations and have a partner or associate who can take over if the adviser is unavailable for more than a day or two. At your initial consultation, the adviser should be able to explain fees and any "extras" that may arise. Recognize that you will be required to pay the agreed fee even if you choose not to follow the advice you are given.

Naturally, and this is of great importance, you should feel comfortable in the adviser's presence.

What can these advisers do for you?

ATTORNEY

It doesn't matter whether you are married to the gambler and are convinced you're staying the course or are an adult child, parent, sibling, or business partner. If the gambling is in any way impacting you financially or legally or the life of someone you care about, you need an attorney who is an expert on the laws of your community and state.

Attorneys can represent you if you ever choose to bring legal action, or if you are called on to defend yourself. An attorney's letter to a creditor may ease some of your obligations. It can protect commingled assets by stopping one-signature withdrawals not only on credit lines but also on joint bank accounts and other financial accounts. An attorney should be consulted before you do anything legally. Acting first and talking with a lawyer later can be very costly.

You are probably wisest to choose an attorney who is a generalist or is in a firm consisting of several specialists. A good generalist will refer you to a specialist such as a marital or bankruptcy attorney when you need one.

You can find an attorney through several referral sources:

- Experienced Gam-Anon members
- Martindale-Hubbell directory found in local libraries
- Local bar association
- Area law schools
- National Organization for Women
- Local public defender or Legal Aid Society (if you qualify under their financial guidelines)

ACCOUNTANT OR FINANCIAL PLANNER

An accountant not only helps prepare tax returns but serves as a financial adviser, helping you to make the best use of your money. This, in turn, can mean lower taxes and greater interest on assets.

Many accountants also can act as financial planners, helping you to assess your financial history and to decide on a financial plan based on your goals and objectives.

These kinds of financial and tax advisers have various levels of certification and licensing. It is probably best to consider a certified public accountant (CPA), a title that indicates he or she has passed a rigorous national examination given by the American Institute of Certified Public Accountants and has worked for a public accounting firm for at least two years. A public accountant who is not certified may be licensed in your state and may also be able to advise you.

A financial planner should be a member of the International Association of Financial Planning (IAFP) or the Institute of Certified Financial Planners (ICFP). Many financial planners are either attorneys, CPAs, or a chartered life underwriter (CLU). A financial planner who is giving advice on securities, use of the stock market, or the value of securities over other investments should also be registered with the federal Securities and Exchange Commission (SEC) or a state agency.

Be sure to discuss fee structure with an accountant or financial planner at your first meeting. Like attorneys, they may charge either a flat or hourly fee.

You can find a CPA or financial planner through the following sources:

- State licensing or control board
- Local and state associations
- International Association of Financial Planning
- Institute of Certified Financial Planners
- Friends or trusted professionals such as an officer of your local bank or your attorney
- Yellow Pages directory—then check credentials with one of the above

See the appendix for names and addresses of national associations that can provide you with a referral.

BANKER OR FINANCIAL CONSULTANT IN BROKERAGE FIRM

An officer in your local bank, or the financial counselor (often called a broker) in a brokerage firm can be a vital member of your advisory team. These advisers can help you set up a new account that cannot be accessed by anyone else, including and most especially the gambler. The banker or broker may also be able to advise you about opening a trust or custodial account for someone else, such as a child or parent, that is secured from the gambler. In addition, this adviser will be able to tell you about any existing accounts and what is needed to "freeze" an account.

INSURANCE AGENT OR BROKER

Insurance agents represent and can help you choose policies from one or more insurance companies. An insurance broker represents the client, acting more like a middleman, advising you on which company will offer you the insurance that best meets your needs. Since most agents and brokers are licensed to do both, there is barely any difference.

An insurance adviser can help you sort out what insurance you have—explain to you exactly what coverage you now have and help you define your present and future needs. As we have indicated earlier, it is not unusual for gamblers to be grossly underinsured, so it is advisable to seek professional help to examine your present coverage.

To select an insurance agent or broker, ask a trusted friend or other professional adviser for a referral, or call the nearest office of any major insurance company. You can also consult the Yellow Pages under insurance and insurance consultants and then contact your state insurance department to be sure the individual you are considering is in good standing.

GAM-ANON MEMBERS

Although Gam-Anon members are not professional advisers, they are certainly experienced in the problems you are facing and can often give you practical advice. They can, with a good degree of accuracy, predict the effect that some of your actions may have on the gambler. They have "heard it all" and know, perhaps better than any professional adviser, how difficult it is to keep the gambler from devouring your assets and creating havoc in your financial and legal life. Be sure that you go to a Gam-Anon meeting, and if there is none near you, you can talk over the phone with an experienced member. Some Gam-Anon members (they are mostly women) have been in the program since the early 1960s and are ready to lend an ear and help you with specific or general problems.

Look in the white pages of your telephone directory to see if there is a listing for Gam-Anon; if there is none, see the appendix.

STEP SIX: PROTECTING YOURSELF

Protecting yourself involves both preservation and acquisition of money and rights.

To aid in preservation, you're going to make good use of your advisory team. And you are going to stop the bailouts.

But that's not easy. To provide themselves with money, gamblers can think of the most creative ruses to get money directly from you or to get you to pay for things.

Invariably you are presented with this request when you are preoccupied, in a rush, or perhaps after what you perceived as an especially warm and intimate situation. You've "been had" but won't realize it until much later.

From now on you're going to cautiously protect yourself and not bail out the gambler.

You're not going to give the gambler any money for *anything*.

You're not going to cosign any loans or other obligations.

You're not going to sign anything the gambler asks you to sign without checking with your advisory team.

You're not going to give the gambler access to any of your assets or credit.

You're not going to be intimidated by your family members or others who question your motives. You are going to resist the pleas of everyone. You're going to be strong.

STEP SEVEN: ESTABLISHING YOUR FINANCIAL IDENTITY

Many women have never established a financial identity of their own, even if they have jobs and deposit a weekly paycheck in the bank. All their bank and credit accounts (even if the wife was issued a credit card with her own name) were listed "Mr. and Mrs." instead of with her individual name.

A woman without a checking account, credit card, or a history of debt repayment in her own name is a woman with no financial identity, and thus with no credit or means of obtaining it in the future. Is this you?

Financial identity may not have been a high priority for you if you have been living "hand to mouth," or merely reacting to the money that passes through your hands.

But financial identity is the first step toward your future financial independence whether or not you stay closely connected to the gambler. It is essential that you have credit in your own name because it plays such an important role in providing purchasing and borrowing power. A line of credit can help you meet financial emergencies and build and preserve credibility in many areas of life. You need credit for convenience: to rent a car, check into a hotel, buy airline tickets, or even shop in a store that doesn't take personal checks. It allows you to not carry cash with you at all times and can also give you access to cash when away from home.

If you don't already have checking and savings accounts, open them as soon as you have the needed minimum. When you can, take out a small loan from your bank and repay it.

Next, apply for a credit card. Look carefully at the annual fee, interest rates, and grace period between when you receive a bill and have to pay it to avoid costly interest payments. Beware of advertising on radio and television that assures you credit *even* if you have been refused. There's usually a catch, and it will cost you money.

When you get your credit card, use it, even for small purchases that you could afford to buy with cash. Put the money aside, so you will have it when the bill comes. Then pay it promptly. This will help you build a good credit history.

A credit card can be wonderful. You may feel liberated by having so much accessible to you and begin using it recklessly. Be careful, because "plastic" can be very expensive. If you have developed poor budgeting habits or are letting "money talk," you can get into deep trouble.

STEP EIGHT: STAYING ON GUARD

The problem gambler *may* be stopped in his tracks when you put on the brakes, but the compulsive gambler is less likely to stop. You must stay on guard. Gamblers are very ingenious in finding sources of money: remaining alert and vigilant will help you keep your own money safe and avoid any of the gambler's financial obligations.

When the pleas or ruses begin and you feel you are about to hand over money, remember to "just say no."

Courage to say no will come from a growing feeling of self-worth and hope. Believe you are not alone but have a loving, caring Higher Power as a companion. Believe that the future holds good things for you. Even miracles. They can and do happen.

You've come a long way. Now it's time to tip your hand.

CHAPTER 10

Putting It on the Line

Confronting the Gambler

Chances are you've faced more than a few crises since the gambler entered your life, or since the person in your life began to gamble too much. You are growing more to believe that you have little power over the gambler. You are learning that you didn't cause the problem, you can't control it, and you can't cure it, but you are coming to realize that you have the power to manage your own life.

You are determined to stop the bailouts and are no longer willing to stand between the gambler and the consequences of his gambling. If you have a problem with alcohol and drugs or any other compulsion or addiction, you should be working toward your own recovery. At the same time, you will gain courage to move ahead and that places you firmly on the road *to* and even *beyond* personal survival. You know that until the gambling stops, your relationship to the gambler will remain unsatisfactory. The gambler's denial prevents him from recognizing that he is on a self-destructive path, but *you* know where the road is likely to end.

You are ready to do something that will help the gambler *now* rather than to wait interminably for him to hit bottom and perhaps take you with him. It is time to begin the process of a confrontation with the gambler in which you will communicate the following:

- Evidence that the gambling is out of control
- Your plans to protect yourself
- Your nonnegotiable demands, including his abstinence from gambling
- Information about specific professional and self-help programs available to him (such as GA or a professional therapist who specializes in gambling)
- What you will do if he does not meet your demands

Sometimes you can get the desired result by talking to the gambler in a calm, factual, and empathetic manner without making any demands of him. It is possible that the gambler may not recognize that the gambling has gotten out of control until you present him with the information and the knowledge you have gathered. It is also possible that he may be relieved to have you bring the issue out in the open because he is aware of his problem but feels too anxious, guilty, or embarrassed to admit it.

A direct and frank discussion works with some gamblers but more often it is met with denial, disagreement, or other forms of resistance. Sometimes the gambler agrees that there is a problem and even expresses anguish about his lies, schemes, and manipulations. He will promise to stop gambling, and actually believe it. But his obsession/compulsion about gambling sends him back to the card table or bingo hall or off to buy lottery tickets. Some gamblers make promises they *never* intend to keep. They simply go "underground," becoming more secretive. As soon as the pressure is off, they return to the "action." Before long you will see that nothing has changed and everything is back to where it was before your discussion.

If the confrontation is carefully planned, it *can* have a marked effect on even the most resistant gambler. Such a confrontation may need to be repeated a few times, but it should always be done at the right time, when you are composed, collected, and firm in your convictions. It can be the first step to breaking through the gambler's illusion of control and denial, leading to recovery.

ENLISTING OTHERS

You may have already discussed your feelings and shared your plans about financial detachment with a friend, Gam-Anon member, or counselor. This may have given you strength and determination.

Consider some of the other people who enable the gambler: spouse, parent, sibling, grandparent, adult child, cousins, friends, coworkers—the list can be endless.

You may feel that you have a responsibility to some of the other people who enable the gambler, so you may think about opening up a discussion on the topic with them. Because gambling is so often hidden, you may find that some of these people had no idea that the gambling was going on almost under their noses. Or if they did know, they might not have understood its progressive nature. You may find that you have to educate them, as well as provide specific information about this particular gambler.

You also may want to discuss your feelings and plans with them because you feel there is just so much you can do alone, and you want support from them. Although you know you have no control over other people's behavior, you may inspire them to stop their enabling and even consider confronting the gambler.

You may be gratified to find that your words fall on receptive ears. Some enablers may have been waiting for someone else to confirm and support their feelings, but were just too ashamed to discuss it, too overwhelmed to do anything, or didn't have the courage to stop. So they continued to enable. You may find that they become strong allies.

However, you cannot depend on getting this response. You will find that there are many people, especially friends or relatives, who don't think the gambling is a problem, or blame you for everything, *even* after you have discussed it with them. They may work at cross-purposes to your plans. For instance, they may continue or even increase their bailouts, because it makes them feel virtuous or important, or because it helps maintain their otherwise tenuous connection to the gambler. Or perhaps their denial is so great that they just can't hear you.

Relatives can be particularly tricky to approach. Families are complicated, emotional, and often volatile. They are composed of various alliances and antagonists; some members get along well, others just tolerate one another, and some are always quarrelsome. Your input may be misunderstood and your intentions misinterpreted for their own purposes, obstructing yours. It is very important to consider the ramifications of discussing the problem with family members before you actually confront the gambler.

With this in mind, tread gently when informing *auxiliary enablers* (such as siblings, cousins, aunts or uncles, or even parents) that *you* are planning to stop all bailouts. If you ask for their support and participation you may find them uncooperative. They may be fearful of being disloyal or of getting involved in what they think isn't their business. Try not to take this as a personal affront.

Secondary enablers (those who "help" the primary enabler) may see the primary enabler as a defenseless victim of the gambler. They resent your suggestions that they stop their enabling because they do not label their helping as such, nor do they see it as a bailout for the gambler.

When you broach the subject with a *primary enabler*, such as the gambler's parent or wife, you may find this person is uninformed, in total denial, or just adverse to discussing the subject. Tell this primary enabler what you have learned about the gambler's loss of control and say that you are planning to detach yourself financially and emotionally. Your suggestions may be met with open hostility by this person because they have threatened the status quo, and you may be perceived as having betrayed both the gambler *and* the enabler.

This may be particularly difficult for you, especially if the primary enabler is your sibling or child. This primary enabler, who is usually female, may feel like a powerless, longtime casualty of the gambler's behavior. She may see you as adding to her distress with what she perceives as your uncaring, punitive, and unfeeling ways. This primary enabler will probably try to gain your sympathy as she has before or angrily distance herself from you.

Stand firm. Trust in yourself and in your motives. Have faith. Be patient. When the time is right, you can talk about it again. In the meantime, let this enabler know you remain loving and constant. Someday she may see things differently and agree that you did the right thing. And even if she doesn't come to that conclusion, you will know that you had no control over the situation but that you did everything you could to stop the bailouts.

Don't be discouraged if you can't reach primary, secondary, or auxiliary enablers. No matter how you struggle to get everyone in the gambler's network of family, friends, and coworkers to cooperate with you, there may be one or more holdouts. Don't dwell on it. Eventually they may all come to say, "Enough is enough."

With or without the support of others, you can confront the gambler in an attempt to bring him to a point where he seeks help *before* disastrous consequences bottom him out.

THINKING IT THROUGH

You may have repeatedly pleaded, cried, cajoled, or angrily stormed out of the house in an attempt to get the gambler to face up to what he was doing to himself, to you, and to others.

None of that worked, did it? So why in the world will the confrontation have a different outcome?

In a confrontation you will act with deliberation not out of desperation. You will objectively discuss the consequences of the gambling instead of attacking, intimidating, and trying to punish him. In a loving, calm, but firm manner you will present the facts: how the gambling affected you and others. The gambler will learn that you mean business and that you will be pulling in your financial and emotional reins: no more bailouts.

If that doesn't seem to get through, you will let the gambler know the next step you will take to manage your own life.

You may have second thoughts about doing this. Confronting the gambler may bring up your earliest fears about disapproval, ridicule, desertion, and abandonment. You may be fearful that you will push him too far and that the relationship will end forever. This is always a possibility, but it's one that exists in all relationships, and it is a risk that you ultimately will have to take.

Many people find that they need some counseling and support at this juncture. You will find the courage you need soon, if not right now.

You know you are emotionally and mentally prepared and ready for a confrontation when:

• You have come to accept that the gambling is out of control because the gambler has either an emotional problem or suffers from an addictive illness, and you no longer personalize it as something he is "doing to me."

• Your chief motivation is to take charge of and make changes in your life, not to denigrate or punish the gambler because of *your* anger, self-righteousness, sense of betrayal, frustration, or hurt.

• You are able to identify and make realistic demands of him.

• You are confident that when you say "I'm going to . . ." you can stick to your guns.

• You understand that the gambler may have a complex enabling system and that you have no power over these other enablers.

• You are prepared to suggest that the gambler contact Gamblers Anonymous, a therapist, or a mental health clinic experienced with gambling and can give him all the vital information.

A confrontation will challenge the gambler's illusions. You are basing your discussion on facts, and your straightforward manner may pierce his denial of the consequences of his gambling and motivate him to change.

This is most likely to occur if:

• The gambler is experiencing significant pain resulting from his gambling.

• The gambler understands and cares about what he has done to himself and others.

• The gambler is willing to consider the possibility of living a life without gambling because he knows others have been able to become abstinent.

TAKING INVENTORY

A financial inventory helped clarify one aspect of your life. Now it's time for further inventory. Remember all the times you doubled up on your chores or efforts or gave up something you wanted to do because the gambler wasn't physically present. Remember too the times you choked back tears or put your own desires on a back burner because the gambler wasn't there emotionally. Remember how he lied and "gaslighted" and made you feel like you were stupid, careless, or irresponsible. Look back at part 1 and identify all the tip-offs that triggered your confirmation about the gambling.

Now take an emotional reading. Are you feeling sorry for yourself? Are you still angry or feeling foolish? Do you feel more resolved to do what you are about to do?

Reread chapter 1. Try to understand the gambler in your heart as well as your head. Are you less ashamed than you were? Do you feel less responsible? Are you beginning to really believe that gambling isn't a moral sin or a lack of willpower but an emotional problem or an addiction? Are you starting to feel more compassion for the gambler?

Don't confuse understanding with acquiescence, illness with incurable, compassion with hopelessness. Something can be done. And you can play a part.

Begin to trust yourself. Believe that you hold the power that will make the difference in your life.

Do you feel ready to confront the gambler alone, or do you need support?

Whether you are joined by someone else or you do it yourself, choose the right time for your confrontation.

WHEN TO CONFRONT THE GAMBLER

A confrontation when he's "up" after a win will fall on deaf ears. Instead, plan it when things are going badly or even during a financial or emotional crisis. Striking while the iron is hot can be very effective. A crisis can serve as an opportunity for change because the gambler is more vulnerable and his delusional system is shaken. Don't be swayed by anyone who says, "How can you hit him when he's down?"

Recognize that you're not hurting him but helping: You are intervening when he is least likely to laugh you off and dismiss your statements as nonsense or "gaslight" you by saying something like "You're making a mountain out of a molehill."

Postponing the confrontation only perpetuates the suffering for the gambler and everyone else, causing you to get into deeper debt and delaying the solutions to your problems.

WHEN NOT TO CONFRONT THE GAMBLER

There are times when a confrontation will be counterproductive. Never confront the gambler under the following circumstances:

- You *or* the gambler have been drinking or using drugs.
- You feel out of control and are hysterical.
- You feel enraged, revengeful, and uncaring.
- You have insufficient time to convey your message in its entirety.
- You feel unready to make the demands you think you should and/or to follow through on your commitment to stop the bailouts.

CONFRONT WITH CAUTION

Even gamblers with multiple problems *can* be confronted. Be cautious. Before proceeding seek guidance and advice from a professional on how to do it. It may even be wise to have a professional present during a confrontation with the following gamblers.

- *Someone who is dually or cross-addicted to alcohol or drugs:* Many gamblers are addicted to a chemical substance as well as to gambling. They need to have the chemical problems addressed before the gambling, or possibly at the same time. You will need to learn a great deal more about these addictions. Going to Al-Anon or a similar group may be a good start. Do some reading. Be prepared to accept that he may require detoxification in a hospital or rehabilitation center. This may be followed by a longer period in a rehabilitation program that helps him deal with the spiraling effects of addictions and to begin on the road to recovery. Unless all the addictions are addressed, there is a great risk of *increasing* one dependency when abstaining from another or of substituting one for another.
- *Someone with a history of violence.* A confrontation can trigger violence. If this person has been physically aggressive toward you or anyone else or has ever committed a violent crime, think in terms of your own protection and don't confront him alone.
- *Someone with a serious mental illness.* Confronting someone

who has a serious psychiatric disorder may cause a severe emotional reaction.

• *Someone who has threatened or attempted suicide.* Anyone who has ever attempted suicide or talked about it may be at risk.

• *Someone who is severely depressed or agitated.* Be sure to note if there is any significant change in a person's level of energy or in his behavior. This may signal an emotional disorder.

If the gambler in your life is someone who functions normally in most aspects of life, you can be comfortable proceeding with your confrontation.

KEEP SOME THINGS IN MIND BEFORE YOU CONFRONT THE GAMBLER

In planning a confrontation, you need to keep in mind the psyche of the gambler. You are dealing with a great escape artist who is going to try to turn a deaf ear to anything he finds unpleasant and painful.

The gambler's cloak of invincibility, the attitude of "my way or no way," and his grandiosity make him seem impervious to anything you say or suggest. The gambler's feelings of insecurity cause this appearance of grandiosity. When you look beyond any outward display of charm or warmth, you find someone who may behave selfishly, be arrogant, prideful, opinionated, impatient, stubborn, and often domineering. Thus, the gambler may experience your confrontation about his gambling as an attempt to break his will and destroy his independence, individuality, and pride.

When you tell him you know about the gambling losses and the consequences, you begin to peel away the grandiosity and omnipotence. Don't be surprised if a frightened, indecisive, dependent person emerges. For a long time the gambler's esteem has rested on his identification as a "gambler," which made him feel superior in comparison to nongamblers who he believed led ordinary and dull "straight" lives. If he concealed the gambling from the family, he reveled in this accomplishment. If the family knew, he took satisfaction in being the center of attention, even if it was negative, and his ability to keep others from stopping him.

The gambler sees gambling as a solution to all financial problems. If he can get enough money to stay in action, and he is not truly threatened with the loss of his family or job, the gambler has little motivation to stop. Abstinence offers him nothing and will only be perceived as a major defeat and potential loss of self-worth. He fears that without gambling he will be just like everyone else, a nobody. Without gambling, these men often feel castrated, reduced to wimphood. They visualize a bored, lonely existence, feel envious of others, and no longer have the opportunity to prove they are the "best" or the "greatest." Accompanying or underlying these feelings is often a pervasive sense of anger. Unable to handle anger appropriately, the gambler relies on gambling as an outlet for it. Without gambling he would have to deal with this anger. He fears this greatly.

Because the gambler needs to feel unique, he doesn't believe that any therapist could understand him. He feels that going to a GA meeting or a gambling rehabilitation facility would be useless because the people there would be totally unlike him.

THE FEMALE GAMBLER

Fewer women than men become problem or compulsive gamblers, but when they do they often hit bottom sooner than men. They usually have less access to funds and thus are less able to hide the consequences. A male gambler is more accepted in our society and is often seen by others as a fun-loving, daring, strong-minded character; a female gambler is often looked upon negatively, with pity or disdain. In some gambling circles, however, women are admired for their ability to participate in a "man's world."

Unlike men who like to identify themselves as gamblers and whose self-esteem is often based on that role, the female gambler seldom sees herself that way. She is more likely to be depressed and gambles as an escape from what may be a lonely existence. She quickly becomes overwhelmed with the problems her gambling has created.

A husband who neither gambles too much nor uses alcohol or drugs usually is intolerant of her behavior and often walks out on her quickly rather than continue to bail her out. Thus her enablers may be limited to parents or siblings.

People who enable the female gambler are often hesitant to detach from her or to stop the bailouts because they fear that she will neglect her children, turn to prostitution, or end up in jail.

But there is a brighter side. When the problem female gambler is confronted, she is often relieved and will stop. When the compulsive female gambler is confronted, she more readily accepts help than her male counterpart.

THE YOUNG GAMBLER

If you are the parent or grandparent of a young gambler, it may be especially difficult for you to plan and gain support for a confrontation. Plagued by dissension among various factions of the family, each member of the gambler's enabling system may have a different idea of how he or she should approach the problem.

Parents may fear losing the gambler's affection, love, and admiration and so they will each initially act as primary enablers, providing financial and other types of bailouts.

At some point, one parent (usually the father) spontaneously stops the financial bailouts. The mother, who may be beset with guilt and self-blame and is more likely to be a "soft touch," continues to bail him out. She may do this with or without the father's knowledge. Often she blames the father, seeing him as uncaring and too harsh on the youngster. The gambler manipulates this situation by reminding the mother how "Dad was never there when I needed him" or "I never had what other kids had," and so she continues the guilt trip that fuels her anger at her husband.

The parents argue and tension grows while the gambling flourishes and the bailouts continue. Grandparents are often brought into the picture because they have been a source for bailouts in the past and may become primary enablers. They may enter the battle between parents (taking the side of either their own child *or* the in-law child), and it isn't long before these opposing teams of allies and antagonists are deflecting attention from the real problem of the youngster who gambles too much.

The young gambler, in turn, continues to manipulate this system, keeping himself funded and "in action." He appeals to guilt, pity, and fear and takes full advantage of the conflicts between what he terms good and bad parents and grandparents.

Sometimes the system may focus on the young gambler to divert attention away from other family problems, especially if other members are dependent on gambling, alcohol, or drugs.

Ideally recovery for these family members would take place, but even without this *you* can proceed with your efforts to help the young gambler achieve abstinence.

If you are a parent or grandparent ready to confront a young gambler, it is best if you present a united front. It is difficult for the enablers of adult gamblers to enlist the support of others, and you may find it just as challenging to get help for the young gambler. Educate them about gambling. Teach them what you have learned. Explain that the longer the problem continues, the more entrenched the behavior will become and the greater the debts will be. The young gambler has youth on his side; unlike the adult gambler, he hasn't had his behaviors reinforced by years of gambling.

A grandparent who may not have known about the gambling may say, "Let him sow his wild oats" or "I gambled when I was young and I outgrew it." Another grandparent may say, "It's only gambling—be glad it's not drugs." Still another, shocked by the knowledge, may turn to one of the parents and say, "You were always too soft on him."

Parents may feel the need to defend themselves by blaming each other or grandparents, saying, "You indulged him too much. You never could say 'no' to him. You taught him to get whatever he wanted without ever having to save or wait for it."

This is not the time for accusations or explanations about the causes of the gambling. Right now you have one goal. Confront the young gambler with or without the support of others in the family and make your demands that he stop gambling. Offer him the help he needs to stop: GA or a therapist or a rehabilitation facility experienced in treating young gamblers.

Be strong. Stop the bailouts and urge others in the gambler's network of enablers to do the same.

THE CONFRONTATION

Your confrontation with the gambler requires compassion, empathy, knowledge, determination, and conviction. You know that you will do whatever you can to avoid any opportunity for the gambler to engage you in a dialogue that elicits false promises, apologies, and explanations and that ends with you feeling like you've "been had."

Do *not* offer him a psychological explanation for his gambling. Don't try to get inside his head. If possible, rehearse with someone who can play the role of the gambler while you talk. This will help you anticipate his reactions. If there is no one available, rehearse it alone.

Have faith that you will be able to convey your message. Even if at first you don't *seem* to have made a dent in his armor, you will have *begun* the process.

Find a time when you can be alone with the gambler. If you have children, they should be out of the house or asleep. Put on the telephone answering machine or take the phones off the hook. Avoid a room where the gambler can suddenly switch on the television. Find a neutral territory: Don't choose a room that one of you considers "yours," or a place that is emotionally laden, such as bed. Perhaps you would both be comfortable in the kitchen, talking over a cup of coffee or a soft drink.

If the gambler lives too far away from you to do a face-to-face confrontation, don't lose hope. An individual confrontation can be successfully accomplished on the telephone when it is the only means available. The cumulative effect of several people calling the gambler can have an even greater effect.

In person or on the phone, tell the gambler you need to talk and that he can talk *after* you finish speaking. Bring notes with you or write it all out if that makes you feel more confident. Begin by telling the gambler that you really care about him.

Be as factual as possible, addressing only what he has done and how you feel about it. Describe the consequences you and others have experienced. And let him know that he has received his last bailout from you.

First present evidence that the gambling is out of control, supported by specifics. Use empathetic but firm language like the following:

What I'm about to say is going to stir up a lot of feelings in you. It will in me too, and I'm going to try very hard not to be too emotional. That's why I have brought along some notes. I want you to know I have worked very hard to prepare this. I'm asking you right now to listen and not interrupt me. When I'm finished, you can say what you want.

First I want you to know I love you. I admire your intelligence and how hard you work. I was so proud when you taught the kids how to swim, and I was so grateful to you last year for taking charge when my grandmother broke her hip and my parents were away. You have often been there when I needed you most, and I will always remember that. We've had some very special times together and they have meant a lot to me.

You may not like what I am about to say. It's not that I want to hurt you, but I must tell you what is on my mind. I know you will see things differently than I do, but please try to see and hear it from my point of view.

I want to talk about your gambling, but not the way I have before when I've been angry and upset. I realize that I know only part of the whole gambling picture because it's not possible for me to know the whole story. Because I don't know some things, it doesn't mean I'm not aware of what the gambling is doing to me and others we care about.

For years, I have been frightened when creditors have called on the phone. Some of them said that if you didn't pay up you might be hurt. Last April and then again in September, when you asked me to do it, I borrowed money from my parents, but I never told them why. I felt lousy doing that. Some creditors have already called again this week. I don't know what to say to them any more.

Just yesterday the dry cleaner told me I had to pay cash because two small checks I made out had bounced during the last few months. I don't know how to face people. I'm so ashamed.

I was also very embarrassed when I went to pay for my mammogram with a credit card and the clinic refused it because you had "maxed" the card by taking more cash advances on it.

One of the saddest days in my life was when you didn't come to the PTA meeting when they honored me for my work at the book fair. You said you had to work late, and that's what I told everyone, but I know you were at the sports bar, drinking and betting on the game with your buddies.

I was angry when I found out you had borrowed money from my cousin and had lied to me when you said *he* had borrowed money from you.

The last straw was when you suddenly canceled last summer's vacation, which the kids had been counting the days to, because you had gambled away the money we had set aside for it.

Pause here. If he doesn't respond with a statement that he's ready to do something about the gambling or ask you what you want him to do, continue by explaining your specific plans to protect yourself.

I have finally decided I am not going to allow your gambling to continue to affect me the way it has. I am going to financially detach from you, and I am going to separate my checking account and credit cards from yours. There is no way you are ever again going to get any money from me. If you don't pay the insurance on the car it will be your problem. I'll take the bus. If there's no money for food, I'll take the kids to my sister's for dinner. You can fend for yourself.

What's more, I am not going to be embarrassed again when you don't show up for something. I will no longer keep it from others that your gambling is out of control. I will tell the truth to anyone who asks where you are.

If someone calls and says he'll break your legs if we don't come up with the money, then you will have to face that. I am never again asking my parents or anyone else for money. No longer will I be a buffer zone between you and reality.

I'm sure I'm making myself clear. From this day on, I will not bail you out of any of your messes—financial or otherwise.

Pause again. At this point the gambler is likely to be more convinced that you are serious. If he doesn't make an offer to seek help, present him with your nonnegotiable demands—including his abstinence from gambling. At this time you will also give him specific information on professional and self-help programs available to him.

Finally, I am going to make a nonnegotiable demand. If you want to preserve our relationship, you are going to have to stop gambling. If you can do it on your own, fine. But if you can't, then you will have to get help. This is the name and phone number of someone from Gamblers Anonymous who is expecting your call. He will meet with you and even take you to a meeting. Here's the name of a therapist who specializes in working with gamblers and their families; she expects your call. And here's the name and phone number of a rehabilitation center that can focus on the way you gamble and drink too much. They await your call. You make the choice.

At this point you will wait for the gambler's response. If he says something like "no way," you will say, "Then that's it." A wife can say she's going to see a lawyer about a divorce. A parent can say "move out." Others can simply break off all contact.

If the gambler says nothing, give him time to gather his feelings and thoughts. Wait—even for hours or until the next day. Then ask him if he is ready to take one of the steps you have outlined. If he remains silent or says no, then tell him again what you intend to do. If he doesn't take any positive action, follow through with your ultimatum. If he says he wants to get help, then you can take the steps outlined.

Obviously each confrontation will be different depending on your situation. Your demands may be different. You may not be ready to sever the relationship. However, the basic requirement is the same for everyone. It's time for tough love. It's time for detachment with love. It's time to stand by your commitment and decisions.

THE GAMBLER'S REACTION TO YOUR CONFRONTATION

The gambler actually may be relieved that the "jig is up" and begin on the road to abstinence and recovery. Or he may listen politely and then try to "gaslight" you. When he sees his old tactics aren't working, he may distance himself from you, hoping it will all blow over.

The gambler has a large bag of manipulative tricks, and he will probably reach into it to weaken your resolve and determination. He may challenge your facts and make use of his knowledge of your vulnerable spots. Be courageous. He may threaten to leave you; he either doesn't mean it or will do it eventually anyway. Don't break down.

Alternating with this aggressive behavior will be a more passive style: self-pity, fear, and despair. You may be tempted to jump in to save, comfort, or join him. Don't. It won't help him, and it won't help you. Detach emotionally just as you have financially. Stay strong. Let him have his pain. The more discomfort he feels, the more likely he is to accept help. You may want to soften things because of your fears and anxieties about what you have just said. Don't. Stand firm, and even if your determination wavers, act tough.

He may ask you not to tell anyone else about this: "Don't humiliate me anymore. I could lose my job—then where would we be? Honey, I don't want you to have any more financial troubles." Then, in a manipulative gesture, he may add, "And you know, you will look foolish too if people find out about it."

The greater his dependency on gambling, the greater will be his ingenuity in getting you to stop your demands. He may suddenly sound very gracious, saying, "Look, I'll show you. I'll stay away from the track this whole week" or "I didn't know you wanted a new kitchen floor. We'll go pick it out tomorrow."

Perhaps he will show little response. You may feel as if you've been talking to a stone wall. Don't be tempted to psychologize and tell him you know he's in denial and then begin an explanation of why people gamble too much. His education can come later. Right now, trust that you have reached him and that your confrontation *has* pierced his defenses.

Watch for these reactions either initially or later.

- *Righteous indignation:* "How could you do this to me?" "Are you forgetting all the things I did for your family?"
- *Hopelessness:* "I can't live without gambling." "I have nothing—no friends, nothing but gambling."
- *Blaming:* "If it wasn't for . . ." "I have to play cards with those guys, they're my customers."
- *Guilt-provoking:* "Don't you see what you are doing to our relationship and to the family?"
- *Disloyalty:* "You told everyone." "How could you do this to me." "I trusted you and *you* turned on me."
- *Remorse and hurt:* "I'm sorry." "I don't know how I could have done this to you and especially the kids." "Yes, yes, you're right."
- *Attack:* "You've got nerve." "Look at yourself—it's no wonder I have to get out of here." "You stupid bitch, you don't understand anything."
- *Threats:* "If you mention this again, I'm going to just walk out of this door and you and the kids will never see me again."
- *Blackmail:* "You are telling me that you won't help me?" "You are some parent." "I'll live on the streets." "I'll go to jail."

- *Justification:* "Gambling is the only way to get out from under debts."
- *Financial responsibility:* "It will be your fault if I lose my job (or license or business)."
- *Silence:* The gambler says nothing or simply "Are you finished?" and walks out.

Stand firm. He's just hoping others won't start bugging him. Stop bailing him out. Don't promise not to tell his mother, his friend from work, or anyone else.

This confrontation isn't about your promises *to* him. It's about promises you are extracting *from* him. And it's about promises you are making to yourself.

It's about no more bailouts.

It's about trying to change your life—and his, too, if he wishes.

It's about moving toward recovery.

AFTER THE CONFRONTATION

You've done something courageous and intelligent. Be proud. You have begun to save your life and that of others you care about. Ultimately you may be saving the life of the gambler.

Remember what happens to gamblers? Before they are drowned in debt, they often have heart attacks, strokes, or fall ill with other stress-related diseases. They alienate their families and friends and trash their careers or reputations. Some end up panhandling; others go to jail.

Don't let the cries of anguish or the screams of anger get you down. You've done something that many of the people you met earlier in this book might have done if they had had the courage.

You have that courage. And you used it.

A confrontation accomplishes a great deal, even if it's not readily apparent. Chances are you got through to the gambler at some level, financial or emotional.

He may admit he can't stop, then agree to your demands. Or he may try to bargain, saying he'll cut down.

Perhaps he *doesn't* say this. He may seem to be going along his merry way—gambling openly or behind your back.

Was the confrontation a failure?

No.

The gambler's denial, projections, rationalizations, and other defenses are so strong that only a wrecking ball could break through them. Maybe he just can't believe that you have changed so much. He remembers the old you: the person from whom he could totally or partially hide his gambling. You've been lying down for so long that he just can't imagine you're still not a doormat.

Actions speak louder than words. Yours and his. You hold your ground. You want to see that he is abstinent. But you know that the hidden nature of gambling makes it difficult for you to be totally sure, although anything less means that your demands are not being met.

For now your actions speak louder and louder. You demand that he meet his financial responsibilities to you and those he cares about first. His gambling debts are his concern, not yours. You have a new checkbook. The bank will no longer honor his signature on any of your accounts. The credit card bills are sent directly to him. You're not borrowing money for him anymore. You're not making excuses for his absences. When he stays up all night at a poker game or misses the last bus from the casino and doesn't make it to work the next morning, you don't call the boss to say he was up all night with a virus. Now when he doesn't show up or calls with a lame excuse, his job may be in jeopardy. He sees that his financial resources could dry up.

You are seeing a counselor or going to Gam-Anon. Or both. By getting help for yourself, you are getting stronger every day.

He'll get the message.

Even if he hasn't heard you, you've heard yourself. You said it once, and you believe it. You can confront him again. Change the dialogue a bit, but stay with the theme and try again.

And again.

And again.

Or consider an Intervention.

INTERVENTIONS

An Intervention is the same as a confrontation except it involves a team. Led by a mental health professional, the team can include family members, friends, coworkers, a member of the clergy, and a member of GA. A group of three to five people can be extremely effective. A larger group may cause "information overload"; however, if only a few members are active and the others are there mostly to show their support for one another (by saying a sentence or two) and to demonstrate a united front, it can be very effective.

The purpose of an Intervention, like that of the confrontation described above, is to interrupt the gambling and its related behaviors and to get the gambler started on the road to recovery. Objective and caring, the team members are not there because they want to air their grievances. Instead, they are taking the opportunity to let the gambler know that they care about him. They hope to break through the gambler's wall of defenses by stating how the consequences of his gambling have affected them.

Interventions are not new. Begun as a means to get alcoholics and drug addicts to accept help, they have long proved effective. At one time it was thought that alcoholics had to hit bottom or become self-motivated before recovery was possible, but then it was found that you could "bring the bottom up for them."

Interventions with gamblers also have a good track record. Family, friends, GA members, and professionals have found that a group of people can sometimes break through a gambler's defenses when one person can't. If the gambler is still resistant, his defenses begin to crumble when the enablers stop their bailouts. When the gambler's funds evaporate and are no longer easily replenished, he is worn down by the financial juggling act and is much more amenable to accepting help.

FORMING AN INTERVENTION TEAM

When you initiate the plan for an Intervention, you should meet with a professional who will guide you through the process. Together you draw up a list of potential team members. These people should have experienced some consequences of the gambling even if they didn't identify them as such at the time. You may need to enlighten and educate them. They should also know something about gambling as a hidden problem and progressive illness, the psychological makeup of the gambler, and the rationale behind stopping the bailouts.

People who are considering joining your team often feel they are putting their relationship with the gambler on the line. Some people won't or just can't do this. For instance, an adult daughter of a gambler may say, "I never had any kind of relationship with my father when I was younger. Now that I have children and finally have a relationship with him, I'm not about to jeopardize it."

Talk to her. Share what you know with her. Tell her that sooner or later the gambler will disappoint her and her children. Explain that she will eventually be called on to bail him out, even if it hasn't happened yet. That will certainly strain or sever her relationship with him. Perhaps she will see that joining you in an Intervention is not such a risk after all, especially since it is done with love and care.

But don't push. She may not be ready.

People who join the team should feel comfortable. Don't coerce them into it, or, like those who flatly refuse, they may end up sabotaging your efforts.

THE INTERVENTION

Just as the whole is often more than the sum of its parts, an Intervention is more than just a number of confrontations all done in the room at the same time. It has a far greater impact.

A mental health professional should serve as a chairperson to help organize the Intervention and take charge to keep it from becoming a free-for-all.

People on the team will prepare their own scripts, following the guidelines of the confrontation. They will probably want to read their portions at the rehearsals, as well as at the actual Intervention, although this is not essential.

The chairperson will conduct the rehearsals, choosing someone to play the role of the gambler. You may find it helpful to change actors at each run-through, because each person sees a different side of the gambler and may add to the awareness of other members. This anticipation of the gambler's responses helps team members remain firm about their statements and demands.

Every Intervention is different. The situation, the gambler, and the team members vary. After each person makes a prepared statement of how each of them has experienced the consequences of the gambler's actions, each one announces that they will no longer bail him out in any way. The chairperson makes the request of the gambler that the group has agreed upon. This is usually the same demand you made during your individual confrontation.

If the gambler resists and says no, members still know they have done their best.

Perhaps the next time the gambler will agree.

Even if he doesn't, you and the other members of the Intervention team will have the feeling that you have done your best. You have allies. You are no longer alone.

YOU'VE COME A LONG WAY

You've come such a long way, and we hope that the gambler in your life is on the way to abstinence and recovery. You may feel good about what you have accomplished, but you may still feel scared. You may be wondering: Have I accomplished enough? Will it make a difference? Will I ever forgive? Will I ever forget?

You have started to rebuild your life, but there is still much to do to get back on track, whether or not the gambler is gambling, is abstinent, or is totally out of your life.

PART FOUR

RECOVERY

CHAPTER **11**

The Gambler's Recovery

Most medical dictionaries define recovery as the regaining of health or function. We define recovery as rebuilding your life so that you are no longer locked into the attitudes and behaviors that are associated with being a gambler or having one in your life.

When the gambler stops gambling and admits that he is powerless over gambling, that his life has become unmanageable because of it, he is on the path to recovery. Later, when he is willing to look inward and beyond himself to restore his normal way of thinking and living, he is still further into recovery.

Recovery seldom runs smoothly for the gambler or for you. The twists and turns, ups and downs, and surprises and disappointments are different for each person. Some people may never achieve recovery.

From the minute you opened this book *you* began the process of recovery. You grew in your recognition and acknowledgement that the problem existed. You came to better understand and accept that the person in your life was a problem or compulsive gambler. You also began to focus on the impact the gambling had on your thinking, feelings, and behavior.

As you considered the steps outlined in earlier chapters, you searched for the courage to move ahead in your life. You may have taken some chances, perhaps thinking about or even risking your relationship with the gambler. If you did this, you found hope, and then, if necessary, took further essential steps toward rebuilding your life. When you began to explore ways to establish your financial and legal autonomy and decided to put a stop to the bailouts, you took an even bigger step toward recovery. Even if you haven't done these things yet, you are giving them much consideration, and that is a major step toward your own recovery.

As you further detach from the gambler's problems, begin to understand your powerlessness over others and feel confident, and are able to love and work to your potential, you will be making still *more* progress on the road to reclaiming your life.

You may wonder, Will I ever let go of my anger, shame, and self-blame? Will I ever trust again? Will I really recover?

Yes, you will. Give yourself time.

For now, let's concentrate on the gambler's recovery.

STOPPING GAMBLING

There are some gamblers (like some alcohol or drug users or smokers) who can stop "cold turkey" and never look back. Some may never have a problem with the substance or activity again.

But most problem or compulsive gamblers who stop and do not get help are just a bet away from trouble.

Joyce learned why help from either a therapist or a twelve-step program is usually necessary.

For years it seemed like Paul was never home. He played poker a few nights a week and I used to get mad because it seemed like no matter what I wanted to do, it interfered with his plans. He had this impossible attitude. He thought everything was coming to him, and he would lie about the littlest things. He was moody. Yet I loved him. And the kids loved being with him. Then Paul had this terrible losing streak. We were in real financial trouble and owed money to everyone. Paul got really upset. I guess it was all those calls, and then I was getting on his case. Then suddenly he stopped going to the games. Just like that. I couldn't believe *my* luck.

But nothing else really changed. He was still moody, jumpy, always complaining he was bored, hardly talked and when he did said nothing. And he still lied. Only he was home more. And he never went for help. "Why should I?" he asked. "I'm not gambling anymore."

When lottery tickets became legal everyone I knew would buy a ticket here and there. I did. And so did Paul. I worried a little about him, but I figured, a dollar here or there, what's the big deal?

Then—I just couldn't believe it—he won. Not just a few dollars like usual. But a big win. The kind of win that could really mean something. Not just an extra night on the town but something that would be there for our future.

A few weeks later Paul told me he was going to have to be away for a weekend on business. He said he didn't know exactly where he was going and where he would stay. He said that one of the other guys at the office had made all the arrangements and he was just going along to help close a big sale.

I believed him. Why not? He never called that whole weekend, and when he returned, he looked like hell.

Then he confessed. He had been to the casino on the nearby Indian reservation and went on a binge. He had lost all the lottery money he had won (which was far more than he had told me), plus cash advances on our credit cards.

I was like a mad woman. Remembering how long it had taken us to originally get out of debt and knowing how the lottery winnings had finally given us some savings, I didn't think I could ever forgive him. I felt as if I had been doubly betrayed. First his lie about the winnings, and then those losses.

I told him to get out. I figured I could support myself. Now that the kids were grown, who needed him? I began to think how self-centered he was, with or without the gambling. I was sick and tired of it all. But I was scared too. Could I really manage alone?

Paul knew I meant business when I said, "Get out." He went for help and now he's taking care of his problem.

THE GAMBLER AND THE TWELVE-STEP PROGRAMS

Many gamblers attend a variety of twelve-step programs, such as Alcoholics Anonymous, Narcotics Anonymous, and Cocaine Anonymous, if they are also dependent on chemical substances. They may feel that these programs also help them with their problem or addiction to gambling, although the focus is not on gambling. Gamblers Anonymous is the program that addresses gambling directly.

Worldwide in scope, Gamblers Anonymous, like other twelve-step programs, is a fellowship that encourages abstinence as well as spiritual and emotional growth. The underlying concept is that people with similar problems can help one another, and the only requirement for membership is the wish to quit gambling. The recovery program is based on principles of Alcoholics Anonymous but is not based on or affiliated with any religion.

The first contact the gambler may have with GA is through a member who responds to an emergency call from the gambler or someone on his behalf. This frequently happens at a time of crisis brought about by family confrontation, an arrest, financial crisis, or the threat of violence from the underworld. The gambler usually feels great relief at having someone who understands his situation and himself so completely—even his lies and manipulations.

When the GA member relates his own story and discusses his gambling experiences, including the crises he has survived, he gives courage and hope to the gambler, who begins to think he also can manage to meet these crises and change his life.

At a GA meeting, the gambler may initially have difficulty identifying with others in the room. They may be from different walks of life; some young, some old. The new member may compare his situation to others. Most GA members are compulsive gamblers, but problem gamblers also benefit from the program. Because he so often lies, he's not sure if he should trust the people he hears at the meetings. He finds it hard to believe that listening to the "war stories" that the gamblers tell and the talk about the twelve-steps will help him stop gambling. The gambler is characteristically impatient, opinionated, and argumentative, so the concept of growth through process is foreign to him, and he has little tolerance for it.

Most gamblers find the meetings inspirational, although they usually question the idea of relying on a Higher Power to face the uncertainties of life. They are not yet ready to embrace honesty, gratitude, and humility as ways of living. When they hear, "Keep coming back. It works if you work it," they may decide to give it a chance. And soon the meetings—the room, as it is called— become an important part of their lives. They begin to understand and accept compulsive gambling as an illness and slowly start to work on recovery.

An important part of GA is the "pressure group." This is composed of a few experienced GA members ("trusted servants"), who meet with a new GA member and the spouse or significant other to allow the new member to "come clean" about everything connected to the gambling. The "pressure group" aids the gambler and family in reordering financial life and in preparing a budget. The gambler is encouraged to begin to assume sole responsibility for his debts. The suggestion that he meet with all creditors to promise full restitution and arrange a timely, manageable repayment plan is often met with doubt and fear, or the desire to get debts paid off quickly. The gambler becomes less resistant to the plan when he is convinced that creditors will accept it. The longer the repayment plan, the more likely he is to be able to meet his obligations and the better it is for his recovery because it will remain a reminder of the consequences of his gambling. In some instances, particularly when the gambler is unable to face creditors alone, a member of the "pressure group" will accompany him.

Because the gambler has a history of abusing money (as an alcoholic would abuse liquor) the "pressure group" strongly suggests that the gambler have little or no access to money. Thus, a responsible member of the family (usually a spouse or parent) takes over full control of family finances. He is advised to turn over all ownership of properties, such as a house or car, to someone else and to remove his name from all bank books, checking accounts, and credit cards. The gambler is also advised to turn over all paychecks uncashed with the stub still attached to whoever is managing his money. In addition, the gambler must agree to a daily allowance—just enough to cover carfare, lunch, and any absolute necessities.

The "pressure group" serves as a constant reminder to the family to stop all bailouts and helps the gambler and family maintain openness and honesty with one another.

As time goes by, the GA room becomes more important to the gambler, for it is a source of new friends and support to replace the gambling scene or people from whom he has borrowed money. Week by week, month by month, year by year, he works the twelve-steps.

Family members of gamblers often find similar support as well as recovery at Gam-Anon meetings, which we will discuss in the next chapter.

HELP FOR THE FEMALE GAMBLER

Often a woman feels uncomfortable at GA meetings, where she finds herself in a minority despite the growing number of female problem and compulsive gamblers. Unlike that of men, the female gambler's identity is not usually built on being a gambler; instead, she gambles because of uncertainty about her identity, and the activity fills a real or imagined emptiness.

She may feel more comfortable in individual therapy. If she identifies herself as codependent, the adult child of an alcoholic, or an incest survivor; has an eating disorder; or abuses chemical substances she may also find help in groups that address these issues.

In her recovery she will work on many issues, and she will have many of the ups and downs her male counterparts experience. She may go into great depth about her feelings related to early and later losses, inadequacies, and shame-based issues—those emanating from childhood experiences or from the consequences of gambling too much. It is hoped that she will overcome old roadblocks to confidence, identity, and independence. She will strive to find new meaning to life and gain greater peace and serenity.

HELP FOR THE ADOLESCENT GAMBLER

Recovery for adolescent gamblers is often complicated by the fact that many come from homes where someone—a parent or older sibling—gambles too much. It is difficult to find help that addresses the particular needs of this age group and that won't make the adolescent feel like a "fish out of water." Recovery groups and twelve-step and other programs that are geared to their age group usually focus exclusively on alcohol or drug abuse. Most GA groups are composed of members much older than the adolescent; this makes it difficult for the youngster to relate to or identify with gamblers who may have spouses, children, and careers. However, some young gamblers find that hearing their older counterparts talk about their criminal activities and the consequences of their gambling "scares them straight." Other adolescents are unaffected.

Unfortunately, school guidance programs often overlook and

fail to address gambling problems at either the prevention or treatment level, but this is slowly changing.

According to many experts who work with this age group, the most effective way to treat adolescents who have various social and emotional problems is with group therapy. Many therapy groups focus on substance abuse, and it is usually difficult to find a group that is appropriate for the youngster whose problem is gambling too much. Individual therapy can be very helpful. In addition to educating the youngster about loss of control over gambling, a good therapist can help him or her understand underlying causes of the gambling and alter attitudes and behaviors. Finding nongambling friends and new interests will also aid in recovery.

THE THRILL IS GONE: A GAMBLER'S LIFE WITHOUT GAMBLING

Imagine, if you can, what it would be like if one day you discovered that your food was tasteless, that the music on the radio no longer stirred you, that the sweet fragrances from your garden had lost their scent, and that everything around you looked nondescript, shapeless, and gray. Even your fun-loving companions seemed dull and monotonous, and your favorite pastimes failed to arouse your interest or involve you in any way.

When the gambler first stops gambling, he experiences his world looking and sounding very much like this. He perceives life without gambling as a life that lacks luster. Circumstances now force the gambler into trying to live the unthinkable: a life without gambling.

His recovery will not be easy. It takes far more than willpower and a desire to stop. It takes enormous work, and sometimes means relearning everything he ever believed, felt, and valued. It takes time. Lots of time. There are no magic potions to destroy the urges and impulses.

RECOVERY AND RELAPSE: A FACT OF LIFE

Most people don't progress in their recovery in a smooth, consistent fashion; some have a great struggle. Many gamblers experience an occasional "slip," a short-lived relapse into gambling from which they quickly return to abstinence and commitment to recovery.

If every gambler who entered recovery remained abstinent (without any relapses), life would be so much easier. However, many gamblers who have stopped, gamble again. They either go on a binge or return on a regular basis, meaning they are no longer in recovery. This may occur even after years of abstinence. Relapses like this are an unfortunate fact of life with all compulsions and addictions; they are a sad testimony to an addiction's powerful hold on people. The gambler may lie to others, even to members of his GA group or to a therapist, about his relapse. He lies to avoid disapproval or shame or to keep people from bothering him about it.

Sometimes relapses happen because the gambler never genuinely accepted either his "powerlessness" or the fact that his life had become unmanageable because of gambling.

Usually a relapse occurs during a period of stress in the gambler's life, often in anticipation of, coinciding with, or following some major change. At other times when his self-esteem is threatened, he may find himself having more impulses and urges to gamble. Whenever the gambler feels overwhelmed by personal or work demands, he may turn to gambling again as a distraction and escape from these tensions.

Often the gambler or the family becomes so complacent about his recovery that they become less alert to surrounding temptations. Sometimes the enablers who had stopped bailing him out unconsciously encourage gambling behavior again, perhaps to prevent their having to face their own personal issues. They also may not realize that abstinence is a lifelong struggle even for gamblers who have many years of recovery behind them. At times, the recovering gambler may be unable to resist these urges, especially when he is feeling vulnerable. Like the alcoholic or drug addict, the gambler returns to his addiction at the level at which he had initially quit. Thus, the track bettor who stopped when he was in the habit of betting two hundred dollars a race will go back to betting the same amount instead of placing a minimum bet of two dollars.

There is still hope, even though a relapse can be financially and emotionally disastrous. Slips and relapses can be viewed as opportunities to recognize what has been overlooked in recovery and to work still harder at it.

With the exception of those slips or relapses that occur in many recoveries, the following is a picture of the typical gambler's recovery.

EARLY RECOVERY

During the early stages of his recovery, the gambler agrees that he should not gamble and acknowledges the fact that he might need help to do this. However, he initially remains unconvinced when professionals, GA members, or his family tell him that he has lost control over his gambling and that his life has become unmanageable. He is not yet ready to admit that he may be suffering from an illness that leaves him powerless over his gambling. The rationalizations, illusions, and denial that have been a big part of his character are still operating, although those defenses have been weakened by the many problems facing him. Perhaps he has been forced to think about abstinence because his enablers have said "enough is enough" and stopped the bailouts. Perhaps he is no longer willing or able to juggle his debts or has lost his family, work, or liberty. Even if he is bottomed out, he may remain unconvinced that he must stop gambling *forever*.

From the members of GA or his therapist he hears slogans like "Easy does it," "Let go, let God," "One day or even one minute at a time." At first they seem like strings of meaningless words, but soon he finds them useful and soothing. Each day that passes takes him further out of the fog of his gambling problem or addiction. He begins to see what the gambling has done to jeopardize or destroy all that he has cherished or worked to achieve. He is thinking more clearly and taking stock of himself and his life. Although he may be relieved that his "cover is blown," he finds that he is feeling pain that he never anticipated. Gambling had become his way of dealing with tension. Stressed by the financial and legal mess he has created, he may also anguish over what he has done to others and what it has cost him personally. He may focus his guilt and self-pity exclusively on his losses—lost opportunities as well as lost money. And yet, despite all of this, there is a part of him that still wishes he were back in action.

Continuing in recovery, he discovers that his resistance to the GA program and therapy is fading and its messages are becoming much more meaningful to him. At the GA meetings he discovers, much to his surprise, that he identifies with the other gamblers and that there are more similarities than differences between him and them.

The gambler comes to believe and to say that his loss of control and his powerlessness over gambling mean that he can't gamble anymore. With greater emotional acceptance, he recognizes that his life had become truly unmanageable and that he suffers from a gambling disorder. Memories of the lying, cheating, and stealing sometimes hit him like a bolt of lightning, and he is filled with remorse and shame. He anguishes more and more over what he did to those closest to him, especially his children. Alone or in the presence of others, he denigrates himself, sometimes genuinely, sometimes to gain sympathy. At other times he reverts to his old ways: minimizing, rationalizing, or denying the reality of the impact of his gambling.

Despite his efforts to actively repair the damage caused by his gambling, it may seem to him that his life at home and/or at work is not getting any better. It is possible that his relationship may be in greater turmoil than before, and his financial and legal situation may have worsened. Because he is in less denial, he sees all of this more clearly and realistically, which makes him feel that his problems are more insurmountable than before he entered recovery. Fortunately, his hopelessness is tempered by the encouragement and information he receives from those who have been in his situation. He accepts taking one day at a time.

Through all this he continues to secretly harbor the hope and belief that someday he will be able to return to gambling. But for now such thoughts are frightening, so he fights his impulses and cravings to return to the action. He finds it hard to believe that his cravings will ever subside, but he learns that others have managed to resist the same temptations and urges. He listens to suggestions on how to avoid people, places, and things that are associated with gambling. At first it seems ridiculous to him. He is aware that gambling is promoted or discussed everywhere: in the newspaper, on radio and television, in places he frequents, among his friends, and even in shop window signs advertising lotteries or trips to casinos. He complains that to avoid these reminders he would have to crawl into a cave.

He may rebel against advice about these "triggers," smugly saying he isn't going to restrict his life that way. Claiming that he won't be tempted if he looks at sporting events, shops in the local store where he used to buy lottery tickets, or drives past the track on his way to work, he finds that these associations do bring on "gambling fever." This further distresses him, so he becomes moody and filled with self-pity. He feels there is nothing for him to look forward to and nothing he can do without risking his abstinence and recovery.

Sometimes he retreats and acts and looks as if he's off in another world. And he is. In his mind he's at the track, the football game, or even standing at the crap table. He's "mind betting" and that keeps him busy and in action—and miles away from you. In his sleep he relives the days Lady Luck delivered and the days she turned against him. He wakes up confused, shocked, and frightened.

As time passes, he may become more committed to his abstinence and recovery and believe and accept that he must not gamble. The struggle with his impulses is less intense, but there are still days when the battle rages inside him. For relief he may turn to alcohol or drugs, running the risk of acquiring a new addiction.

Perhaps his abstinence from gambling was not so difficult after all because the cravings lessened or disappeared quickly. He might feel foolish and question why he ever gambled in the first place. He sees himself as "weak" and wonders why he was overcome by the urge to gamble too much.

After he's been away from gambling for some time, a euphoria may set in. He may get complacent about his program or therapy commitment and consciously or unconsciously set out to test himself. He avoids his old gambling patterns, but the former track bettor says, "Why can't I buy a lottery ticket or two? That's not gambling." "I think I will get some exercise and go bowling with the guys," he says, forgetting that those friends always bet on their games. "Why can't I read the financial page or the sports section?" he asks. "What's wrong with taking my son to a hockey game?" he pleads.

When confronted with how ill-advised such a choice of activity would be, he comes to further understand the cunning nature of his denial about his gambling problem or addiction. He now strongly identifies himself as someone whose gambling was out of control, and he knows he must be careful. He wears this identity as a badge, even referring to himself as a "sick" or "degenerate" gambler. He may unconsciously feel this badge allows him to be excused and not held responsible for his past behavior. On the other hand, this badge may make it easier for him to cope with the very real guilt and shame he feels about the hurt and damage he has caused. If he is in "good" recovery, his strong identification as a problem or compulsive gambler is a mark of accepting his past irresponsibility and feeling accountable for his present life.

Sometimes he looks and acts as if he's lost his best friend. And indeed he has: Gambling *was* his best friend. He grieves for the "good old days" as he glorifies particular events and people, including bookmakers and moneylenders. He longs for the times when he was a "big shot" and the center of attention and admiration. He wonders if the euphoria he experienced when gambling can ever be replaced with something as exhilarating and pleasurable. Anger over loss of gambling may be displaced on the family or where he sought help. This may be the time when he grieves for early losses in his life.

SOME THINGS STAY THE SAME

He's still a puzzle. His new openness, honesty, and growing self-awareness may surprise you, but most of the time he remains as tight-lipped as ever about his hurt, fear, and doubts. The lying continues but is not habitual as it was when he was in action. He may consciously recognize that he lies to avoid his pain from conflict and confrontation with others and then may be self-critical or apologetic about it.

At times, in an attempt to make amends, he lays his cards on the table and confesses to past wrongdoings, especially the way he deceived and "gaslighted" you and others. He may be surprised if you become angry instead of being immediately appreciative that he has come clean. He can't understand why people aren't willing to instantly forgive and forget. He may say, "What is past is past." He knows that people are justified in their anger toward him, yet he can't help resenting it. He also notices that you and others check on him, and even though he welcomes it as a way of helping him maintain control at the same time he resents it.

His enduring need for immediate gratification and his sense of omnipotence lead him to believe that all the hurt, stress, and losses will be magically rectified when he wants and expects them to be. Characteristically he may keep silent about these feelings or tell you only what he thinks you want to hear.

Even though he has quit gambling, the stresses and strains in meeting his financial obligations don't let up. He finds that he doesn't seem to be making a dent in his debts; payments barely keep up with growing interest and penalties.

"One day at a time," he keeps telling himself. "Things would be worse if I went back to gambling." Slowly he begins to give up the fantasy that gambling will solve all his troubles. Paradoxically, he may be buoyed up by all his new financial activity and actually enjoy it. Managing his debts, trying to save a few dollars here and there, looking for bargains, covering checks so that they clear, and even working second and third jobs can give him the sense of excitement and challenge that the gambling action once gave him. He may become a workaholic.

Unfortunately, some gamblers have firmly ingrained character defects or personality problems that just don't seem to change even if they stop gambling. They may remain depressed, self-centered, and immature, and have poor interpersonal skills. They may always feel as if they are on the outside looking in. They may even suffer from an antisocial personality disorder, as described in chapter 1, and continue a life of crime.

MOVING ALONG IN RECOVERY

If all goes well, the gambler eventually reaches a stage in his recovery when he recognizes that he doesn't *need* to gamble. Acceptance of his powerlessness over the illness and his loss of control is no longer a slogan, but is more deeply felt and embraced. The gambling and the obsessive thinking about gambling are now parts of his past. He devotes his energy to the continued rebuilding of his career, home, and financial life.

The low self-esteem, poor frustration tolerance, depression, and anxiety that are so typical of the person whose gambling is out of control are addressed, and changes do occur. He learns to deal with his pain and conflicts with a wider range of healthy strategies and to think before he acts on his feelings. His decision making and coping improve, and he also finds he can channel his energies into more acceptable and productive activities: home, family, career, and recovery. Slowly he sees improvements in his life, but because of his impatience he wants these changes to occur quickly. He is not better able to restrain his impulsivity, even when frustrated or anxious, although it remains difficult for him.

Around this time in recovery he discovers something very new to him: relaxation. He seeks out old or new interests as substitutes for gambling. He may find new sources of joy in his life, and pursues them with his usual gusto. He still may miss the gambling highs, but begins to remember those days with a new perspective.

He may feel content, even though he recognizes that some losses, such as life-style and income, are permanent. Eventually he stops looking back. He forgives himself.

Recovery is a lifelong process. The need to gamble fades because of his emotional growth. Ideally he directs his energy and attention to rebuilding the relationships he damaged and to building new and meaningful ones. Sharing his feelings and listening to others' feelings may still be difficult for him, and he may always struggle to achieve mature intimacy with people. However, the gambler at this point is more productive at work and enjoys a more meaningful social life with his family. He feels self-confident and sees his life as emotionally rewarding and spiritually worthy.

LONG-TERM RECOVERY

The gambler feels worthy and more confident than ever before as he looks back at the gains he has achieved since he began his recovery. He may have acquired a new appreciation in faith and spirituality, the basis of which is humility, gratitude, and honesty. He now lives "one day at a time" with the "wisdom to know the difference" to cope with the stresses, disappointments, and pain in his life. He is able to ask for help from others and to call on his Higher Power to face life realistically.

Whether the gambler is in recovery or not, *you* need to recover and reclaim your life.

CHAPTER 12

Common Issues in Your Recovery

(Even If the Gambler Is Still Active)

Occasionally my wife's mother, Sarah, would call me at my office. Swearing me to secrecy, she would tell me she had gotten "a little behind" at the casinos and ask me to tide her over until her luck changed. I would give her the money. She never paid it back, but I figured I could afford it. Besides, she's a good mother-in-law and grandmother to our little boys. But then one day I accidentally learned that her other son-in-law was also regularly bailing her out. It was then I realized she was gambling too much. I stopped the bailouts and got her to agree that she needs help with her problem.

Ray F., age forty-two

I'm a single parent and between my job, the kids, and trying to be available to my elderly mother, I am on overload. I vowed that if my sister Lenora called once more with her story about how business is bad at the beauty salon she owns and needed money I would say no. But then I would worry that she would ask our mother, and I wanted to spare her from learning about Lenora's gambling. So I would help her out. Finally I decided to stop, and I refused her next plea.

Judith S., age fifty-one

My father always gambled, but when I was a child it didn't seem to have an effect on me. But now every few weeks my mother calls and either hints or directly asks if she can come and stay with me, my husband, and the kids for a few days. Dad is off to the casinos, or she's had a fight with him about the gambling and she's looking for a "safe haven." The kids like having her around, but it's often inconvenient. And besides, I hate being caught up in my father's gambling problem and my parents' conflicts. I asked Mom to go for help but she refused, saying, "Your father's not so bad, not like his cousin Ben."

I finally said to my mother, "Nothing is changing, not Dad's gambling or your fights with him, because when you come here it just takes the heat off him and makes it easier for him to keep up the gambling." I said they needed counseling, and I was no longer going to bail her out by allowing her to stay over when they fought over Dad's gambling. Mom is hurt: She doesn't understand what I'm saying and trying to do. But I feel a lot better about things now myself and I hope she'll really get sick and tired of her situation with Dad and do something about straightening out her life.

Rita N., age thirty-eight

My husband, Larry, is a compulsive gambler. For years I put up with a lot, but one day Jay, my college friend, called to say he was sorry about my uncle. He hoped that the money he had lent Larry for the funeral was helpful. I didn't even have an uncle, so I knew Larry had lied to him to borrow money. I was embarrassed and humiliated, but I told Jay the truth. That was it! I couldn't put up with my husband's lying anymore. The stress was too much for me, and my migraine headaches were getting worse. I thought if I had to make one more excuse to his boss about his absences, borrow money from my parents to cover his bad checks, or sit up all night waiting for him to come home I would really fall apart. That's when I decided to call Gam-Anon, and now I'm getting help.

Kate M., age twenty-seven

These people have all stopped bailing out the gambler. Are they in recovery? Perhaps. On the surface it looks as if they are. But have they changed the attitudes and feelings at the root of their enabling? Do they have emotional needs that the enabling fulfilled? Are they beginning to permanently let go of their enabling? Have they healed from the hurt and stress and anger caused by the gambler?

As a general rule the more emotionally and financially involved you are with someone who gambles too much, the more complex and lengthier your recovery will be.

For some, usually auxiliary enablers like Ray F. who only occasionally bail out the gambler, stopping their enabling may constitute recovery. Secondary enablers like Rita N. who bail out or enable the primary or direct enabler of the gambler often have more recovery work to do. Primary enablers like Judith S. or Kate M. who regularly bail out the gambler are directly and negatively impacted by the gambler. Often their view of themselves and the world has become so distorted that healing will take time. Their recovery needs to focus on the anger, hurt, and pain they have suffered, and this will support their decision to end the bailouts. Even if they break off the relationship with the gambler altogether, such as in a divorce, they don't leave the past behind, and anger, hurt, loss of self-respect and trust, disappointment, and betrayal may remain with them for a long time, sometimes forever.

THE STAGES OF RECOVERY

Keep in mind that some people go immediately from one stage to another; others stay in one stage for years without moving on to the next one.

IDENTIFICATION STAGE

This initial stage may start with your total lack of knowledge that the gambling is out of control or even occurring. Perhaps you have some knowledge, but you misconstrue the situation or minimize it because so many others in your family or community accept it as casual, social gambling. When you do recognize that the gambling is problematic, you may *accept* that the issue needs to be addressed or *deny* or *rationalize* its seriousness. Sometimes you first face the reality of the gambling problem when a financial, legal, or emotional crisis occurs. You realize you missed the tip-offs because of the hidden nature of gambling.

When the truth finally hits you, you may blame yourself or other people or situations. This defense mechanism helps you escape the pain and suffering you might experience if you face the reality, and lets you avoid dealing with the fear of upsetting the gambler or ending your relationship with him.

Later in the identification stage you begin to look more objectively at the gambler and the impact of gambling on you and others. You learn that gambling too much may be either an emotional disorder or a serious addictive illness. At first you may have trouble separating the person from his gambling, but later you accept that the gambler is not willfully trying to harm you. You may continue to be overwhelmed and perhaps panic about what has already happened or what lies ahead. But you hope that you will manage the problems in your life. Despite this progress, you are likely to harbor many intense, almost unbearable, feelings of anger, shame, humiliation, guilt, and anxiety. You slowly realize how much you have lost or will lose because of the gambling, and you begin to grieve.

During the identification stage you may want to or even try to bury your head in the sand and take the attitude "what I don't know won't hurt me." This is a poor strategy because you are more aware of the devastation that accompanies having someone in your life who is a problem or compulsive gambler.

ACKNOWLEDGMENT STAGE

You have gone beyond your initial knowledge and understanding of the gambler and his loss of control. You see more clearly the impact it has on you, others, and the gambler himself. Things are really sinking in. You are beginning to accept (rather than just saying it) that compulsive gambling is a progressive addictive illness over which *you* have no control, meaning that you are powerless over the gambler and the gambling. You feel less ashamed and are able to discuss your situation with others. You are in less denial than before and are not as likely to reproach yourself or blame others. Intellectually you *know* you haven't caused the gambling and you can't control it or cure it, but at this point it is a thought you continue to struggle with rather than accept as a deeply felt belief. You are beginning to know the difference between what you *can* change and what you *can't*, and you are mobilizing your strength to change those things you can. You "know the score," and you accept the reality that you and others are behind the 8-ball. You realize more than before that the gambler deceives you and you feel very foolish. Knowing more than before, you're even more frightened about everyone's future: You recognize your role as enabler and perhaps as a codependent to the gambler. There are times when you continue to feel as overwhelmed, angered, confused, and hurt as when you entered the identification stage.

SURVIVAL STAGE

With your newfound awareness and courage, you take steps to protect yourself or others from the consequences of the gambler's obsession. This is an important step in your recovery. If necessary, you take financial inventory and learn more about how gambling has affected your life. You still feel betrayed and are often hit with a wave of panic. As you learn more, you realize that you have known so little about your situation because of the hidden nature of problem and addictive gambling. The gambler's lies and "gaslighting" still confuse you, so sometimes you question your suspicions and findings. But you are now determined to persevere and reach out for help in dealing with the emotional, financial, and legal consequences. You recognize that the gambler must take responsibility for his problem or addiction, and you act on your growing knowledge by detaching yourself emotionally, financially, and legally.

Perhaps you have already confronted the gambler, who may even be getting help. Your education continues as you learn more about the gambler and the enabling system. You begin to learn more about yourself. Perhaps you start to cope with uncertainty by developing faith in a Higher Power and in the attitude of one day at a time. Building on your earlier knowledge and understanding, you start to deal differently with your feelings and life in general. You realize you have come a long way and accept that you still have miles to go.

REBUILDING YOUR LIFE

Your recovery now involves a much more objective view of yourself and your relationship to the gambler. Your feelings and attitudes change as you examine the underlying core issues that led to your enabling. You also reexamine your values, solve your problems in new and better ways, and redefine your relationship to the gambler and others in and out of your enabling system. You feel less shame, anger, and guilt as your past experiences and feelings are validated, and as you come to accept that the gambler suffers from a disorder or an addictive illness. As you continue to learn, you find that you can begin to forgive the gambler, yourself, and others.

You also realize you must deal with your own self-defeating behaviors including compulsions and addictions. You learn more about your relationship to the gambler as well as new ways of coping with your feelings. You find that you can make choices for yourself and others without exerting compulsive control. You no longer feel overwhelmed when you don't try to fix everything. You are able to let go. Your spirituality has evolved, and despite the uncertainties in your life, you find comfort, perhaps by calling on a Higher Power. There is more honesty in your life. You experience far less shame, confusion, anxiety, and fear about having someone in your life who gambles too much. At times your anger and outrage about the gambler's lying (which may continue even if he is in recovery) may erupt but subside more easily. You are becoming less reactive and more active as you take charge of your life. You have greater self-esteem, hope, faith, and confidence as you manage the stress. Forgiveness starts to come easier to you. You begin to reach out to help others who are starting their journey to recovery.

LOOKING AHEAD—AND BACK

At this point, you may feel as if your recovery is well under way. You are rebuilding your life—with or without the gambler.

In reviewing your life you will be aware that at times you bring your past hurts and fears into your current life-style and relationships, including those with the gambler. These injuries to your inner well-being may have come from early emotional or physical traumas, deprivation, or neglect. Although common sense would dictate that you would avoid a replay and not re-create these early experiences or similar relationships, you find you have done so, even against your will. As a child you thought your unhappiness or unsatisfactory life resulted from *your* faults or shortcomings, and so as an adult you unconsciously believed and hoped that this time you would make it come out right. You also believe (again, unconsciously, as when you were a child) that things will turn out better because you wish it to be so. The purpose of all of this is to get what you always wanted and needed: unconditional love and understanding.

Exploring these issues and overcoming the earliest hurts constitute the next stage of recovery, which may or may not be essential for you.

RECLAIMING YOUR LIFE

Would you be different if you had been fortunate enough to be raised in an environment that was perfectly tuned to your needs? What would you be like? How would you function spiritually, emotionally, and intellectually in your roles as parent, partner, lover, worker?

Chances are that if you had this kind of optimal rearing you would be the very best you could be. Few of us have this "perfect" rearing, for even with the best intentions, parents make errors, and many factors beyond their control can make their roles difficult to fulfill.

You can still do something to make up for these early experiences. You can reclaim your potential by focusing on the early injuries and damage that continue to hold you back. It will mean understanding and then offering comfort to what has been referred to as the "inner child." It is long, hard, but rewarding work.

Psychotherapy and self-help support can provide you with the experiences that will help you address these painful feelings. It will help you nurture the part of you that is underdeveloped and it will challenge the basis of your negative self-image, such as low self-worth, excessive shame, and guilt. This work requires that you learn to identify those feelings and needs that you may have avoided, denied, or displaced onto others. Gradually you will learn to tolerate and accept these feelings and be able to express them appropriately to others. You will grow in self-acceptance, self-worth, and caring of others.

The deep distrust you once felt as the result of your early hurtful experiences will fade into the background, becoming part of your history. Your capacity for intimacy will grow.

As you reclaim this "inner child" your fears of abandonment will lessen. Being alone will seem less frightening because you recognize your ability to nurture and care for yourself.

You will blossom in other ways, becoming more productive, wiser, and serene. You will feel entitled to the joys of your life.

ILLUSION TO REALITY

As you move into the recovery process think of it as moving from illusion to reality. Like the gambler, you suffered from some illusions. As you go through the process of recovery you will give up the following and other illusions:

- The gambling isn't a problem.
- The gambler will be able to stop after recouping his losses.
- I can stop the gambler from gambling.
- If the gambler stops, everything will be all right.
- The gambler will *never* stop and my life will *never* change.

Then, as you move deeper in recovery, reality sets in. You know:

- The person is gambling too much.
- Maybe the gambling will stop, but chances are *everything* won't be all right.
- I can't make the gambler stop, but I can help break down his denial by stopping the bailouts.
- The gambler may *never* stop, but I can change *my* life.

By reading this book or receiving help from others, you may move from illusion to reality quite quickly. Initially you may have to make a conscious effort to do things differently. In time and with effort your new behavior will become spontaneous and natural to you. The same is true of how you cope with your feelings and attitudes. See your recovery in terms of small specific goals such as not checking up on the gambler's whereabouts or, when he played cards all last night, refusing to call work to tell his boss that he's going to be late. Also see your recovery in terms of longer, more complex goals, such as being able to be more loving and less angry at the gambler. Always take time out to acknowledge your achievements and the efforts you are making as you strive toward recovery. Don't expect miracles, but trust that eventually you will achieve greater peace of mind and feel comfortable with the truths of your life.

HELP WITH RECOVERY

It's possible to travel the road to recovery alone, but you don't have to. Gam-Anon and other twelve-step self-help groups are there for you. You also may choose to get professional help by joining a group led by a mental health professional or having individual, marital, couple, or family therapy.

SELF-HELP OR GROUP THERAPY

A group setting can be particularly effective in reducing your isolation and in providing support for you to make changes. This is especially important for a family member or friend of a gambler because of the stigma and misunderstanding about problem and compulsive gambling. You will feel validated and understood by the other members who have had similar experiences. They can encourage and support you as you take the risks necessary to move on with your life. They will also help you when you unknowingly "slip" and fall back into an enabling role. The members understand how difficult it can be to give up familiar roles and behavior *even* when it perpetuates your suffering.

This acceptance may be particularly meaningful to you at this vulnerable time if you are subject to criticism from those who "knew" about the gambling and can't really believe that you didn't. If others around you seem to resist or sabotage your efforts, a group experience offers an effective counterbalance and helps to give you the support to "stick to your guns."

You will also find that a group provides an excellent setting for working out family problems because there you learn and get a chance to practice different ways of interacting.

In a group you have an opportunity to help others too, and this can heal your eroded sense of self-worth. There is a "yes, you can" attitude in a group, and this in turn helps empower you to do what you know you should do.

INDIVIDUAL THERAPY

You may opt for individual therapy instead of or in addition to a group experience. In a one-to-one setting with an experienced mental health professional you will find new ways to rebuild and reclaim your life. You may wish to begin with individual therapy, especially at a time of financial and emotional crisis to help you sort out and manage the many problems you face. Or you may begin with a twelve-step program and then find that individual therapy will help you delve further into your own historical issues. If you are so overwhelmed and flooded with feelings that you are not yet ready to discuss them in a group, you may prefer the undivided attention of a therapist. You will identify your feelings, get help in expressing them appropriately, and then act on them with the assurance that you are doing something good for yourself and your situation.

JOINT, COUPLE, OR MARITAL THERAPY

You and your spouse, live-in, or close friend may find joint therapy especially helpful in changing the interactions necessary to rebuild your lives together. Even if the gambler is in "good recovery" the relationship may still be fraught with conflict and distrust. Since there has been so much hurt, anger, blame, and even fury, the foundation of your relationship to the gambler has been severely eroded. Perhaps the only "glue" that holds you together is your emotional dependency on each other.

Poor communication may threaten both the relationship and your individual recoveries. You may find that you are working at cross-purposes, the result of old power struggles. You might need guidance to learn to listen to each other so that you can work together cooperatively.

You and the gambler may have become isolated from friends and other family members and need help in reentering the social system and in finding new friends and interests you can share. Joint therapy provides an excellent opportunity to help each of you take responsibility for hurts you have caused and to forgive the other for hurts received. It can help you both redefine your relationship and make it more satisfying.

FAMILY THERAPY

A gambling problem or addiction is a family affair. As we have seen, even though only one person may be a gambler, others are impacted. Some families are so relieved when the gambler goes into recovery that they minimize or deny this impact. However, until the resentments, distrust, hurt, pain, shame, disappointment, and humiliation are acknowledged, addressed, and resolved, family life cannot proceed and recover. Even if the gambling was well hidden and family routines such as meals, traditional events, weekend activities, or vacations were not disrupted, members feel the impact. Secrecy, deceptions, occasional consequences, or crises affect the development and perpetuation of trust and well-being. When family members (especially children) see, hear, or feel that something is going on but no one confirms or acknowledges it, they are still affected. This can result in long-term problems with anxiety, self-doubt, shame, and guilt.

Based on each member's perceptions and emotional resources, the entire family is helped to heal its past inner wounds. In these family sessions, open communication is encouraged, and permission is given to members to let go of bottled up feelings and thoughts. This helps to bring truths to the surface and rebonds the members, often with increased love and understanding. These sessions also support the individual gambler's recovery as he "makes amends" and explains his "character defects" to the others. Your recovery can also be assisted during these sessions, in which you have an opportunity to say what is on your mind.

If the gambling was hidden in your family, the children and other family members may blame you rather than the gambler for tension or arguments in the household. If the gambling was open, they may still "blame" you for making such a fuss about it. You may have stood alone everywhere, unsupported by extended family, friends, or community. This emotional isolation coupled with having been the target of the gambler's behaviors for so long may have made you extremely hostile. If you have become increasingly angry and hysterical, it is possible that no one even listens to you anymore. In the calm of family sessions, you can vent and correct misunderstandings as well as make amends for the times when feelings of unhappiness, frustration, and stress were displaced onto other family members. If you were physically, verbally, or emotionally abusive, this is where it can be safely discussed.

These family sessions provide an opportunity to reexamine values, find new ways to arrive at decisions, and support individual and collective goals to growth.

RESISTANCE TO YOUR CHANGE

It is human nature to resist change in many areas of life, even when you know it is for the best. You may resist changing now to protect whatever happiness or fulfillment you have in your life. You may also resist giving up your enabling or codependent role, even though it is painful and you feel like the gambler's victim.

Perhaps you recognize that change in one part of you, your family, or group of friends will have a ripple effect. This can be unsettling, stressful, or painful. Change can make your life feel unsteady and therefore unsafe.

You may find some family members and friends are uncomfortable seeing you change even though they agree that "something needs to be done" or "you don't have to put up with that." At the same time, they don't want to "upset the apple cart" so they may unconsciously or even consciously push just as hard to keep you from changing. Your actions or words may be telling them things they don't want to hear or feel and would rather push under the rug.

The gambler may resist your change because it is threatening to the status quo that allows him to continue to be in action, and challenges his grandiose perception of himself and his view of your relationship to him. Highly sensitive to what others may think of him, he may feel uncomfortable about your newfound openness in speaking to others (in or out of therapy) about his gambling. If you and others identify him as a problem or compulsive gambler, he may be frightened, insulted, or angered because this pierces his denial. The gambler alternately fears and seeks dependency on you or others, but paradoxically wants you to be dependent on him. Your growing autonomy thus makes him uncomfortably fearful. You may be away from home more, perhaps at school or work, as well as emotionally distant. Without your undivided attention, the gambler begins to have to face his emptiness and dependency issues. He may feel like an abandoned child.

Families often resist change until their members can find new ways to accommodate to it. The family is actually a very structured organization with specific stated and unstated rules and roles for each member. There are rules for how the family communicates and makes decisions and for how members are to behave. The roles and rules of a family represent its beliefs and values.

In a healthy family these rules and values are designed to meet the needs of all its members, to make them feel safe and productive and to keep the family working as a unit. The parents' role is to provide nurturance, economic and emotional protection, and leadership. Children's roles are to be nurtured, grow, play, learn, and gradually assume appropriate responsibilities to prepare them for their adult years.

In some families the rules and roles are vague and confused, unpredictable and difficult to understand. In others they are overly rigid and difficult to live with or follow. These families are commonly referred to as dysfunctional family systems.

Most families are a mixture of healthy and dysfunctional elements. No family is perfect. Regardless of whether the family is healthy or not, it is thrown out of balance if one member changes, even if that change is for the better. You can get a sense of what would happen if you picture four people walking briskly along arm in arm in unison. If one of them slows down or stops or suddenly moves ahead faster, the others will be thrown out of step.

Your recovery or the gambler's may be resisted by other family members for one of these reasons:

• It may cause a change in the structure of the family, affecting particular role assignments—who is in charge, who is cared for, and so on.

• It may challenge various rules, such as those about secrets, avoiding painful or confrontational discussions, how money is spent, or how leisure time is organized.

• It may challenge how other members have bolstered their sense of importance and competence or managed their emotional needs, perhaps by being needed by others or by gaining sympathy by being viewed as a helpless victim.

RESISTANCE TO THE GAMBLER'S CHANGE

Some people will resist your change *and* the gambler's change, especially if your change challenges their enabling role, and they are not ready to give it up. This may complicate your recovery.

Some people are unable to let go of their perceptions of the gambler as the Black Sheep, the Happy-Go-Lucky, or the Big Sport, and have an interest in seeing that the gambler stays the way he is. Siblings of the gambler often feel this way.

Surprising as it may seem, you may find *you* also resist the gambler's change and recovery for these or similar reasons:

• You secretly or unconsciously admire his recklessness or lack of respect for rules and authority.

• You privately share his omnipotent or grandiose fantasies and ideas.

• You would rather "mother" the gambler and continue to see him as a needy, problematic child than relate on an adult level.

• You want to protect the power and control you currently exercise over your life or others.

• Your attention and response to the gambler helps you to avoid your more powerful and uncomfortable "inner child" issues.

At times you may find that you sabotage the gambler's recovery. Use these experiences to discover more about yourself, the gambler, and your relationship.

Remember that each step toward self-awareness and self-acceptance creates energy, desire, and motivation to counter your resistance and move you closer toward your recovery goals.

WILL I EVER FORGIVE THE GAMBLER?

Everyone knows bitter people who are old before their time. Often they haven't forgiven someone who has destroyed, abused, or betrayed their trust. Perhaps this person "gaslighted" them into such confusion that they distrust everyone, even themselves. Holding on to their hostility and resentment, they wear a mask of coldness or hatred that keeps others at arm's length and does nothing to enhance their lives.

Forgiveness is such an essential part of your recovery, whether or not you stay involved with the gambler, that without it recovery is impossible. It is not self-righteous, holier-than-thou forgiveness or forgiveness given grudgingly to avoid arguments and confrontation. It is not forgiveness that is motivated by "selflessness." It is *true* forgiveness.

You need to forgive so that you can let go of the past and go on with your life. To forgive, you need not forget, excuse, accept, or tolerate the hurts the gambler has caused you. Instead, you must fully and honestly acknowledge how you were hurt and feel the pain. The pain will pass and then you will be able to genuinely forgive.

To soften the ongoing pain you may be experiencing, you will separate the gambler from his actions. You will allow yourself to grieve for the losses and the dreams and hopes that were never realized. You may need to look at others whom you have loved, admired, or even exalted who knowingly or unknowingly aided and abetted the gambler as they played out their enabling roles. You may have to admit your own role or your naïveté that made it easy for the gambler to lie and gaslight you. For recovery, you will need to forgive yourself as well as others.

How will you know when you have forgiven the gambler?

• When you are no longer totally preoccupied or obsessed with the gambler or the gambling and its effect on you.

• When people are no longer saying "get on with your life."

• When you no longer feel revengeful, spiteful, and filled with malice toward the gambler and those people, places, and things you associate with the gambling.

• When you can form new relationships with new patterns.

• When you can recall the hurts and disappointments caused by the gambler, but feel the power to wish him well or even feel truly loving toward him.

CHAPTER 13

Your Own Journey to Recovery

Specific relationships raise different problems and concerns in recovery. As the spouse of or someone in a relationship with a gambler, you may feel in conflict about starting your recovery journey. You imagine the risks it poses to your present life and relationship to the gambler. You fear that you and the gambler will grow apart if you change.

This may indeed happen, especially if the gambler doesn't change along with you. But many people close to a gambler have learned that their own recovery can present an opportunity to heal the relationship, gain even greater closeness and mutual respect, and normalize their life together. This can happen to you.

Perhaps you are so unhappy and life is so miserable for you, your children, and others that you know something must change; it is a necessity, not an option. This change and recovery are complicated by the kinds of ties (once comforting but now strangling) that bind you to the gambler: familial, economic, legal, social, and emotional. You wonder if you can make changes without cutting all the ties. At times you feel as if you are constantly giving but receiving nothing in return. The hurt and exhaustion from dealing with the consequences of the gambling make you ready to totally bail out of the relationship. Perhaps cutting these ties is the only route you can take that will put an end to your devastation.

If you choose to do this (and many spouses or partners do), you may need emotional as well as legal or financial help in the process. Will you need recovery work? Probably, for it will help you avoid carrying the issues and pain from this relationship into future ones.

Even if you formally end the relationship with the gambler you may still find yourself bound to him in some way. Perhaps you have legal obligations for debts. If you have children together, you may find that the connection never ends, for after children are grown grandchildren may hold you together. Your recovery will be similar to but far less complicated than that of those who stay in the current relationship. You still need to heal the hurts and anger as you deal with your grief over your losses of what never was and what never will be.

The choice to stay in the relationship means you will have to face daily the problems associated with gambling. At the same time, you will be severing your financial ties and adjusting, untangling, and even strengthening other ties to the gambler. You may doubt that this can be done, but you will learn from others that it is possible.

Although you are not responsible for the gambler's recovery, it will be helpful to both of you if you understand his and if he understands yours. During this period, you will find that you continually experience contradictory feelings and desires. As you move ahead in recovery, this will continue, sometimes becoming so intense that you may feel immobilized. The family's and the gambler's resistance and the gambler's tendency to exploit your feelings may make your recovery even more difficult. You maintain a difficult balancing act as you struggle to make decisions or avoid acting on impulses that may work against achieving longer-term goals. You will be asking much of yourself now, a task made still more difficult because you have been so emotionally bruised. Understand and accept that your recovery, like the gambler's, will have its setbacks and plateaus. Be kind to yourself and be patient.

At this time, you may overreact as the gambler "comes clean" by becoming erratic, impulsive, or even violent. Each new deception uncovered feels like another assault to your self-esteem.

You again feel betrayed. You wonder whom you can trust. It is natural to feel angry with yourself, the gambler, and others, especially those who have enabled the gambler or kept his secret. The more you know and the less you deny, the more you will feel anger and pain, and the more you may want to punish and strike back at the gambler, feeling your rage is justified. Intellectually you realize that hurting the gambler will only cause more tension and pain. Although it may feel immediately satisfying, it will put a strain on his ability to abstain from gambling and also make it harder to eventually mend your relationship. You continually struggle with these conflicting and contradictory feelings.

At times the problems may seem insurmountable and you may be tempted to throw them back into the gambler's lap: "See what you've done. It's your problem, it's your addiction, you fix it." Or you may figuratively throw a blanket over your head to forget everything and leave it all behind you. But now you know better. So instead you struggle to stay detached, but remain aware and realistic about your situation. With guidance and experience, you will begin to find your efforts rewarded.

With support from others—your therapist or the members of Gam-Anon, or other groups—you feel less alone. Still you struggle to accept your powerlessness and to remain in touch with your feelings and your experiences. Although you better understand the gambler, you still have alternating feelings of anger and sympathy toward him, and these never-ending contradictory feelings cause guilt and stress. As you begin to examine your own role— that of enabler or codependent—you tend to blame yourself and feel that some people will also blame you.

"What about me?" you want to wail. "Aren't I suffering? When will it be my turn to be understood?" You mistakenly feel that you are being pressured to put aside your feelings and needs once again and that the gambler is getting "bailed out" in a new way. Now he's off the hook because his "bad" behavior has been redefined as "sick."

Slowly but surely your recovery takes place. As you begin to take responsibility for your own and the family's financial and legal needs and establish your financial independence, your self-esteem increases.

Your experience with the GA pressure group leaves you more at ease because you now know the score. You are hopeful because your financial problems seem more manageable. The repayment and budget plan they help you devise serves to settle some of the conflicts you are having with the gambler over money. You also learn about your own attitudes toward spending and saving and realize how they have contributed to your enabling of the gambler and your situation.

You are now more in charge. Having the upper hand gives you a sense of power and peace of mind. You and the gambler may confuse this control with keeping him in line, against which he most likely will rebel. You feel bitter and resentful that it has come to this, and you long for the day when someone will take these responsibilities off your hands and take care of you.

Just as things are settling down and your life becomes more predictable, the gambler may disclose more problems or even suffer a relapse. It may feel like day one of recovery all over again. All the old fears, resentments, rage, and even hatred flare up. You feel out of control and vulnerable. You learn, once again, that there are no guarantees, especially when there's a gambler in your life.

You may tighten your controls on the finances, checking to see if the gambler has found any loopholes he can manipulate. Your distrust heightens. There are fewer illusions as you face life with a gambler more squarely, but you are frightened as you look to the future.

Although you accept that you are powerless over the gambler and that he must take responsibility for his own recovery, you might find yourself struggling with becoming his watchdog. Every move he makes is seen with alarm. You monitor his television viewing, inspect the newspaper to see what he's been reading, listen in on phone calls, look through his pockets, check out his wallet, and keep constant tabs on his whereabouts. You keep checking to see if he has switched from gambling to alcohol or drug use. You recognize that this is contrary to everything you are learning about in therapy, but you find it difficult to restrain yourself because of your fears about the devastation the gambler can bring on you and your family. You may find that these behaviors are indicative of your codependency. Whatever the reason, you take greater comfort in turning to a Higher Power and letting go.

Soon you become less of a watchdog and less harsh with yourself when you do slip back into old controlling behaviors. You see yourself and your relationships with the gambler and others in your past more clearly. You no longer think of the gambler's actions as something done just to upset you. You further understand his psyche, and you emotionally accept and appreciate his struggles with his problem or illness and how they may even be complicated by other dependencies on alcohol or drugs. You are much more aware of the complexities of your enabling, realizing that you may have been and are still occasionally bailing him out, if not with money with time and emotions. You understand this is natural, and you are less self-critical.

You still check on the gambler but less as you develop emotional detachment. You also check yourself and your actions. Am I too trusting or too distrustful? Am I being too assertive and aggressive or am I too passive? Then you begin to examine your motives. Do I say no to the gambler because what he is asking is a bailout or just to punish him and make his life difficult?

Sometimes you aren't sure if you are being fair to him. You are happy he is getting help with his recovery but then it seems to you as if he uses his recovery to gain attention. As he begins to share responsibilities with you in the household or with the children you feel he is infringing on your turf. Perhaps you are accustomed to being alone and now in his sudden desire for more togetherness he smothers and crowds you. In contrast, you may feel abandoned because he's attending frequent GA meetings or working a second or third job to cover debts.

There may be fewer fights about gambling or money, and the volatile atmosphere at home diminishes. Your life feels more normal and for this you are grateful. But now you are learning that gambling wasn't the only source of your unhappiness. Other issues surface. For instance, he may want more or less sex than you do. He may still lack warmth, respect, and enthusiasm for anything other than gambling, and he may still be unable to express feelings in an honest, open fashion. You are disappointed and recognize that even though you intellectually understand his psyche you still harbor the illusion that "if only he stopped gambling, he would be perfect and all I could want."

If he becomes more emotionally available, this closeness may make you want to move away. Perhaps for the first time you recognize that you may have problems with intimacy and may have been initially attracted to him because he kept an emotional distance.

Slowly you examine your own participation in the "insanity" that often goes along in a household in which someone gambles too much. You look at how you have coped and possibly at your own dependencies on alcohol, drugs, or something else. You feel great remorse for what you may have said or done during the heat of your frustration, and you attempt to make amends to those you hurt, especially the children. You interact with family and friends with more honesty and directness, and where appropriate you ask for forgiveness. You will know that you are reaching the final stages of recovery when:

• Your feelings, sense of worth, self-esteem, shame, and general well-being no longer depend on the gambler or his behavior.

• You develop new interests apart from the gambler.

• You no longer feel dread, terror, guilt, panic, or other acutely uncomfortable feelings when you think of detaching from the gambler financially, legally, or emotionally.

• You no longer spend most of the time with the gambler feeling miserable, consumed with fear, frustration, anger, disappointment, neediness, and guilt.

• You have decided that since the gambler is continuing to gamble you are taking steps to detach and disengage yourself.

• You are willing to take healthy risks to change and improve your life.

• You are more open, honest, and direct with others.

Like Megan S., whom we met in chapter 6, you will be able to turn your life around. As you read Megan's story, note that her identification stage comes as a sudden revelation, that she spends considerable time just "knowing" but not moving on to the acknowledgment stage. Too insecure to move on, but never thrown into a financial crisis, she spends several years in a chronic unhappy state. Al, moody and difficult, is always either working, playing golf, or off gambling, and she feels as if she is rearing the children alone. When a school guidance counselor suggests she seek counseling regarding one of the children, she also enters therapy, and then is able to truly acknowledge that Al is a problem gambler. It is then that she is able to enter the survival stage, where she builds courage and goes back to school and starts to take charge of her financial life. As she rebuilds her life, she gains still more courage and makes a major decision.

I was frightened and angry when I discovered that Al had been gambling all those years. It was like finding an important piece to an unfinished puzzle. How could I have been so blind? What was going to happen to us? What else was hidden from me?

Al's gambling explained a lot of the things I could never understand about him, like how he would bark at me and the kids for no reason at all. He was so moody and at times he was a million miles away. Now a lot more made sense, like the way he had trouble sleeping and his problems with his stomach. I thought about all the times I felt he was lying but was too frightened to challenge him.

It dawned on me that I was living with a stranger. I wondered what other secrets he was keeping. This frightened me so much I just kept it to myself for a long time. Then when I began therapy I started asking myself a lot of questions about myself, my life with Al, and the part that his gambling played in all of it. At first I spoke to the therapist only about my concerns for my daughter and my dissatisfaction with my life in general, especially with my relationship to Al. I didn't even mention the gambling because I was embarrassed to admit that I had been overlooking it for years. But after I began to trust my therapist more, I discussed it in my sessions. As I learned more about the problem, it became easier to talk about it, and I became less hard on myself.

I tried bringing up the subject to Al many times, but he would get so angry and accuse me of being all sorts of things: selfish, nagging, castrating, hysterical. Then he would attack my therapy and call it psychological "garbage." I wasn't getting through to him, and after a while I stopped trying.

I realized that his anger and defensiveness were clues that he was trying to hide still more from me. I set out to find what that was, partly to satisfy my own need not to be fooled as I had once been and also because I was concerned about the kids' and my futures.

Although Al kept his bank statements and bills in a drawer, I knew he had a file with other things in the basement. Surprisingly, I had never looked there before, probably because I really didn't want to know more than I did. But now I needed to know. In that file cabinet I found everything about our finances: old tax returns, bank statements, and stock sales. It wasn't difficult to understand. I realized that despite Al's substantial salary and other perks from the family business and a life-style that should have left us with plenty of surplus, we had little savings and no investments. Al had only basic life insurance and our medical insurance was inadequate. We had very little to cushion us in the event of an emergency or if something happened to Al.

I was angry and hurt all over again as I realized I had been fooled into complacency, thinking that despite Al's gambling my life was secure. Now I confronted Al again, this time with greater conviction. As usual, it got me nowhere. Although I saw through his lies, he made no effort to stop gambling or to change his ways.

By that time I had returned to college and was studying to be a nutritionist and also had started my own savings account from my earnings as a lab technician. My sense of worth grew with each achievement in school and my growing financial independence. In therapy I became more aware of myself, recognizing that I had always felt inferior to Al and others and had never questioned or asked too much of people.

By now Al didn't even pretend he was away on business when he went to Las Vegas. But when I discovered that for the last year he had been taking other women with him, I decided to end the marriage.

Being a single parent with a limited income is not easy. My fourteen-year-old daughter is still angry with me because she misses her father living at home and feels he needs his family to help him settle down. I know she will understand when she's older. Sometimes after a long day when I am tired and lonely, I ask myself if I did the right thing.

My answer is always the same. Yes.

Do I have any regrets? Yes, just one. I wish I had gotten his parents to help me confront him in a formal Intervention so he might have gotten help.

Cynthia B., whom we met in chapter 2, married to William for twenty-five years, made a suicide attempt, the cumulative result of the stress of having grown up in a gambling household, being married to a compulsive gambler, and experiencing problems with her children—Bill, who gambled and drank too much, and Anna, who was distancing herself from her mother and was critical of her.

I didn't realize how crazy our life was. William was gambling so much that he even lost a good job because of it. He had had that job for years. We constantly fought over bills, money, and the kids, but I always broke down in the end. It was not in my nature to fight. I am really a very quiet person. My life was a mess but I really thought everyone lived like us. After all, my parents had lived the same way.

I guess I couldn't take all the pressure and that's when I wound up in the hospital and that's where I started therapy. It took me a long time to feel comfortable to talk about myself, William, and the kids. It was still embarrassing, even after I learned that William was a compulsive gambler. I always knew he gambled too much but never dreamed he was really addicted or that he was as sick as an alcoholic or a drug addict.

At first I refused to go to Gam-Anon as my therapist suggested but then I spoke to Barbara C., who became my sponsor. She took me to my first meetings. I was terrified that I would have to speak, but she reassured me that I didn't have to until I was ready. I was amazed that I could identify with the other members, and it felt good to finally feel that other people understood what it was like to be the wife of a compulsive gambler.

The talk of the twelve steps sounded so religious at first. I couldn't possibly see how following them could help me. How was praying going to pay the bills, decrease our debts, or stop William's lying and Bill's drinking? I found the first step particularly difficult—admitting that I was powerless over the problems in my family. Goodness knows I already *knew* I was powerless. Hadn't I been struggling long enough to change William and everything else in my life? But as I listened I gradually began to realize that accepting powerlessness rather than fighting it as I had been doing made me feel free. I began to think about other things and concentrate on myself.

I had a lot of trouble with the idea of a Higher Power. I had once been a churchgoer but had abandoned my faith because of my anger and disappointment at home. It took a while before I started calling on my Higher Power and relying on the serenity prayer. I began to learn the wisdom to know the difference between what I can and cannot change. Now I feel secure about leaving the rest of my life to my Higher Power. It's in good hands.

Week after week I went—and still go—to my meetings. They became a place where I could be myself. With the help of Gam-Anon and my Higher Power, I was able to stick to my guns with William. The stronger I got the less he could bully me. Finally I told him that if he didn't go for help for his gambling he could just pack his bags and get out. That time I meant it. And William really believed me. With the help of Barbara's husband, who had been with GA for years, he went to a meeting and he hasn't stopped going since. He's had his slips, but then he returns to work his GA program even harder. When he relapsed, I also fell back into my old ways until I was able to regain my senses and rely on my faith.

Our relationship is better than ever. I mean, we have arguments, but at least we can talk to each other to settle things. I have gotten to know him better since he is in recovery. He is really kind of shy and insecure. I have changed a lot. I'm much more assertive now and can speak my mind. I truly feel I deserve to have more kindness from others than I thought I did. I'm also learning to live with my emotions and I no longer think it's wrong to have feelings.

I have a long way to go, but whenever I get down on myself, I remember program slogans like "easy does it" or "progress, not perfection." I'm very active in Gam-Anon, and I'm now a sponsor and helping others.

I got my high school equivalency a few years ago and then got a job as a teacher's aide in my local school. I really enjoy it and feel confident working with the kindergartners. I feel appreciated there, something I never thought would happen. I won't pretend that everything is fine with William and me. But we are still married, and our daughter Anna is in therapy and doing well. Our son Bill still drinks and gambles too much, but I have stopped enabling him, and now the only thing I can do is pray that he finds his own path to recovery.

RECOVERY FOR PARENTS, PARENTS-IN-LAW, AND GRANDPARENTS

Of all those related to the gambler, possibly the parents and grandparents have the most difficulty detaching financially or emotionally. Even if they are able to do it, their recovery is likely to be complex and rocky.

It's not surprising. One of the most memorable days in most people's lives is the day a child or grandchild is born. Do you remember how you felt when you first set eyes on each child? Remember how it felt to hold these children in your arms and the dreams and hopes you had for their future?

Perhaps you wanted them to match your achievements or you hoped that they would have all the things that had passed you by. You viewed each milestone with such pleasure, from the first smile and step to various achievements in school and elsewhere. Your heart swelled: that's my boy, that's my girl!

You also may have experienced disappointments if the child didn't live up to your expectations. Still, you had confidence that things would work out in the future, and your love remained steady. But the consequences of gambling may have a huge effect on your relationship with your children or grandchildren. As in any recovery, you will go through the stage of identification, acknowledgment, survival, and rebuilding your life.

Whether this child is a teenager or middle-aged, you feel great disappointment as well as fear and pain. You may have already seen this boy or girl turn from great promise or hope for the future into a person who is decaying morally and spiritually.

Ashamed and saddened by the gambler's behavior and your participation as an enabler, you may feel as if *you* have been inadequate. These feelings may be heightened or reinforced by other family members who criticize you for how you raised your child or how you responded to the gambling.

Fearing further humiliation, you might reject help from all sources until anguish over the situation or related circumstances leaves you with no options. You seek help from a twelve-step program like Gam-Anon or another group that addresses family problems or from a counselor or therapist. The support from others is comforting, but at times you become distressed when you hear others complain about or blame gamblers' problems on their parents. You may find yourself overidentifying with these comments, feeling increased responsibility and guilt that can interfere with your recovery work. To avoid this, seek out a self-help group specifically for parents of gamblers or people with other dependencies or addictions.

If the gambler is young, you may have been tempted to think that it is just a "stage" that he will outgrow. You grieve for the financial, emotional, educational, and career opportunities sacrificed for the gambling action. You still try to reason with the gambler, attempting to impart your life's wisdom about the gambling and other things. Even if the gambler agrees with you, he may not be ready yet to move into recovery, so these efforts are fruitless and frustrating.

You regret overlooking clues about the gambling, but you also recognize that the gambling was so well hidden there was no way to have known, especially if you didn't live with the gambler or, even if you did, if you had respected his privacy.

All the "should haves" and "shouldn't haves" seem to haunt you. Maybe you have spent years or decades cushioning your child from suffering the consequences of the gambling. Now you are acknowledging your role in the problem.

At this point, you have more understanding about the gambler's loss of control and your "powerlessness" to do anything beyond ending the bailouts. The support you get makes it easier to refuse to be your child's enabler, and you are beginning to resolve your conflicting feelings of responsibility to the gambler.

Seeing your child in pain produces pain in you, but you are learning that without it there is no chance for change. You may look into the possibility of a formal Intervention so that the gambler will accept help soon. In the meantime, you learn the importance of having faith that your gambling child will remain safe until he finds his way toward recovery.

You still chastise yourself because you closed your eyes to the problem or the potential consequences and didn't "do something" before difficulties or a crisis set in. As you learn more, you are easier on yourself, recognizing that in some families "helping the younger generation" and "being there" when they need you are the expectations. It is easy to confuse such rules and roles with enabling. It is also possible that the roots of your enabling may be codependency.

During this part of your recovery, you will begin to identify these different issues. Perhaps you fought against acceptance of the gambling problem or addiction to avoid family problems. You or another family member may have been dependent on substances or gambling. The gambler may have exploited conflicts and division within the family to get bailouts.

Your decision to stop the bailouts may continue or increase conflicts with your spouse or others in the family. It may remain an issue of control that the gambler exploits. Each member in his or her own way must eventually accept that everyone is "powerless" over the gambler's behavior. There may be struggles with a spouse or others who still do not see the gambling as serious or accept it as an emotional problem or illness. They may feel anger or sympathy toward you, but at the same time they may resist your efforts. You may feel alone and unsupported, or you may find that you have strong allies in the family.

Perhaps now the gambler is in recovery or you may already

have stopped the bailouts, but it has been difficult and you may sometimes give in. But more often you are able to say no not only to financial and other bailouts but to other inappropriate needs the gambler identifies. You appreciate your own growth. You question the mistaken belief that you are letting your child down by not giving in to him or making his life easier. You manage your own fears by relying more on what you *know* than on what you *feel*. You don't let guilt from the past influence your decisions.

You are more aware of what issues motivated you to enable and bail out your child, and you identify and overcome them. Still, you continue to harbor some of the following feelings:

- Guilt or a sense of failure for past mistakes or neglect
- Ambivalence toward the child
- Inability to tolerate having your child feel discomfort, disappointment, or pain
- You are not deserving of happiness or kindness
- Your financial aid is the solution to helping the gambler
- Viewing the child as an infant prince, needy and unable to make his own way and/or special or entitled to have everything his way
- Assuming total responsibility for the gambler's emotional problems, and therefore accepting that you have to "fix it"

As you share more with others in therapy, your evolving spirituality helps to anchor you in the present and guide you in determining what you now need to do for yourself, the gambler, and others. Your feelings about financial and emotional detachment are still in conflict, but over time the gambler's manipulations like "I'll lose everything if you don't help me" or "Why can't I come to you if I need help?" are less effective in keeping you in the enabling role.

You may see the gambler's life collapsing but steel yourself against rescuing attempts. Even if the gambler goes into recovery, there is still a great deal of work to do to rebuild your damaged, faltering self-esteem and your family relationships.

It may be difficult for you to resolve the damage to family relationships caused by conflicts over the gambler and the part that others perceived you as playing. The gambler's siblings, aunts, uncles, and grandparents, who are *your* relatives too may still heap blame on you, even though *you* have stopped blaming yourself. Perhaps they will see things differently someday. Your recovery may open up new channels of communication that can help solidify the family.

You are more able to accept that you cannot turn back the clock and that you shouldn't even try. You know you can't "make up" for those things that were beyond your control or ability to provide for your child during critical periods of his or her growth. You know that even if you overindulged or neglected the youngster, you didn't do it with the idea that it would someday cause problems.

Your sense of responsibility undergoes further revision as you become more educated about the multiple factors—emotional, biological, and cultural—that cause someone to turn to gambling to cope with feelings.

You begin to be good to yourself. You know you did your best under the circumstances. If the gambler child or others tell you your best wasn't good enough, you refrain from becoming defensive. You learn to make amends appropriately, not with more bailouts but by saying "I'm sorry for the past" and showing your children you are getting on with your life. You have faith that they too will recover.

If the gambler enters recovery or you have detached successfully and are now rebuilding your life, other issues may emerge and other problems in your life may be highlighted. For instance, you and your spouse may have had a common bond, focusing much of your energy on the gambler and the ensuing problems. The gambling problems may have helped you avoid your own emotional problems or a marriage that is shallow, empty, eroded, or depleted. Major conflicts caused by disagreements over whether or not to allow the gambler to experience the consequences of his gambling may have been hurtful, leaving each partner resentful and in pain. One parent may have continued the bailouts, unknown to the other, thus undermining trust and respect.

Even the best of marriages can be left weakened long after the enabling and the gambling end. Reviving this relationship is an important aspect of recovery and has positive effects for the whole family. Mutual support of each other will aid in facing the future.

You may find that you have achieved many of your goals, but

shame and guilt continue to trouble you and undermine your sense of worth. These may be chronic feelings, separate from being a parent or grandparent of a gambler. It is never too late for you to change. You can resolve these feelings and thus prevent your own sense of shame and guilt from being transmitted to your children or grandchildren. Through therapy you will work on the renewal or development of self-appreciation and pride in the most difficult but most rewarding job in the world—caring for children.

Adam T., whom we met in chapter 2, was born to an affluent family. His natural father died when he was young and his mother and paternal grandparents were never able to refuse him anything. His mother married Brad when Adam was five. Brad became a loving but critical father who always had great expectations for Adam.

Adam began gambling in high school, and my wife, Emily, and I saw it as a temporary problem, so we paid off his loans. When Adam got into deep trouble at college, I felt we should let him take the consequences. But Emily disagreed. She said Adam seemed so contrite she was sure he had learned his lesson. There seemed little point in my arguing, because I could never really get through to Emily and Adam's grandparents about the way they overindulged him and never let him pay the price for his escapades.

Emily was sure that Adam had stopped gambling, but I had my doubts. She wouldn't listen to me, so there was little I could do. Adam had money of his own that he had inherited from his late father's estate, so he seldom asked me for anything. But I knew that Emily was giving him money.

Adam became an accountant and was doing well—at least that's what we thought. I was outraged when Emily bought him a new car to replace the second-hand one he had that was running fine, and I thought it was ridiculous when his grandparents gave him the down payment for a condo. When I stated my opposition I was outvoted. Even though I had adopted Adam and loved him as if he were my biological son, I hesitated to assert myself because I didn't really feel I had the same "rights."

Often when we were with Adam, I would notice that he was very jumpy. He never seemed to be able to sustain a conversation. He was beginning to be careless about his appearance, and he had lost a lot of weight. We didn't see him as often as we would have liked, but Emily kept saying, "He's working so hard." I wasn't so sure that was the reason. I knew we could always be sure of hearing from him when he needed anything, which was more often than it should have been.

One Thanksgiving we had some of the family over for dinner, and Adam drank too much. We refused to let him get in the car and drive home, so he stayed over. The next day Adam was still in bed at noon. Emily went in to see if he was all right. She couldn't wake him. She panicked as I called for help.

The EMS technician took one look at Adam and knew that he had overdosed. They took him to the hospital, and for the rest of that day we thought he wouldn't survive. Emily and I did a lot of soul-searching.

Even though I had long suspected something was wrong, I was jolted to learn that Adam was using drugs as well as drinking too much. We also realized that there had been a number of clues that the gambling had never stopped.

A few days later we confronted him about what had happened. He was initially resistant, but then he told us he owed a great deal of money and began drinking more and using cocaine to deal with the stress. He asked if we would bail him out again. "Not this time," I said. Thank goodness Emily agreed. We told him that he had to go to a rehabilitation facility. He made a fuss, saying he could straighten himself out, and focused more on his gambling debts. Emily was ready to give in, but I said it wasn't negotiable and that we would get help to see how he could handle his debts himself.

Adam did well with his rehabilitation. In the family education program we learned a great deal about Adam and our role in his addictions. After Adam was discharged from the inpatient program, he went to Narcotics Anonymous and Gamblers Anonymous. We joined a program for parents, and we all went into family therapy. Adam's grandparents, now in their late seventies, joined us for several sessions.

Although we had identified the gambling problem almost ten years ago, we never acknowledged the seriousness of Adam's addictions until we almost lost him to an overdose of cocaine. We were ready to do everything we could to help him, and that meant we had to come face to face with ourselves, our relationship, and even our way of looking at life. At first we all did a great deal of blaming. Adam's grandparents blamed "the accident" (as they insisted on calling it) on Adam's "no good" friends, the drug dealers and the loan sharks. They asked us not to tell the rest of the family.

Emily and I blamed each other. I complained about her overindulgence and her tendency to show tenderness and love through gifts and with money. She countered with accusations about my unrealistically high expectations for Adam and my reliance on logic and lack of feeling. At times our accusations got really nasty and we both thought our marriage might be over.

Until we accepted that Adam was to take responsibility for his addictions and his life we continued to fight bitterly and were also unrelentingly harsh on ourselves.

Nevertheless, in the process we discovered feelings we were never aware of that had a big impact on us. Emily became more in touch with the guilt she felt for emotionally abandoning Adam during his toddler years when his father was in and out of the hospital and later when she was grieving. She also confessed that at the time she wished she didn't have Adam because he was a burden. She discovered on a deeper level that this rejection was about her fear of having to face another possible loss. Her honesty helped me to express my ambivalence about Adam as a demanding little boy and as a problematic adult. I shared my disappointment about not having my own children. I saw that my unresolved grief about my mother who died before my fifteenth birthday made me see Adam as I saw myself after my mother's death: a heartbroken, lost little boy.

Emily and I realized that much of our willingness to give in to Adam had more to do with fulfilling our needs than Adam's. Now we knew we had done the best we could, and our actions required no apologies.

For several years after Adam went into recovery, Emily and I relied on each other and our friends for the strength to avoid temptations to give in to Adam when he needed financial help and to turn his life back over to him. He has had his ups and downs in recovery, but through it all Emily and I have grown closer to each other.

A few years ago Adam married a lovely young woman and we have a wonderful granddaughter. For this we are so grateful.

RECOVERY FOR SIBLINGS, STEP-SIBS, AND SIBS-IN-LAW

If you are the sibling of the gambler, you may have any one of a number of conflicting feelings. These are shaped by early and current relationships with the sibling, parents, and other family members.

The gambler may be the sibling you always looked up to, the one you took under your wing, or the one you always resented and envied. In any sibling relationship you are likely to have some conflicting feelings: intense loving *and* not-so-loving feelings.

Right now you may not feel very sympathetic toward your sibling, even though you have acknowledged your brother or sister suffers from a gambling problem or addictive illness.

Perhaps you were the first to notice that the gambler had lost control. When you attempted to call it to your parents' attention, they dismissed your observations and warnings because they denied, misunderstood, or had long ago labeled you as "too cautious and conservative."

If your parents see you as spiteful, unsympathetic, or ungiving because of your stand against bailing out your sibling, you will feel rejected. These feelings may be heightened by your parents' involvement with the never-ending problems and crises of your brother or sister. "What about me?" you ask yourself.

Perhaps you alerted others: your sib's spouse, grandparents, aunts, uncles, or cousins. Because of their own resistance, they also disregarded or minimized your warnings.

Hurt by these responses, you may find yourself "acting out" in hopes of calling attention to yourself. Or, trying to remain aloof, you become a sideliner. This attempt may have fooled others, but you know you felt frustrated, powerless, and furious. Over time these feelings may fade, and you may begin to question your perceptions and reactions to the gambler. "Did I misread the tip-offs?" you ask yourself. "Did I overreact and misjudge the gambling?" you wonder. "Am I still holding a grudge because my sibling has always been the 'favorite' child?"

Maybe you have only recently realized that your sibling gambles too much, and that, unknown to you, you have been a primary, secondary, or auxiliary enabler. You might have begun bailing out the gambler from a sense of family loyalty or to protect your aging, vulnerable parents or because you have always taken on the role of the "responsible child." If the gambler is your spouse's sibling, you may have done this for the same reasons or for the sake of your spouse, parents in-law, or nieces or nephews.

Like those of other family members, your recovery needs will depend on your ties to the gambler *and* the gambler's ties to others in your family system.

As you go through your stages of recovery, you further identify and acknowledge the impact of the gambler on you and other family members and better understand the gambler's addictive thinking, emotional life, and relationships to others, especially your parents. In time, this will become clearer to you, and you will be able to take whatever measures needed for your own personal survival and move on to rebuilding your life.

During this recovery period, you will see the gambler in perspective and will feel less hurt and angry. In your own recovery program, you will understand how your birth order, gender, individual characteristics and your parents' relationships to you and other children in your family have shaped your feelings and behavior. As you understand more about your family constellation, you will move even closer to recovery.

This self-exploration serves to mend the relationship to your sib, even if the gambler and your parents are not in recovery. You will see the gambler more realistically and be able to accept this sibling for who he is: a human being with strengths and frailties. Your growing self-love and kindness toward your family will make others more loving too and may spread throughout the family.

Judith S. finally refused her sister Lenora's plea for a bailout. It was a difficult decision for her because she didn't want to upset her elderly widowed mother. Judith was conflicted and made the decision to stop enabling Lenora only because she was worried about her own finances.

I constantly worried that my mother would learn about Lenora's gambling and become very upset. Some months after I refused Lenora her last bailout, I was helping Mom straighten out her checkbook. I cannot begin to tell you how shocked I was to see she had been giving Lenora money regularly over the last year. When I questioned Mom, she told me that Lenora could not meet her monthly bills because of business reverses, so Mom was helping her out for a while.

Calmly but firmly, I told her that Lenora's "business reverses" were gambling debts. From the embarrassed, guilty expression on Mom's face, I knew she had known all along why Lenora needed money. I was furious. It stirred up all my old resentments about Lenora being Mom's favorite, and I also felt betrayed.

I had been in therapy since the breakup of my marriage, and I had often discussed my hurt about being the overlooked child. Now I began discussing Lenora's gambling and how I felt about that too.

For a long time I remained angry with my mother and with Lenora. I kept thinking that if my father were still alive things would have been different. He and I really understood each other. I was probably his favorite.

I would argue with my mother, trying to explain that gambling was a disease and that the longer she bailed out Lenora the worse things would get. But Mother just couldn't turn down Lenora's requests, pleas, and even threats to hurt herself, saying she could not turn her back on her daughter, especially if she was sick. Then Mother would tell me that I didn't understand and accuse me of being unfeeling. I kept trying to get through to her, and sometimes I thought I did. But then Mom would continue to complain about how Lenora was asking more and more of her and how listening to all of Lenora's worsening problems was making her so unhappy and affecting her health. However, Mom continued the bailouts.

"What can I do?" she would say, and then in the next breath complain that she soon would have no savings.

Things just didn't change. Discussions about Lenora always ended in an argument. My mother felt misunderstood and I felt frustrated and angry.

It has been very difficult for me to emotionally detach from Lenora and my mother. I have come to understand that I initially enabled Lenora because it made me feel superior to her and it gave me a chance to be protective of my mother, which in turn, let me feel close to her. I had always loved my father, and I missed him. By taking care of my mother I somehow felt I was doing what my father would have done and would have wanted me to do. And that softened my grief.

I am working on these issues in therapy, and I am beginning to be more comfortable about telling Mom that I refuse to discuss Lenora until she stops the bailouts or Lenora goes for help. I now feel less stressed in dealing with both of them. And I realize that no matter what I do I will never have the picture-perfect family I always wanted.

RECOVERY FOR CHILDREN OF GAMBLERS

If you are married to a gambler and have children at home, or if your grandchildren or nieces or nephews live with a gambler, you may be troubled about the effects of gambling on them.

Twelve-year-old Tim's father gambled too much.

Lately I've been asking a lot more questions about my father. I remember that when I was in kindergarten he lied to me and told me he was a policeman. Why did he do that? I remember that I would go up to every policeman and ask if he knew my father. I saw it upset my mother, but she never told me why. My mother used to talk to my uncle about him very quietly so I wouldn't hear. But sometimes I would hear, and I remember they once spelled the word j-a-i-l. I knew it meant jail. When I asked them about it, they looked at me sort of weird and explained that my father was going to be a policeman in the jail and not live at home for a while. I started crying and asked them who would take me to the park and who was going to teach me to ride my bike. My mother kept telling me not to cry, that she or my uncle would teach me.

The next thing I remember about my father was when I started second grade; I came out of school and there he was waiting for me and carrying a baseball mitt and a box of baseball cards. I was so excited. I still have the mitt. I never asked him about working in jail. I guess I wanted to forget all about it.

After he came home, my mother always seemed angry, even at me. They fought a lot about money and his going to the track and then he went to live with my grandmother.

When he comes around now we always have a lot of fun. Sometimes he takes me to baseball card conventions and buys me great cards. But he doesn't come around a lot. Sometimes he comes when we don't expect him, and other times he says he will come and he doesn't. It bothers my mother but not me, not anymore. It doesn't really matter. I know he will bring me more cards.

Gerri, now sixteen, tells her story.

This is the second time we've moved since I started high school. The house is OK but smaller than the other one. My mother says it's in a better location and to be thankful for that. Things around the house need fixing and straightening up, but when I ask Mom she tells me not to worry, it will get done. Lately that's my mother's answer for everything.

My mother has a gambling problem, and although she never hits me physically, she beats me mentally. This is the worse kind of beating to take. Mind games are very hard on a child of ten or eleven (that's when I started to see what was going on) because you don't know what exactly is going to happen to you and your parents. My mother's mood can change from hot to cold just like that. My father is sweet and quiet most of the time, but he has a temper, especially when he argues with my mother about her gambling.

I remember wishing that she would win when she gambled because then she would be in a really good mood and maybe she would take us shopping for clothes or fix us one of her special dinners when she came home. When she is like that she is a really cool person. I think I can tell when she is on a losing streak because she usually smokes more and yells all the time and bangs the pots when she gets settled down to making dinner. Sometimes to calm her down I help her out by doing something extra special. Sometimes it works.

My mother and my older sister Anne never got along. Anne just dropped out of school and comes and goes as she pleases. Anne is still angry at her because my mother took our baby-sitting money we were saving and lost it at the track. She never did make it up to us—not all of it.

Sometimes she tells us she is going to cut back a little on the gambling. I think that if she really loved us all enough she would stop. It's not good for her either, but she wouldn't believe me.

Once when I told my grandmother I thought my mother didn't love me she said, "Your mother loves you, she just has a funny way of showing it."

I don't want the funny way. I want the normal way. I know I can't count on my mother or ever really trust her, but I do love her. I guess I will always have to watch out for myself.

Children living in a gambling household too often live in a world of lies, deceptions, and illusions. There may be no emotional validation, environmental stability, or parental predictability. For some families the gambling is short-lived; well-separated from the family. It has little impact on the household until a crisis occurs. For others, gambling is a chronic problem that influences every aspect of daily life. Even if this is the case, the children of gambling households may not be affected.

No one can predict for certain what impact Tim's or Gerri's or any child's experiences will have on them as adults. The effects of the gambling depend on many factors. Positive influences of family and community resources as well as each child's own inner resiliency can counter any negative effects. Children who live in a gambling household are more likely to have difficulties and problems if the following stresses are also present.

LACK OF EMOTIONAL VALIDATION

Children of gamblers often have a sense that their feelings and experiences are not confirmed, accepted, or noted by authority figures, especially parents. This makes it difficult for them to identify or trust their own feelings and thoughts and causes them confusion about their perceptions and knowledge of the world. Doubting their perceptions makes it all the more difficult for them to judge, evaluate, and cope with events around them. Lack of confidence in themselves makes them feel insecure and fearful.

For instance, Tim had a hunch that his father wasn't a policeman. His family wanted to "protect" him from this knowledge, so they pretended otherwise and no one validated Tim's pain about his father's leaving. Gerri's grandmother also wanted to be helpful but actually "invalidated" Gerri's feelings when she said that her mother had a "funny way" of showing love.

LACK OF ENVIRONMENTAL STABILITY

Children need emotional and intellectual consistency: Events should happen in familiar patterns. The routines and rules of the family can be used as experiences to help the child learn gratification through work and persistence and toleration of frustration. Stability gives children an opportunity to practice what they learn about the world and makes them feel safe knowing that what they have today will still be there tomorrow. Children feel extremely stressed in a household in which gambling consequences undermine family rules and routines of daily living and threaten relationships.

Gerri's household revolves around her mother's mood swings rather than clear-cut rules and routines. Tim experienced traumatic separations from his father. Both children were stressed because they didn't know what to expect and therefore felt constantly vulnerable.

LACK OF EMOTIONAL PREDICTABILITY

Children's sense of themselves as well as their expectations of others is based in large part on how their parents react to them. Ideally, parents should respond to a child with clear messages of approval and love, and meet their needs appropriately, with neither too much nor too little gratification.

The gambling parent may be excessively indulgent and stimulating, or physically absent and so self-focused as to be emotionally unavailable, or just ungiving. To cope, some children may deny the pain of the parent's unavailability by identifying with the most exciting, glamorous aspects of the gambler. Like the gambler, they may continue to engage in magical thinking and believe in magical solutions.

The stress and confusion may be reinforced or compounded by the other parent who may also be emotionally unavailable or volatile because of the stress of living with the gambler.

Both Gerri and Tim lacked emotional predictability in their lives. Gerri could never predict her mother's mood, and Tim saw his father as very giving, but always deserting him.

Like children who come from homes where alcohol or drugs are abused or from families strained by other types of chronic problems like mental or physical illness, the children of gamblers may become depressed and anxious, reacting to these stresses in a variety of ways. For instance:

• They don't learn to trust themselves or others.
• They internalize their angry feelings *or* act them out.
• They have difficulty tolerating tension and frustration and rely on action and immediate gratification, strategies they learn from the adults in their lives.
• They develop problems with schoolwork.
• They express their anxieties and pain with physical complaints like stomachaches or headaches.
• They become either overly responsible and serious for their age or extremely irresponsible.
• They have difficulty maturing and developing autonomy.
• They have a strong sense of shame and guilt.
• They don't develop an ability to tolerate feelings.
• They become loners, or, in contrast, they refuse to be alone.
• They have trouble sleeping.
• They take unnecessary risks or are overcautious.

Other problems and issues more specific for the children of gambling households result from the hidden nature of the gambling problem or addiction as well as from interactions with a parent who gambles.

OVERVALUING MONEY AND MATERIALISM

Money may be seen as an expression of love, especially in families where the gambler is sporadically very generous. Children manipulate parents who are self-preoccupied and absorbed with problems. They may demand money or gifts as visible proof that they are loved and approved of.

Children may not fully understand the fighting and arguments about money if their basic needs are being met, especially if they are young. Often they perceive the nongambling parent as being unreasonable and the gambling parent as the victim. It is not unusual for a child to offer to give a parent money from his own savings or piggy bank. Children who have had their money "borrowed" with or without permission may feel proud and important to be helpful, and are confused by the nongambling parent's angry reaction. Sooner or later these children will feel betrayed. As a result, they may be wary of ever trusting again, and may spend the rest of their lives feeling the parent is in their debt.

GUILT AND SHAME

Gamblers' children are often unable to identify the cause of the unhappiness and tension in the home, so they blame themselves. Gamblers' children are confused by their parents' disappearances to gamble and may feel unlovable or think they did something wrong that caused the parent to prefer gambling to being with them. Often children think that this abandonment is meant to punish them.

SUSPICION AND DISTRUST

Children of gamblers may become overly suspicious of the gambler's every move because of their own experiences with the gambler's lies and deceit or because they mimic the nongambling parent's behavior. They may respond to the gambler's "gaslighting" by becoming confused, anxious, and hurt.

BLAMING THE NONGAMBLING PARENT

Often the gambler, who is erratic and emotionally unpredictable, is excused for his behavior, especially if this parent is perceived by the child as exciting, generous, or special. Children unconsciously know that the gambler's ties and affection are tenuous, so they direct their anger and frustration onto the nongambling parent who they feel is more consistent and trustworthy. They may also believe that the nongambling parent's unhappiness and anger are the causes of much of the gambler's behavior, including physical and emotional absence. Some children are extra good in an attempt to keep the gambler from "abandoning" them.

DISAPPOINTMENT

Gamblers in the process of deceiving themselves and others make promise after promise, only to break them over and over again, leaving children constantly disappointed. Many children eventually form opinions based on the gambler's actions rather than words. Expecting little, these children may disengage, and perhaps find other sources of support. Others refuse to give up their illusions about the gambler's emotional capacity and consistency and will learn to tolerate the disappointment.

FEAR

Children may fear, perhaps appropriately so, that there won't be enough money for something they want or even for necessities. They may also fear for their safety and well-being and those of the family because of the gambler's dealings with criminals.

ISOLATION AND HUMILIATION

Children may be humiliated by the legal and social consequences of the gambler's addiction, or they may be perplexed by the family's self-imposed isolation or by being shunned by others.

LOSS

The financial consequences may be acute and sudden, and the children may lose all that is familiar: their home, family leisure activities, school, and life-style.

DISREGARD FOR LAW

Children may be aware of a parent's connection to the underworld, arrests, or jail sentences, but because of their need to love and respect a parent may begin to believe that they too are exempt from the law.

WHEN A PARENT IS IN RECOVERY

If the gambler goes into recovery, you may expect the children to be relieved and pleased. But be prepared for the youngsters to be even more confused because the gambler, full of remorse, may now be overly attentive, trying to "make up" for lost time spent gambling. Or perhaps the gambler has suddenly become the child's "favorite" because he has finally fulfilled their fantasy of a caring and interested parent. In addition, children may see the gambler as a great hero who is overcoming his illness and becoming a "better" person. This can create problems in the children's relationship with you. Even though you are happy that the gambling has stopped, it is natural for you to feel some envy and resentment that this "undeserving" parent is now accepted or even revered by the children.

There seem to be so many problems and issues that you may be wondering if you or anyone else can help. Indeed you can. Whether or not the gambler is recovering, it is extremely important that you yourself, if you are the other parent, go into recovery. If you are a grandparent or other concerned adult, urge the nongambling parent to get help. Remember, however, that some children will need little help and still emerge from the gambling household emotionally intact.

You can do other things to help slow the roller coaster effect for a child whose household has been in constant and chronic turmoil, or if it has collapsed into disarray because of a sudden crisis.

VALIDATE

Validate the child's feelings and provide an emotionally predictable and structured environment. It will heal the child's sense of well-being and build trust.

Stimulate discussions about their conflicting feelings toward the gambler and others. Validate accurate perceptions and correct misperceptions. If you have "covered up" or lied about the gambling in the past, admit to your own untruths and explain that at the time you felt you had the child's best interests at heart.

Encourage the youngsters to learn to check out the facts instead of accepting everything that goes on as if it were etched in stone. They will begin to reexamine their values, many of which were shaped by the gambling behavior. For instance, unpredictability may be described by a child as "spontaneity," but not really experienced that way. Many families, especially those with someone who drinks or gambles too much, have an unwritten code of honor: Don't talk about the family to anyone else. Gamblers are especially secretive so the problem may have been hidden even from the family. Children recognize that this is a home where you don't ask too many questions, and if you do get answers you don't tell them to others. To help children gradually give up the rule of secrecy, seek help so you can be open and honest with yourself and better encourage the children to share their feelings and thoughts with you or understanding others.

Difficult as it sometimes is, explaining and being truthful with children at a level that they can understand helps to plant trust that you can be depended on not to "hide" things from them. It lets a child know that even though one parent may betray them, other people won't.

EDUCATE

Educate the child about the problems of gambling and how it is similar to other addictions, such as alcohol and drug abuse. Most children learn about addictions in school and may have been given written materials that explain this. If not, you can obtain them. Children like many adults may need time to understand and accept that someone can be as addicted to an activity as to a substance. Explain the addictive potential of gambling to a child. Be sure that the child understands that compulsive gambling is an illness. Children may have trouble understanding this concept, but it is important that they recognize that their parent is someone who needs help, not someone who is "bad and uncaring." It also helps a child to understand that denial is part of the illness, and the parent's refusal to go for help is not stubbornness but another aspect of the disease.

COMPENSATE

You and others can help to compensate for many of the problems that arise in the gambling household by providing many predictable experiences: A weekly routine of watching a television show together, muffins every Sunday for breakfast, a special weekend at Grandma's once or twice a year, and regular (even if monthly) attendance at church or synagogue can give a child a sense of continuity and stability. By seeking help yourself, you can get a better handle on your own feelings and thus more easily provide an emotionally stable atmosphere for the child. This is not enabling—you are not assuming the gambler's or the primary enabler's responsibilities.

PROFESSIONAL HELP

Whether or not the parents are in recovery, children will often benefit from another safe place where they can express their feelings and discuss their experiences of living with someone who gambles too much. School counselors and other mental health professionals who work with children can be a big help (providing they are knowledgeable about gambling as a problem or an illness) in getting a child started and then staying on the road to recovery. Some of the issues addressed may be children's distorted values and perceptions of reality and faulty or abnormal roles they have assumed. They will begin to understand that they are not responsible for either parent's behavior and that *they* cannot do anything to change their parents. Many children, especially those whose parents are not in recovery, also may need the opportunity to grieve for those things that will never be. Children can be helped to find good role models within and outside of the family and encouraged to become involved in healthy activities, such as after school programs.

Despite the effects of gambling on children, it is heartening to know that many of them—with or without help—will survive emotionally unimpaired, and even be strong. The children you care about deserve that extra edge: Give the help yourself or find it elsewhere.

RECOVERY FOR ADULT CHILDREN

Louise J., now thirty-two years old, sat in the office of her therapist talking about her new job:

> I guess I feel good about it, everything is going so well, but I have my doubts about that salary offer. I am always second-guessing myself. Maybe I have these mixed feelings because I expect even more of myself. And besides, I don't know if it will even work out. It never fails: I am always waiting for the other shoe to drop. When something good happens, I know that something bad will happen next.
>
> Funny, I just thought about my father. Next week is the fifth anniversary of his death. I miss him and wish he was here. There is so much I would say to him—things I could never have said when he was alive. I would tell him, "I love you, Daddy. I've always loved you very much. When I was a little girl I thought you were the greatest. It was so nice when you hugged me. You were so affectionate and warm. I remember you used to make up stories about me and all my dolls. You were the one who bought me my first doll, and then all the others. Remember how you would wink at me when you came home from work, and that was your signal that you had bought me another one. Mom would get really mad at you and say, 'Doesn't that child have enough dolls? She has more than she can play with.'
>
> "Mom was right, but it was fun seeing you give me that secret wink.
>
> "I knew you were the bravest firefighter in the city, and I think you made captain when Arthur was born. I was six years old and Barry was finishing junior high school. I still can see you in your uniform: my hero. I was sure you would be there to protect me always, your little girl.
>
> "I used to think our luck changed because Arthur was born. But it was gambling that changed everything. I remember you and Mom arguing a lot about your staying out to play cards. It would confuse me because I also saw how happy you both were when you went on those weekends to the casinos. Grandma would stay with us, and that was fun for me. She used to say, 'Your parents are going away to have some fun too.'
>
> "I guess you gambled for years. You didn't have to work nights or

weekends anymore, but I know you seemed to stay away from the house more than ever. You never really talked to me except to just joke around. Where were you all those years?

"Mom was always yelling and having her headaches and always worrying. I used to get those cold compresses and sit with her when she had a really bad attack. Arthur, of course, your 'little betting buddy,' as Mom called him, seemed to run the house. He was such a little monster and you or Mom didn't do anything about it. No wonder he is so immature and impossible now. He never learned any respect.

"There were times when Mom would sit with the bills in front of her, complaining that there would never be enough money to pay the rent and the next thing we knew you were coming home with a new television set. Mom would scream, and you would say, 'Don't treat me like I am one of the children. I'll do what I want.'

"I knew, and so did Arthur and Barry, that when you acted remorseful it was the best time to ask you for something. I always felt guilty about being so manipulative.

"For years things seemed to go along OK. Barry was almost finished with medical school and I was in college. Mom would call me with complaints about you, and I would tell her things like 'you know how he is,' and sometimes I would even say, 'Why do you put up with it?' Then she would also tell me about another problem with Arthur. I felt too guilty to tell her I didn't really give a damn, and I didn't want to hear about it.

"Barry hardly ever called me, but one day he called to say that there were 'missing funds' and that you had mortgaged the house without telling Mom. I couldn't believe it, and still really don't. But when I came home during Christmas break and told you that the college had notified me I couldn't register for the next term until the tuition was paid, you said, 'College is overrated.' You didn't look me in the eye that whole time I was home. You knew how upset I was.

"A few months later when you had that first heart attack, I thought it was guilt that did it to you."

It wasn't easy growing up in a household with a parent who was a problem or compulsive gambler. If your feelings were not encouraged and validated and emotional predictability and environmental stability were not provided, you may find you are still having problems, particularly around issues of trust and intimacy. Both you and the therapeutic community (adult children groups and individual therapists) may have overlooked the impact of gambling on your life.

During your childhood you may have taken on various abnormal roles that served to deny or minimize the gambling situation and your feelings about it. Children as well as adults in the family will sometimes assume these roles or a combination of them out of well-meaning but misdirected love and personal needs. Similar to roles assumed by members in an alcoholic family, they may also have further enabled the gambler. Although it may not have been evident to you or others during your childhood, these roles were "internalized" and may be affecting you now.

Perhaps your parent also abused alcohol or other substances. You may be coping with this aftermath too. Acknowledging your experiences is crucial for recovery. Only then can you work toward rebuilding and reclaiming your life.

You can explore many of these issues in a group for adult children of gamblers or for those who grew up in addictive or otherwise dysfunctional families, or in family or individual therapy. To provide you with the help you need, group members or a therapist should understand that gambling is a problem or illness.

To begin to understand how the gambling affected you, see if you can find yourself in one or more of these roles either as a child or as an adult. These roles were first described by many experts in the field of alcoholism.

HERO

You might have become a Hero, trying to get attention by being extra good and doing more than would normally be expected of a child your age. Sadly, you might have gone unnoticed despite these high achievements, confirming your own sense of low self-esteem. You seemed to have abundant energy, taking on leadership roles at school and always being helpful to others. Through it all, you tended to act happy and pleasant, and everyone liked you. Nobody suspected that you felt like a failure and were often filled with guilt and humiliation.

CARETAKER

You might have been a Caretaker both to the gambling and nongambling parent. Perhaps you were privy to the gambler's secret and even went along to the track or other places where the gambler found action. Or maybe you were a "courier" for the gambler, delivering money and picking up winnings from a bookie. You also may have become the nongambling parent's confidante, rescuing her from unhappiness. Perhaps you assumed parental and adult responsibilities, such as preparing dinner or caring for younger siblings when Mom was late getting home from bingo or the casinos or because the gambler or the nongambling parent was emotionally unavailable. You may have appeared to be above it all, denying what was going on and acting as if nothing bothered you. You may have become a peacemaker, always trying to find a way to compromise your own needs or help others work things out.

LOST CHILD

Perhaps you were a quiet, nonassertive, passive Lost Child, emotionally and physically isolated from other family members and schoolmates. You may have appeared to others to be adjusted because you never caused any trouble. When an argument developed in the family, you simply "disappeared" from sight. You probably appeared not to be affected by the gambling and may even have denied it to yourself, but you were greatly pained. Feeling powerless, you were a worrywart, always ready to believe the worst, so you were never able to enjoy being "in the moment." Maybe you were a child who questioned everything and were full of guilt about what was going on around you as well as about any of your own "good luck" or achievements.

SCAPEGOAT

Perhaps you were a Scapegoat, angry and defiant, who in an attempt to get the attention you needed got into trouble at school, with friends, or at home. You also may have been demanding, self-centered, and materialistic. You blamed others and thought that everything that went wrong in your life was the fault of someone or something else. Through it all you felt rage, and you may even have hidden your sense of failure and guilt by acting like a bully or a big shot.

COMBINED ROLES

Perhaps you played different roles in different places or at different stages of your life. In school you were a rebel, but at home you were a caretaker. You were an "angel" in elementary school, but "acted out" in junior high. Although all children have some elements of each role, the child who assumes them as a way of coping with life is likely to have problems in adulthood.

You may still be living with a parent who presently gambles or did at one time, or you may live far away from the gambler, or the gambler may have died. Still the emotional consequences remain with you. You may be a puzzle to yourself as well as to others. One moment you are counting up your money, convinced that no matter how much savings you have accumulated it will never be enough, and the next minute you're financially bailing out someone else. You may be attracted to gambling or be afraid of *any* kind of risk taking. Your legacy may be one of self-fulfilled prophecies. Expecting to be let down you always are. Unable to make decisions, you wonder why your life is out of control.

A number of traits are often seen in adult children of gamblers. In any one family, each adult child may differ greatly from the other. As you identify and acknowledge your traits (and perhaps note those in your siblings), you will have a good foundation on which to rebuild and reclaim your life.

• *Shame:* A pervasive sense of being flawed and less than adequate envelops you, and it is unrelated to how you behave. This feeling is one of the most common among children who were reared in a family with chronic problems.

• *Pessimistic:* You always feel that the worst will happen and that at any moment the rug will be pulled out from underneath you.

• *Worrisome:* As a child you may have worried about adult problems, and even now you excessively and unrealistically worry about everyone and everything.

• *Injustice collector:* Excessive feelings of betrayal cause you to keep an inventory of the injustices that others and the world in general have heaped on you.

• *Secretive:* You tend to form relationships that exclude others and are unwilling to share information that other people would not consider special or private.

• *Distrustful:* You find yourself unable to trust your own feelings as well as the motives or feelings of others. You have a pervasive sense that you have been fooled and turn this anger onto yourself.

• *Fear of abandonment:* The lack of consistent and appropriate parenting can result in excessive dependency needs and fear of abandonment. Any early problems with separation may continue to plague you.

• *Mediator:* Like the child peacemaker, you may still be a mediator, often called on to negotiate peace treaties between your gambling and nongambling parent.

• *Workaholic:* If you have denied your childhood and current dependency needs, you may have trouble relaxing today. Instead, you compulsively bury yourself in work and activity.

• *Ambivalence:* At the root of current relationships with others are your early mixed feelings toward the gambler. Then, like now, you alternately idealized or denigrated the gambler.

• *Risk confusion:* You have difficulty in differentiating healthy from poor risk taking, and alternate between ultraconservatism and recklessness.

• *Hidden anger:* You are afraid of your own anger and impulses, so you turn them inward, appearing to others to be passive and depressed.

• *Optimistic:* You feel that "hope springs eternal," and like the gambler, you wait for the big payoff or the big hit.

• *Poor decision-making ability:* Because your childhood was unstable and unpredictable you feel that you are always struggling to control your life. Consciously or unconsciously, you feel that any decisions you make will not work out.

• *Belief in magical solutions:* Identification with the gambler, whose belief in magic was at the core of his psyche, can result in your illusion that every problem will have a magical solution.

• *Excessive need to have feelings validated:* If your feelings were not validated or accepted as a child, you will not be able to identify them now. You only guess at your feelings and this affects your judgment.

• *Confused sense of self:* Having grown up with a lack of validation and emotional predictability, you are left confused about who you are.

Your recovery work may begin with the identification stage when you either initially identify the gambling or identify its impact on you. In the acknowledgment stage, you recognize that the impact has extended into your current life, even if the gambler is no longer active or you no longer have contact with him. At this time you better understand and acknowledge why you perceived and experienced the impact differently than your siblings or other members of the family. You recognize the variables: age, maturity, prior experiences, other social interactions, information and messages parents share with you, and your own inborn personality. Your recovery work will focus on discovering who *you* are and how you became the person you are now. You will explore issues of your relationship with both the gambling and the nongambling parent, and look for familiar patterns in your current relationships. Did you replicate them or avoid them? Are you able to form and sustain satisfying relationships? Do you avoid them altogether? Are you still searching for that "perfect" person to make your life better? Are you still puzzled about your parents' relationship, then and now, and your role in it? Are you concerned that your children have some of the same "traits" that you saw in yourself, a sibling, or your gambling parent? Is your career on track?

As you address these issues you will move into rebuilding your life. It will be hard work, and there will be times when you will want to lash out at your gambling and nongambling parents. There may be times when you will want to embrace them and say, "I understand."

You will detach from the gambler financially. If you enable one parent who enables the gambler by providing financial, emotional, or time bailouts, you will stop. If they are still "pressing your buttons" you will work on detaching emotionally from both of them. For now this may even cause estrangement. Try to maintain your belief that in time you can become friends again.

If your parents are still alive and well, you will have the opportunity to make peace with them. If they are not in recovery, you will maintain your faith that they will someday rebuild their own lives. If they *are* in recovery, you will have the chance to say all the things that many family members never say to one another and perhaps build a relationship that is precious and beautiful.

But this may not be possible. The gambler who has destroyed the family and all relationships may be difficult to reengage. The gambler who is no longer alive cannot be confronted or embraced. In your therapy, in a journal, or simply in your mind and heart you can "talk" to the gambler. You can draw pictures. You can look at photographs and try to remember. Remember the pain and remember the good times. You will be able to accept your past and forgive, so that you are no longer controlled by it.

Take one day at a time. Keep faith. You will rebuild and reclaim your life.

Afterword

From the day you recognized and accepted that someone you care about—a spouse, a partner, a parent, a child, or a sibling—gambles too much to the time you begin to rebuild your life, you embark on a journey that has many detours, side roads, and dead ends, sometimes overlooking cliffs. At times you feel as if the odds are against you and that the obstacles placed in your path are formed by fate, the gambler, enablers, and others who for reasons of their own resist your progress.

It isn't easy to seek help or to make changes in your life. It takes courage and the belief that you are entitled to a better life. You are taking one step at a time. See what you have already done and how you have changed.

1. *Recognition.* You have already recognized that gambling is a problem in your life. Reread the beginning of this book. Convince yourself that you aren't "overreacting" and that the recognition and discoveries you have made have given you power. Although you don't have power over the *gambler,* you do have power over *yourself.* You have learned that if you don't take steps to change your life things will get worse. Recognizing the extent of the gambling and its effects on you is an ongoing process, but you have already taken an important first step.

Your change: You have gone from ignorance to knowledge.

2. *Hope.* Real hope is different than the false hope that the gambler holds. It is based on (a) knowledge that others have faced the same problems and triumphed and (b) belief and faith that someone or something is out there giving you strength and watching over you. You don't have to make any major changes yet. They will come later.

Your change: You have moved from pessimism to optimism.

3. *Acknowledgment of feelings.* Acknowledging feelings can be overwhelming, making you feel more vulnerable and powerless than before. But this is already motivating you to change. Until you acknowledge your feelings, illusion and self-deception will govern your life.

Your change: You are no longer bottling up your feelings, and you are living with fewer illusions.

4. *Assessment of financial and legal problems.* You have considered what might happen and what has already happened to you.

Your change: By understanding all the ramifications of the gambling you can decide what to do about them.

5. *Permission.* You have spent your life "doing the right thing," following the family rules, keeping the secrets, and believing the myths. You are now giving yourself permission to question these guidelines and develop new goals and new ways of coping.

Your change: You are looking at things differently and reordering your priorities.

6. *Comfort.* You need and deserve comfort, nurturance, and protection as you deal with the emotional, legal, and financial consequences of the gambling. Your support system (composed of experts, survivors, or people you already know) is already comforting you so that you are able to consider the changes that are crucial to your survival.

Your change: You know and believe that you can accept help and you won't have to be alone.

7. *Practice.* You put everything you have learned into a plan of action. It involves developing tasks and practicing them to achieve your goal of making changes.

Your change: You act instead of react.

We hope that you have begun to take these steps, and that this book has served as a guide to inform and support you on your road to recovery. Having read it, you are better able to appreciate the complexities of your circumstances and how far you have come in your recovery.

And while you continue to assess the progress you have already made and consider the distance you still want to travel, remember that you are quite resilient. Remind yourself of your strength, the strength of your family, and the potential strength of the gambler.

Like so many others you can overcome the obstacles created by having someone in your life who gambles too much. In moments of anguish or fear, remember the courage you showed in other situations.

Whether or not the gambler is willing to change, you can cope with the hardships and uncertainties of life, and you can rebuild and reclaim your own life without illusions.

Be brave, have faith, and keep your convictions. You now know the score and are becoming more courageous. You can emerge from the shadows behind the 8-ball.

The Gamblers Anonymous Questionnaire

TWENTY QUESTIONS

1. Did you ever lose time from work due to gambling?
2. Has gambling ever made your home life unhappy?
3. Did gambling affect your reputation?
4. Have you ever felt remorse after gambling?
5. Did you ever gamble to get money with which to pay debts or otherwise solve financial difficulties?
6. Did gambling cause a decrease in your ambition or efficiency?
7. After losing did you feel you must return as soon as possible and win back your losses?
8. After a win did you have a strong urge to return and win more?
9. Did you often gamble until your last dollar was gone?
10. Did you ever borrow to finance your gambling?
11. Have you ever sold anything to finance gambling?
12. Were you reluctant to use "gambling money" for normal expenditures?
13. Did gambling make you careless of the welfare of yourself and your family?
14. Did you ever gamble longer than you had planned?
15. Have you ever gambled to escape worry or trouble?
16. Have you ever committed, or considered committing, an illegal act to finance gambling?
17. Did gambling cause you to have difficulty in sleeping?

18. Do arguments, disappointments, or frustrations create within you an urge to gamble?
19. Did you ever have an urge to celebrate any good fortune by a few hours of gambling?
20. Have you ever considered self-destruction as a result of your gambling?

Most compulsive gamblers will answer yes to at least seven of these questions.

For Further Information

The National Council on Problem Gambling, Inc., established in 1972, is a non-profit health agency whose mission is to disseminate information about problem and pathological (compulsive) gambling and to promote the development of services for those afflicted with the disorder

For further information on membership and referrals to professional treatment programs, contact The National Council on Problem Gambling, Inc., or an affiliate council near you.

The National Council on Problem Gambling, Inc.
NATIONWIDE HELPLINE 1-800-522-4700
PO Box 9419
Washington, DC 20016
10025 Governor Warfield Parkway Suite 311
Columbia, MD 21044
410-730-8008
Fax 410-730-0669
www.NCPGambling.org
E-mail: ncpg@erols.com

AFFILIATE COUNCILS OF THE NATIONAL COUNCIL ON PROBLEM GAMBLING, INC.

Arizona Council on Compulsive Gambling, Inc.
PO Box 23896
Phoenix, AZ 85063
602-212-0278 Fax 602-212-1725
Helpline: 800-777-7207
Web site: www.azccg@azccg.org
E-mail: azccg@infinet-is.com

California Council on Problem Gambling, Inc.
121 S. Palm Canyon Dr. Suite 207
Palm Springs, CA 92262

760-320-0234 Fax 760-416-1349
Helpline: 800-Facts 4 U (322-8748)
Web site: www.calproblemgambling.org
E-mail: califcpg@bigplanet.com

Colorado Council on Compulsive Gambling, Inc.
PO Box 280265
Lakewood, CO 80228-0265
303-220-1911   Fax 303-220-8107
E-mail: ccgam@aol.com

Connecticut Council on Compulsive Gambling, Inc.
47 Clapboard Hill Rd., Suite 6
Guilford, CT 06437
203-453-0138 Fax 203-453-9142
Web site: www.ccpg.org
E-mail: ccpg@problemgambling.org
Helpline: 800-346-6238

Delaware Council on Gambling Problems, Inc.
100 West 10th Street Suite 303
Wilmington, DE 19801-1677
302-655-3264 Fax 302-984-2269
E-mail: dcpginc@magpage.com
Hotline: 888-850-8888

Florida Council on Compulsive Gambling, Inc.
Box 3487
Longwood, FL 32779-0487
407-865-6200 Fax 407-865-6103
E-mail: FLCCG@aol.com
Hotline: 800-426-7711

Georgia Council on Compulsive Gambling
2300 Peachford Rd. Suite 1111
Atlanta, GA 30338

Illinois Council on Problem Gambling, Inc.
PO Box 6489
Evanston, IL 60204
847-296-2026 Fax 847-296-2094
Web site: www.ncpgambling.org/state/il.htm
E-mail: catex @aol.com

Indiana Council on Problem Gambling
10104 Manhattan Circle

Ft. Wayne, IN 46825
219-489-0506   Fax 219-489-0506
Helpline: 800-994-8448
E-mail: drwrphil@aol.com

Iowa Problem Gambling Council, Inc.
1544 2nd Ave.
Des Moines, IA 50314
515-282-7322   Fax 282-7336
Hotline: 800-238-7633

Kentucky Council on Compulsive Gambling
PO Box 1043
Frankford, KY 40602
502-227-8995   Fax 502-227-8986
E-Mail: justann123@aol.com
Helpline: 800-Gambler

Louisiana Association on Compulsive Gambling
820 Jordan St. Suite 415
Shreveport, LA 71101-4581
318-222-7657   Fax 318-222-3273
Helpline: 800-749-2673

Maryland Council on Compulsive Gambling, Inc.
503 Maryland Avenue
Baltimore, MD 21228
410-788-8599   Fax 410-730-0669
E-mail: Jeffnik@erols.com or IPGMD@aol.com

Massachusetts Council on Compulsive Gambling, Inc.
190 High St. Suite 6
Boston, MA 02110
617-426-4554   Fax 617-426-4555
Helpline: 800-426-1234
E-mail: gambling@aol.com

Michigan Council on Problem Gambling
18530 Mac Ave #552
Detroit, MI 48235
313-640-4110   Fax 313-640-4172
Helpline: 800-270-7117
E-mail: caselinik@aol.com

Minnesota Council on Compulsive Gambling, Inc.
702 Torrey Building

314 W. Superior Street
Duluth, MN 55802
218-722-1503 Fax 218-722-0346
888-991-1234
Helpline: 800-541-4557
Web site: www.nati.org

Missouri Council on Problem Gambling Concerns, Inc.
5128 Brookside Blvd.
Kansas City, MO 64112-2736
816-889-4662 Fax 816-881-5087
Helpline: 800-bets off (238-7633)
E-mail: moprobgamb@aol.com

Mississippi Council on Problem and Compulsive Gambling, Inc.
PO Box 1784
Jackson, MS 39215-1784
601-353-4010 Fax 601-353-2807
Helpline: 888-777-9696
Web site: www.msgambler.org
E-mail: mcpcg@netdoor.com

Nebraska Council on Compulsive Gambling
2003 Galven Road
Bellevue, NE 68005
402-291-0980 Fax 402-291-4605
Helpline: 800-560-2126
Web site: www.neccg.org
E-mail: rezlep@ixnetcom.com

Nevada Council on Problem Gambling, Inc.
3006 S. Maryland Parkway Suite 405
Las Vegas, NV 89109
702-369-9740 Fax 702-369-9765
E-mail: carolo191@aol.com

New Hampshire Council on Problem Gambling, Inc.
PO Box 13
West Chesterfield, NH 03466
603-256-6262

Council on Compulsive Gambling of New Jersey, Inc.
1315 W. State Street Suite 1
Trenton, NJ 08618
609-599-3299 Fax 609-599-9383
Web site: www.800gambler.org/

E-mail: ccgnj@800gambler.org
Helpline: 800-426-2537

New York Council on Problem Gambling, Inc.
The Dodge Building
119 Washington Avenue
Albany, NY 12210-2292
518-427-1622   Fax 518-427-6181
E-mail: NYCPG@global2000.net
Helpline: 800-437-1611

Council on Compulsive and Problem Gambling of North Dakota, Inc.
PO Box 7362
Bismarck, ND 58507-7362
701-255-3692 Fax 701-255-2411
Helpline: 800-472-2911
E-mail mchand@btigate.com

Ohio Council on Problem Gambling
Box 41220
Brecksville, OH 44141
Helpline: 888-869-9600

Oregon Problem Gambling Program-Commission GAT Clinical Division
1201 Court St. N.E. PO Box 866
Salem, OR 97308
503-230-9654   Fax 503-239-5953
E-mail: pdpotter@concentric.net
Helpline: 800-233-8479

Council on Compulsive Gambling of Pennsylvania
1002 Longspur Rd.
Audubon, PA 19403
215-744-1880 Fax 215-879-2443
Hotline: 800-848-1880

Rhode Island Council on Problem Gambling, Inc.
PO Box 6551
Providence, RI 02940
401-724-8552 Fax 401-322-7169
E-mail: nobettors@aol.com
Hotline: 877-9-GAMBLE

South Carolina Council on Problem Gambling, Inc.
1201 Main Street   Suite 1980
Columbia, SC 29201

803-748-1313 Fax 803-748-1288

South Dakota Council on Problem Gambling, inc.
3818 S. Western Ave. Suite 177
Sioux Falls, SD 57105
605-987-2751 Fax 605-987-2365
Helpline: 888-781-4357

Texas Council on Problem and Compulsive Gambling, Inc.
PO Box 835895
Richardson, TX 75083
972-889-2331 Fax 972-889-2383
E-mail: tcpcg@ruff. com or suecox@sicembears.com
Helpline: 800-742-0443

Vermont Council on Problem Gambling, Inc.
PO Box 381
Brattleboro, VT 05302
802-257-7785 Fax 802-258-3791

Washington State Council on Problem Gambling, Inc.
PO Box 55272
Seattle, WA 98155
206-546-6133 Fax 206-542-8981
Helpline: 800-547-6133
Web Site: www.wscpg.org
E-mail: wscpg@mail.gr.cc.us

Wisconsin Council on Problem Gambling
1825 Riverside Drive
Green Bay, WI 54301
920-437-8888 Fax 920-437-0694
Helpline: 800-426-2535
E-mail: wcpgamble5@itol.com

Associate Councils

Canadian Foundation on Compulsive Gambling (Ontario)
505 Consumers Rd. Suite 801
Toronto, Ont. M2J4V8
Canada
416-499-9800 Fax 416-499-8260
Helpline: 888-391-1111
Web site: www.cfcg.on.ca/

E-mail: cfcg@interlog.com

Canadian Foundation on Compulsive Gambling (Saskatchewan)
2505 11th Avenue   Suite 207
Regina, Saskatchewan S4POK6
Canada
306-352-9988   Fax 306-352-2266

Other Sources of Help

Institute for the Study of Gambling and Commercial Gaming
University Of Nevada-Reno
Reno, Nevada 89557-0016
702-784-1477   Fax 702-784-4337

The Institute for the Study of Gambling and Commercial Gaming serves to encourage and disseminate research relating to economic, social, political, and technical implications of gambling and commercial gaming throughout the world.

Gamblers Anonymous
PO Box 17173
Los Angeles, CA 90017
213-386-8789   Fax 213-386-0030
Web site: gamblersanonymous.org
E-mail: isomain@gamblersanonymous.org

Gamblers Anonymous (GA) is a fellowship in which people share their experiences, support and hope to stop gambling and build better lives. To learn about a Gamblers Anonymous meeting near you, look in your telephone book or call The National Council on Problem Gambling or the National office for Gamblers Anonymous.

Gam-Anon
PO Box 157
Whitestone, NY 11357
718-352-1671

Gam-Anon is a program for family members and friends of gamblers. it is completely separate from but closely allied to GA, and they cooperate with each in every way. To learn about a Gam-Anon meeting near you, look in your local telephone book under Gam-Anon or Gamblers Anonymous or call the National Council on Problem Gambling or Gam-Anon's national office.

To find information on help for gamblers and family members outside of the United States, you can contact the national GA office or the National Council on Problem Gambling or The Institute for the Study of Gambling and Commercial Gaming.

National Self-Help Clearinghouse
25 West 43rd Street Suite 620
New York, NY 10036
212-354-8525 and 212-642-1956
(They prefer that you send a self-addressed stamped envelope with your request for information)

American Self-Help Clearing House
c/o Northwest Covenant Medical Center
25 Pocono Road
Denville, NJ 07834-2995
973-625-7101
Web site: www.cmhc.com/selfhelp
E-mail: ashc@cybernex.net

Both of the above self-help clearinghouses have lists of local clearinghouses throughout the country that can refer you to a variety of self-help groups in your area. The latter one lists them on their web site.

Institute of Certified Financial Planners
3801 East Florida Avenue   Suite 708
Denver, CO 80210
800-322-4237 303-759-4900
Web site: www.icfp.org

International Association For Financial Planning
5775 Glenridge Drive NE   Suite B300
Atlanta, GA 30328
800-945-4237   404-845-0011
Web site: www.iafp.org
National Association of Personal Financial Advisors
800-366-2732

These three organizations can provide you with the names of financial planners in your area.

For Further Reading

The Journal of Gambling Studies is the official Journal of the National Council on Problem Gambling and is co-sponsored by the Institute for the Study of Gambling and Commercial Gaming. It publishes articles by the foremost researchers and clinicians in the field of gambling behavior. Subscriptions are available along with memberships in the co-sponsoring organizations or from the publisher, Human Sciences Press, 233 Spring Street, New York, NY 10013-1578.

Some of the following books may not be immediately available at local libraries, bookstores or even through the bookstores on the Internet. Contact your nearest State Affiliate or Associate of the National Council on Problem Gambling who may have information on availability.

Beattie, Melody *Codependent no More: How To Stop Controlling Others and Start Caring For Yourself.* San Francisco: Hazelden/Harper 1987

Beattie, Melody *Codependents" Guide to the Twelve Steps.* New York:Prentice Hall, 1990.

Black, Claudia *It Will Never Happen To Me.* New York: Ballantine, 1987.

Chamberlain, Linda L. and William McCowan, *All Bets Are Off: The Dynamics and Treatment of Compulsive Gambling.* New York: John Wiley, 1998.

Crockett, Marilyn Hope, Diane Terman Felenstein and Dale Burg, *The Money Club: Is Your Financial Future Safe? What Every Woman Should Know.* New York: Fireside/Simon and Schuster, 1998.

Custer, Robert L. and Milt, Harry. *When Luck Runs Out.* New York: Facts on File Publications, 1985.

Eadington, William R. and Judy A. Cornelius (editors) *Gambling Behavior and Problem Gambling.* Reno, NV: U. of Nevada Press, 1995.

Eadington, William R. and Judy Cornelius (editors) *The Downside: Problem and Pathological Gambling.* Reno, NV: U. of Nevada Press, 1997.

Eadington, William R. and Judy A. Cornelius ed, *Gambling: Public Policies and the Social Sciences,* Reno, NV: U. of Nevada Press, 1997.

Gamblers Anonymous. *Sharing Recovery Through Gamblers Anonymous.* Los Angeles: Gamblers Anonymous Publishing. 1983.

Hannon, Kerry *Suddenly Single: Money Skills for Divorcees and Widows.* New York: John Wiley, 1998.

Heineman, Mary *Losing Your Shirt: Recovery for Compulsive Gamblers and Their Families* Minneapolis, MN: CompCare, revised 1996.

Johnson, Vernon E. *Intervention: How To Help Someone Who Doesn t Want Help.* Minneapolis, MN: Johnson Institute, 1986.

Leonard, Robin *Rebuild Your Credit.* Berkeley, CA : Nolo Press, 1993.

Leonard, Robin *Money Troubles: Legal Strategies to Cope With Your Debts.* Berkley, CA: Nolo Press, 1997.

Lesieur, Henry R. *The Chase: Career of the Compulsive Gambler* Cambridge, MA: Schenkman Publishing Company, Inc. 1984.

Lesieur, Henry R. *Understanding Compulsive Gambling.* Center City, MN: Hazelton, 1994.

Lewis, Judith MD. and Herman, Judith Hehrman *Trauma and Recovery,* New York: Basic Books, 1997.

Mays, June *Women s Guide to Financial Self-Defense* New York: Warner Books, 1997.

Mundis, Jerrold, *How to Get Out of Debt, Stay Out of Debt and Live Prosperously.* New York: Bantam Books, 1988. reissued 1990.

O 'Brien, Timothy L. *Bad Bet: The Inside Story of the Glamour, Glitz, and Danger of America s Gambling Industry.* New York: Times Books/Random House 1998.

Orman, Suzie *The 9 Steps to Financial Freedom.* New York: Crown, 1997.

Schaef, Anne Wilson *Co-Dependence: Misunderstood, Mistreated.* San Francisco: Harper, reissued 1990.

Seixas, Judith S. and Geraldine Youcha *Children of Alcoholism: A Survivor s Manual.* New York: Crown, 1985.

Saunders, Carol Silverman *Straight Talk About Teenage Gambling.* New York: Facts on File, 1998 (a book for ages 9-12).

Spanier, David *Inside the Gambler s Mind* Reno, NV University of Nevada Press, 1994.

Twerski, Abraham, MD *Addictive Thinking: Understanding Self-Deception.* San Francisco: Harper/Hazelden Book, 1997.

Twerski, Abraham MD *I 'd Like to Call For Help, But I Don t Know The Number: The Search For Spirituality In Everyday Life.* New York: Henry Holt, 1996.

White, Shelby *What Every Woman Should Know About Her Husband s Money.* New York: Random House, 1992.

Whitfield, Charles *Healing the Child Within.* Deerfield, FL.: Health Communications, 1987.

Yablonsky, Lewis *Emotional Meaning of Money.* Mattituck, NY: Ameron, Ltd., 1991.

For Young Readers
Dolan, Edward F. *Teenagers and Compulsive Gambling.* Danbury, CT: Franklin Watts, Inc. 1994.

Haddock, Patricia *Teens and Gambling: Who Wins?* Springfield, NJ: Enslow, 1996.

Hautman, Peter *Stone Cold* New York: Simon and Schuster 1998.

Index

LINDA BERMAN, M.S.W.

Linda Berman, M.S.W. is a recognized expert in the field of gambling addiction. She is a consultant to Westchester Jewish Community Services, a large non-sectarian family mental health agency, and is sought after as a consultant and speaker throughout the country. She has appeared on numerous radio and television programs.

Ms. Berman earned a master's degree from The Fordham University School of Social Work, is a National Certified Gambling Counselor, and a member of the National Council on Problem Gambling in addition to various other professional organizations.

Her private practice of psychotherapy is in Westchester County and in New York City, New York where she sees individuals and families with a wide variety of problems.

MARY-ELLEN SIEGEL, M.S.W.

Mary-Ellen Siegel, M.S.W. holds the faculty rank of Clinical Instructor in the Department of Community and Preventive Medicine (Social Work and Behavioral Sciences) at Mount Sinai School of Medicine in New York. She is the author of the following:

Her Way: A Guide to Biographies of Women For Young People
More Than a Friend: Dogs with a Purpose (coauthor: Hermine M. Koplin)
Reversing Hair Loss
The Nanny Connection (coauthor: O. Robin Sweet)
The Cancer Patient's Handbook
Finger Tips (coauthor: Elisa Ferri)
Dr. Greenberger's What Every Man Should Know About His Prostate
Safe in the Sun
Feeling Dizzy: Understanding and Treating Dizziness, Vertigo, and Other Balance Disorders (coauthor: Brian W. Blakley, M.D., PhD.)
Living With Shingles (coauthor: Gray Williams)

She is in the private practice of psychotherapy in New York, is a member of the National Council on Problem Gambling in addition to various other professional organizations. She has co-chaired and moderated academic conferences for health and mental health professionals as well as for the general public and has made over 150 national radio and television appearances.